Change One

Published by
The Reader's Digest Association Limited
London • New York • Sydney • Montreal

The **Breakthrough**
12-week Eating Plan

Change
One

Lose Weight Simply,
Safely and **Forever**

John Hastings

with Peter Jaret and Mindy Hermann, RD

This edition adapted by
Norma MacMillan and Fiona Hunter

Contributors

John Hastings is the US senior staff editor for health at *Reader's Digest*, the world's largest consumer magazine. He has worked as a journalist covering medicine, nutrition and fitness for 14 years.

Mindy Hermann is a registered dietitian, and a speaker and consultant on weight loss and nutrition. She has written for *Family Circle*, *Men's Health* and other magazines, co-authored the US Reader's Digest book *Live Longer Live Better*, and was the nutrition writer for the American Medical Association *Family Health Cookbook*.

Peter Jaret is a frequent contributor to *Reader's Digest* magazine. His work has also appeared in *National Geographic*, *Newsweek*, *Vogue*, *Glamour* and *Harper's Bazaar*. He is the author of the US Reader's Digest book *Heart Healthy for Life*, and has also received an American Medical Association award for medical reporting.

Norma MacMillan is a food writer and editor. Originally from the USA but now based in London, she has written a number of American cookbooks, including *In a Shaker Kitchen* and *Traditional American Cooking*, and collaborated with top chefs on collections of their recipes. She is particularly interested in healthy eating and was editor of the Reader's Digest series *Eat Well, Live Well*.

Fiona Hunter is a nutritionist and food writer. She writes regularly for the *Daily Mail*, *Good Housekeeping*, *Slimming* and other newspapers and magazines. Her books on eating for health and special diets include *Power Juices* and *Weight Loss Cookbook*. She was nutrition advisor on the Reader's Digest *Eat Well, Live Well* series.

Food photography Elizabeth Watt and John Freeman

Exercise photography Beth Bischoff

Portraits George Kamper, except page 56 Gary A. Morehouse

Cover photograph Leland Bobbé

ChangeOne began life in the United States as a programme designed to help anyone to achieve the weight and health that they deserve. It was conceived at a time when more and more people are, for a multitude of reasons, having trouble controlling their weight and when obesity-related disease is becoming ever more common. I am delighted that it has been adopted as the authorised Reader's Digest diet.

The theory and techniques that lie behind *ChangeOne* have been proved successful many times over, but I and the team involved in the creation of the book thought it crucial to give the programme a rigorous trial run before putting it into print. In the pages of this book you will find the inspiring personal success stories of many of those who volunteered to test the 12-week *ChangeOne* programme.

I am delighted that it has been possible for the original *ChangeOne* programme, including the eating suggestions, recipes and menus it contains, to be adapted for readers in Britain, making it possible for you to gain all the benefits of the programme in your own environment.

I sincerely hope that, along with other dieters, you too will be encouraged to use this extraordinary weight-losing tool to good effect, and to view yourself and your life, in a new and positive way.

John Hastings

Contents

Part 2
ChangeOne Resources

Winning at losing

How many diet plans have you tried? High protein? High carbohydrates? Low fat? Only eat things that are white? Don't eat anything white? Only eat grapefruit, or cabbage? You know the feeling. For a few weeks the latest fad seems to be working. You lose a few pounds, feel better about yourself and life in general, and then bang – the weight comes back like a boomerang, and with a vengence. Now you're left with two problems: you still have those pounds to lose, and you feel like a failure.

Well, *Reader's Digest* wants to help you. That's why, for the first time ever, we have created a diet of our own. You will lose weight without giving up the foods you love to eat. And you'll be stronger – in body and mind. By using some of America's top nutritionists and dietary specialists and adapting their advice for the way we live and eat in Britain, we have come up with this completely new eating plan that takes the weight off…and keeps it off. In only 12 weeks – with just one simple change each week – you will win the weight-loss battle. *ChangeOne* is easy. It's different. And thanks to the testing we've done, we know it works.

Regain control over your eating *without* giving up the foods you love.

There's so much more at stake than simply looking good. Nearly half the men and a third of the women in the country are overweight, numbers that have nearly doubled since the mid 1980s. Obesity is now a national health crisis, causing preventable disease in young and old. For instance, an increasing number of children are contracting Type 2 diabetes, largely because of obesity. It has even been estimated that nearly two-thirds of cases of Type 2 diabetes in men and three-quarters of cases in women could be avoided if no one was overweight.

But that should be no surprise. Eating is a national pastime. In towns and cities, you can find breakfast, lunch and everything in between. In shopping centres everywhere restaurants and retailers combine shopping and eating as a full-time hobby. On the road, fast-food outlets and pubs with restaurants are legion. And let's not forget that merely shopping for food can be fattening. In many supermarkets, chocolate bars and savoury snacks are placed close to the checkouts, making them almost impossible to resist. And this at the same time as you're being tempted by two-for-one or half-price offers, great value bags of cakes and an ever-expanding array of speciality breads, cheeses and meats.

It's time for us to regain control of what we eat. With *ChangeOne*, you don't have to give up the foods you love. You don't have to learn to like tofu. And you don't have to eat dry, tasteless fat-free snacks or enormous quantities of lettuce. You just have to change one eating habit at a time, starting in Week 1 with breakfast. Then it's on to lunch, snacks, supper, eating out and beyond as you watch the weight melt away. Simple. Stress-free. Sensible.

Behind all the recipes, tips and nutritional guidance is one very special idea: we'll be with you throughout this 12-week programme. Every page of *ChangeOne* is designed to make it easy on you, to answer your questions and keep you motivated. Think of this book as your diet companion, a trusted friend who's been through it all before. All we want is for you to feel healthier, have more energy and, finally, fit into the clothes that make you feel fantastic. We know you can do it. Make the change!

Part 1

Change One

The Programme

The *ChangeOne* Quick-Start Guide

ChangeOne eating

The central theme of our 12–week programme is that all foods are allowed in appropriate amounts. Most people will eat about 1300 kcal a day on this plan. Larger or more active people can add roughly 300 kcal through extra servings of grain or protein each day. Here's an overview of the first four weeks:

Week 1: Breakfast

Around 300 kcals

Eat a healthy breakfast and love it, even if you don't normally eat anything.

The basic menu

- **One grain or starch** – roughly a cricket ball of ready-to-eat cereal; a slice of toast; or a roll (tennis ball).
- **One dairy or high-calcium food** – 250 ml (8 fl oz) milk; or 200 g (7 oz) yogurt.
- **Fruit** – one piece or an equivalent amount of melon or berries.

Variations: champagne brunches, smoked salmon and bagels, even a morning parfait are fine if done the *ChangeOne* way.

Week 2: Lunch

Around 350 kcals

You'll learn to recognise a sensible lunch that fits your lifestyle and tastes.

The basic menu

- **One grain or starch** – two slices of sandwich bread; a tennis ball-sized potato or a bread roll; or a serving of pasta or rice.
- **One protein** – thin palm-sized slice of cheese; a small fast-food burger; a stack of 3 CD-sized pieces of cooked meat.
- **Fruit** – one piece or an equivalent amount of melon or berries.
- **Vegetables** – as much as you want.

Variations: soups, salads and wraps can all work fine with sensible portion sizes.

Week 3: Snacks

Up to 200 kcals

Yes, you can have cake and eat it too – twice a day, if you watch yourself.

- **Salty** – a handful of crisps, savoury biscuits, nuts in the shell or popcorn
- **Sweet** – a palmful of M&Ms, jelly beans, malted milk balls, raisins, boiled sweets; a mini chocolate bar.
- **Baked** – 2 small biscuits; 1 fairy cake; or a 5 cm (2 in) square brownie (½ a business card).
- **Frozen** – 2 golf balls worth of: frozen yogurt, sorbet or reduced-fat ice cream. Half a tennis ball-worth of regular ice cream. A fruit juice lolly.

Week 4: Supper

450 kcals

A full day's worth of dieting begins this week, and you'll never look back.

The basic menu

- **One protein** – a tennis ball's worth of prawns, scallops or crab; a deck of card's worth of chicken fillet, beef or salmon. Or a serving of white fish the size of a chequebook.
- **One grain or starch** – a tennis ball-sized serving of rice, pasta, noodles or bread.
- **Vegetables** – as much as you want.

Variations: braises, Chinese buffets, grilled kebabs, stir-fries, barbecues.

The key principles

1. Make one change at a time. You can't become a new person overnight; lasting change requires a measured approach.
2. The secret of weight loss is understanding portion sizes, not maths. If you don't want to count calories for the rest of your life, don't diet that way.
3. All foods are allowed. Let your meals be a source of healthy pleasure and never skimp on flavour or pleasure.
4. Eating for a healthy weight is the same as eating for health. Think of *ChangeOne* as a way of life, and this will be the last time you *have* to lose weight.

ChangeOne living

While the first four weeks cover meals, the next eight weeks offer essential health lessons. Each week takes on an aspect of daily life that influences how you eat.

Week 5: Eating Out

We'll ask you to go out for meals at least twice this week (yes, you *have* to visit restaurants) to practise ordering, and eating, only what you want.

Week 6: Weekends & Celebrations

Plan to get together with family or friends, and not only will you be able to enjoy yourself, you'll learn to gracefully say 'no' when your mum or aunt turns into a food pusher.

Week 7: Fixing Your Kitchen

Take a hard look inside your refrigerator and your storecupboard. Is the food you see going to help you lose weight or undermine your efforts?

Week 8: How Am I Doing?

Everybody take a deep breath. You're two months into the programme so it's time to stop and assess your progress and clean any blockages.

Week 9: Stress Relief

Stress has a way of sneaking up on you and eating often serves as a coping mechanism. We'll help you identify and relieve those hidden pressures.

Week 10: Staying Active for Success

Well, you knew you couldn't avoid exercise. This week you'll learn the only foolproof way to keep weight off.

Week 11: Keeping on Track

If the pounds start to return, they won't do it all at once. Your goal is to devise your own 'First Alert' programme that will help you contain the gain.

Week 12: *ChangeOne*...For Life!

You made it! So don't let boredom ruin the new you. Here's how you can make great food an ongoing source of pleasure – and maintain your loss.

Welcome to *ChangeOne*

You've opened this book for one simple reason: you want to lose weight. Maybe a little, maybe a lot. Maybe you'd like to improve the reflection looking back at you from the mirror. Maybe you're hoping to fit more easily into an old pair of trousers or jeans. Or perhaps you simply want to be healthier and feel better.

Whatever your goal, *ChangeOne* will help you lose weight – and keep it off.

That may sound like a big promise. But there's really no mystery to dieting, despite the bewildering number of plans out there. Want to know a little secret? They all work. You can lose weight on almost any diet because only one thing matters in the weight-loss game: eat fewer calories than you burn. All diets, even the seemingly crazy ones, restrict your calories and that's why you lose weight. Eat sensible amounts of food and the weight will melt away.

Honest, sensible weight-loss

So you won't find any silly gimmicks in *ChangeOne*. We're not going to make you become a vegetarian, a strict carnivore, a caveman or a goddess. But we're radically different in one crucial way. *ChangeOne* asks you to approach dieting one meal at a time, one week at a time. (*ChangeOne* means just that – one change at a time.) We won't overwhelm you on day one. Most diets ask you to throw out the way you eat overnight and adopt a new plan. The biggest problem with that kind of approach is that people will eventually go back to their old ways and gain back the weight they lost.

Imagine a psychologist who expects depressed patients to be happy after one visit. Or a language teacher who announces on the first day of class that students will be able to speak fluent French the next day. It sounds laughable because making a significant change takes time; new skills require practice. Yet instant change is what most diets ask for, which could explain why so many people end up regaining the weight they've lost.

ChangeOne slows dieting down so you can experiment and learn. But don't worry, the weight will start coming off right away.

In the first week, you'll make just one change to your diet: overhaul your breakfast, following one of the five suggested *ChangeOne* breakfast menus. Don't worry: we've counted the calories for you. All you'll have to do is learn to recognise reasonable portions.

In the second week, while you stick with your new habit of eating a healthy, low-calorie breakfast, you'll move on to lunch. Again, we offer a variety of simple menu choices. All you do is choose one each day during the week.

The *ChangeOne* team

To put *ChangeOne* to the test the team that made the original book in the USA recruited volunteers from around America – people just like you, who wanted to lose weight to look and feel better. Many of them worked in the offices of **Reader's Digest in Pleasantville, New York.** When we offered people the chance to try the programme, we had an overwhelming response. The results were just as positive. Over the 12 weeks, our volunteers lost an average of 8 kg (17 lb). Just as important, they honed skills and strategies that have helped them keep the weight off. Throughout this book, you'll hear first-hand how they shaped the *ChangeOne* approach to work for them.

In the third week, you'll focus on snacks. What do snacks have to do with dieting? Plenty. Snacks will keep you from getting too hungry, strengthening your willpower. We'll offer you satisfying choices that will help, not derail, your diet.

In the fourth week, with breakfast, lunch and snacks up and running, you'll move on to what's typically the biggest meal of the day: supper. You'll find a tantalising variety of great-tasting supper menus and tried-and-true strategies for keeping portion sizes under control.

Voilà. By the end of the fourth week, you will have reworked your diet, reduced calories and fat, and discovered new ways to enjoy good nutrition and great-tasting food. And you'll be watching the weight melt away.

This measured approach makes it easy to experiment with each meal, allowing you to incorporate food that you enjoy into your diet. By focusing on one meal at a time, you'll discover more about the way you eat. You may find that eating a reasonable breakfast and lunch is easy, but at supper you go overboard. Or maybe snacks are your biggest stumbling block. You'll also gain confidence as you succeed in getting each meal under control. Then in the following

continued on page 19

Dieting as a tennis match

Reading the health sections of newspapers and magazines could make you feel as if you're at Wimbledon. One day you'll read that carbohydrates are terrible and fat is fine; the next day, you'll hear the opposite. What's the real answer? It'll be years – even decades – before the scientific debate over low-carbohydrate and high-carbohydrate diets is resolved.

But maybe it doesn't matter. Consider a recent study that tested two very different diets. The first was low in carbohydrates and very high in fat (15 per cent of the calories came from carbs, 53 per cent from fat and 32 per cent from protein). The second diet was high in carbohydrates and low in fat (45 per cent of calories came from carbs, 26 per cent from fat and 20 per cent from protein). The only thing the diets had in common was that each totalled 1000 calories a day. When the two groups of volunteers stepped on to the scales after six weeks, guess what? On average, all of them had lost nearly the same amount of weight and body fat.

High fat, low fat, high protein, low protein – none of it made a whit of difference on the scales. What mattered was calorie intake. The key to losing weight is as basic as that.

> Ultimately, the protein vs carbs debate is missing the point.

Ready, steady...lose

Yes, you want to lose weight. But before you start, it's worth checking to make sure you've got what it takes to succeed. To test your readiness, answer these 10 questions by circling the appropriate number in the right-hand column.

1. Which term best describes your attitude towards losing weight?

Enthusiastic	4
Positive	3
Lukewarm	2
Resigned	1

2. How much weight do you want to lose?

4.5–9 kg (10–20 lb)	4
9.5–18 kg (21–40 lb)	3
18.5–27 kg (41–60 lb)	2
28 kg (61 lb) or more	1

3. How would you rate your chances of reaching your goal?

Excellent	4
Very good	3
So-so	2
Poor	1

4. How do you feel about being physically active?

Enjoy it	3
Don't really mind it	2
Hate it	1

5. Which of the following statements best describes you?

Once I make up my mind to do something, I get it done	3
My intentions are good, but my will power is sometimes weak	2
I tend to get discouraged easily	1

6. How important is losing weight to your health?

Very important	3
Somewhat important	2
Not very important at all	1

7. How well do you deal with stresses and strains in your life?

Very effectively	3
So-so	2
I get frazzled easily	1

8. How much time do you spend in front of the TV on a typical day?

Less than an hour	4
One to two hours	3
Three to four hours	2
Four or more hours	1

9. Which of these statements best describes your knowledge about losing weight and keeping it off:

I know what it takes	4
I'm pretty sure I know	3
I'm confused by conflicting advice and diet plans	2
I have no idea where to start	1

10. Think about the people closest to you. How are they likely to react to your decision to diet?

Very enthusiastically	4
Somewhat positively	3
Sceptically	2
Negatively	1

Turn to the next page to add up your score.

Quiz score

Now add up your score. If you had a total of 22 or more, you're ready, but a lower score is no cause for alarm. Many dieters feel grim about their chances early on. Look for the ones or twos in your responses, then read the answers below to boost your readiness.

1. Enthusiasm doesn't guarantee success, but it does help. If yours needs a tune-up, draw a line down the middle of a piece of paper. In the left-hand column, write all the benefits you expect to get from losing weight. In the right column, jot down all the obstacles you anticipate. Finally, begin thinking about ways you could get around those obstacles in order to achieve the benefits you've listed.

2. Experts say your first goal should be about 10 per cent of your current weight. With a reasonable goal, you're less likely to get discouraged before you reach the finishing line. It may not seem like much, but people who lose 10 per cent look better, feel more confident and energetic, and are ready to set their next goal.

3. Despite discouraging words to the contrary, many people do lose weight and keep it off. Researchers at two American universities have been keeping track, in the National Weight Control Registry, of people who succeed at weight loss. We'll share many of the strategies that spell success for these successful slimmers.

4. Not everyone likes to get hot and sweaty. But you'll stand a better chance of succeeding if you become more active – walking, swimming or playing football with the kids, riding a bicycle round the neighbourhood, gardening, taking the stairs instead of the lift.

5. A lot of frustrated dieters want to put the blame on will-power failures. The surprising truth is that you don't need a rock-solid will to lose weight. You need strategies that will spare you from having to rely on will power all the time. You'll find them here: ways to ward off hunger; ways to navigate restaurants; ways to satisfy your sweet tooth on fewer calories.

6. Better health is a bonus for *everyone* who sheds excess weight. Carrying around too much weight increases your risk of diabetes, heart disease and some cancers. The changes in *ChangeOne* are designed not only to help you lose weight but also to become healthier.

7. Too much stress can undermine even the most determined dieter's plans. All of us face stresses and strains in our lives. What matters is how you deal with them. In *ChangeOne* we'll introduce you to effective ways to take the sting out of stress – techniques that will help you get through even the rockiest times.

8. The more television people watch, studies show, the more they're likely to weigh. Ask yourself this: would you be willing to give up just half an hour of TV three times a week to lose weight and feel a whole lot better? If so, you've just jump-started your chances of success.

9. Feeling a little unsure of the facts? Don't worry. In *ChangeOne* we do more than just tell you what to do. We explain why, based on the latest research. The more you know about gaining and losing weight, the better your chances of meeting your goal.

10. The support of family and friends makes a big difference when you're trying to make a change for the better. But they may not be as supportive as you'd like. If that's true for you, remember that you are the only person whose opinion matters. You can do this on your own.

continued from page 16
eight weeks you'll tackle the big issues dieters face, such as how to eat prudently at restaurants, manage stress and exercise for long-term success. Best of all, you'll learn skills that will help you eat sanely for the rest of your life. Losing weight is something you want to do only once. With *ChangeOne*, you'll take the time to get it right.

The numbers behind *ChangeOne*

The meals and menus you'll find in the following pages are more than just delicious. They've been designed to offer maximum nutrition with a sensible number of calories. That's important. When you're cutting back on calories, you certainly don't want to cut back on vitamins, minerals, fibre and the other health benefits of good food. The beauty of *ChangeOne* is that you don't have to weigh every gram or calculate every calorie. We've done that for you. The *ChangeOne* meal plans are designed to meet the following daily guidelines:

- **Calories:** from 1300 to 1600
- **Calories from fat:** approximately 30 per cent
- **Saturated and hydrogenated fats:** no more than 10 per cent
- **Fibre:** at least 25 grams
- **Calcium:** approximately 1000 milligrams.
- **Fruits and vegetables:** at least 5 servings a day

The calorie target of 1300 to 1600 a day is the one used in most diet programmes run by experts in the field of weight loss. Not everyone needs the same number of calories, of course. A large person uses up more calories than a small one. A very active person uses more than someone who doesn't get around much. As you'll discover,

What you'll find inside

On the following pages you'll find regular features packed with dozens of helpful tips and plenty of advice based on the latest weight-loss research, including:

ChangeOne Menu

Meals and recipes that will help you cut calories without sacrificing flavour or the pleasures of eating. And our photos are accurate – the portion sizes you see pictured reflect what you'll be eating.

Help!

Trouble-shooting tips to help you overcome many of the most common obstacles along the way to successful weight loss.

First Person

Insights from people who have used the *ChangeOne* approach to shed weight and keep it off.

Fast Track

Optional strategies to help you to speed your progress.

ChangeOne is designed to let you set your own calorie target and adjust it along the way to suit your needs.

You'll also notice that *ChangeOne* meals don't cut fat to unrealistically low levels. In fact, you may be surprised to find that some of our meal plans contain slightly more than the level of 33 to 35 per cent calories from fat that top nutritionists recommend. The latest research shows that diets with a decent amount of fat – the healthy kinds, of course – are actually more successful than diets that restrict fat to an absurd minimum. Another key to success is foods that are higher in fibre, which help people feel fuller longer. We've made sure the meals we offer include both fats and fibre, as well as all the other nutrients you need.

> The key is to eat enough so that you do *not* feel hungry.

ChangeOne is designed to help you to slim down gradually, from 500 g to 1.5 kg (1–3 lb) a week. People who lose weight at a steady, moderate pace like this are the most likely to keep it off. But many dieters are impatient to slim down. If you are one of them, *ChangeOne* offers 'The Fast Track' features with suggestions to help you drop pounds faster.

Sound simple? We hope so. That's the goal of *ChangeOne* – to take the mystery and frustration out of weight loss.

Getting started

The basic *ChangeOne* meal plans you'll find in this book contain about 1300 kcals a day. That's a reasonable goal for many people who want to lose weight. But if you're very active or weigh more than about 86 kg (190 lb), you may want to set your target at 1600 kcals. People who are physically active burn more calories minute by minute than people who are sedentary. People who are heavy burn more calories than lighter people because they use more energy carrying around the extra weight.

What's the ideal target for you? Here's what we recommend:

Aim for 1300 kcals if:

- You're a woman who usually does less than half an hour's worth of physical activity (including walking and other everyday activities) most days.
- You're a fairly inactive man who weighs less than 85 kg (190 lb).

Aim for 1600 calories if:

- You get at least half an hour's worth of vigorous exercise most days of the week.
- You weigh more than 85 kg (190 lb).

Keep in mind that you can always adjust your calorie target up or down during the programme. If you aren't losing weight as quickly as you'd like, you can decrease your calorie level. (We don't recommend going below 1300 kcals a day, however, because a diet that is skimpy is likely to fall short on vitamins, minerals and other nutrients you need.) If you feel too hungry on most days, you can increase it. The key is to *not* feel hungry. Researchers have found that dieters quickly adjust to a lower calorie level, so if after a few weeks you're still starving, eat a little more. Once you reach your weight goal we'll help you find a calorie target that balances the energy you take in with the energy you burn.

The 1600 Club

If you decide to go for 1600 kcals a day instead of the basic 1300 *ChangeOne* plan, don't worry about counting every extra calorie. Here's all you have to do:

- At breakfast, double your portion of cereal, toast, bagel or bread roll.
- At lunch or supper, double your portion of protein (that is, your meat, chicken, fish or tofu serving). Or, at supper, double your portion of starch or grain.

Real rewards

Most people on a diet want to see changes on the scales. That's natural. We recommend that you weigh yourself once a week, preferably every Monday (it will help stay honest over the weekend). Use the same scales, and choose the same time of day. Keep a log of your weight.

But remember, logging weight loss on the scales is only one way to measure your progress, and not necessarily the best way. If you're losing fat and adding muscle, for instance, your weight may remain the same but you'll look and feel a lot better (and your waistline is likely to slim down). One of our *ChangeOne* volunteers actually stopped lifting weights when the numbers on the scales weren't dropping as fast as he would have liked. But he looked great, and the strength training had a lot to do with that. We convinced him to start exercising again and to pay less attention to the scales and more to the way he looked and felt.

That's good advice for anyone beginning a diet. Keep an eye on your image in the mirror, your clothes size, your energy and the notches on your belt, and you'll enjoy all the rewards of slimming down.

Breakfast

How does this sound? This week you'll start *ChangeOne* by eating breakfast every morning.

Maybe you don't eat breakfast. Plenty of hopeful dieters forgo the first meal of the day. What better way to make my weight-loss diet work, the thinking goes, than not eating? People reckon they'll end up taking in fewer calories that way.

In fact, it works the other way round. People who skip breakfast often end up consuming more calories during the day. Those who start the day with a healthy meal, meanwhile, are more likely to stick to healthy eating throughout the day.

In this chapter you'll find several great breakfasts, along with simple ways to adapt them to your own tastes. Every day this week, help yourself to whichever *ChangeOne* breakfast strikes your fancy. Experiment – and don't worry if you try something that doesn't fill you up. The rest of the day you can eat the way you normally do. That's all there is to taking your first step towards losing weight – and keeping it off.

Egg on a roll

1 egg, scrambled, poached or hard-boiled

1 small wholemeal roll, about 50 g (1¾ oz) (tennis ball)

115 g (4 oz) fresh fruit salad (2 golf balls)

150 ml (5 fl oz) skimmed or semi-skimmed milk

kcals 300, fat 10 g, saturated fat 3 g, cholesterol 242 mg, sodium 419 mg, carbohydrate 40 g, fibre 4 g, protein 16 g, calcium 187 mg.

Instead of	Try
Egg	100 g (3½ oz) low-fat cottage cheese 60 g (2¼ oz) wafer-thin ham
Wholemeal roll	1 English muffin 1 small pitta bread 1 slice wholemeal toast
Fruit salad	175 ml (6 fl oz) orange juice 1 orange 1 banana 1 apple

Time-saver
This is a breakfast you can make at home to eat straight away or take with you. Or ask a café or sandwich bar to make it for you. Even fast-food places can prepare this, using an English muffin. If you're making scrambled egg at home, remember you only need to use a small amount of butter – about ½ teaspoon should be enough.

Pancakes with berries

4 pancakes

1 tablespoon maple syrup
(1 to 2 syrup bottle caps)

85 g (3 oz) strawberries, sliced
(2 golf balls)

200 ml (7 fl oz) semi-skimmed milk

kcals 300, fat 8 g, saturated fat 3 g, cholesterol 73 mg,
sodium 229 mg, carbohydrate 47 g, fibre 1.5 g,
protein 13 g, calcium 390 mg.

PANCAKES

Makes 16 pancakes to serve 4
75 g (2½ oz) self-raising flour
1½ teaspoons caster sugar
¼ teaspoon bicarbonate of soda
175 ml (6 fl oz) buttermilk
1 tablespoon vegetable oil
1 medium egg
½ teaspoon pure vanilla extract

1. Whisk the flour, sugar and bicarbonate of soda in a bowl. Make a well in the centre. In another bowl, whisk the buttermilk, oil, egg and vanilla extract until blended. Pour into well in the flour and whisk until moistened. Allow batter to stand for 5 minutes.

2. Meanwhile, coat a large non-stick frying pan with cooking spray and set over medium heat until hot but not smoking.

3. For each pancake, pour 1 tablespoon batter into the pan. Cook for 3 minutes or until bubbles appear on the surface and begin to burst. Turn and cook for 1 to 2 minutes or until the other side is golden.

4. Make 4 pancakes for yourself. If not cooking for others, you can cover the extra batter and keep in a fridge for the next day. Or cook all the pancakes, wrap extra in foil and keep in fridge for a day or freezer for a week. Reheat wrapped pancakes in a 180ºC (350ºF, gas mark 4) oven for 10 minutes.

Instead of	Try
4 pancakes	1 slice pain perdu/eggy bread or 1 slice cinnamon toast (standard bread slice)
Maple syrup	fresh fruit coulis

Why breakfast is key

If you usually skip the morning meal, you may need a little convincing to get you started. Many of the volunteers who tested *ChangeOne* weren't breakfast eaters either. What they discovered was that starting the day with a healthy meal was the single most important change they made. 'I was amazed, really amazed,' one *ChangeOne* volunteer told us. 'Starting to eat breakfast changed the way I ate all day long. It really made the difference.'

Don't just take our word for it. In an experiment conducted at Vanderbilt University in Nashville, Tennessee, researchers recruited overweight women who usually skipped breakfast. All the women were put on a 1200-kcals-a-day diet. One group divided calories between just two meals: lunch and supper. The second group ate those meals plus breakfast. Twelve weeks on, the breakfast eaters had lost 7.7 kg (17 lb); the women who skipped breakfast had shed 5.9 kg (13 lb).

Wait a minute, you might say. Weren't both groups consuming the same number of calories? No, the researchers concluded. The women who ate breakfast were more likely to stick to the 1200-kcals diet. Those who went hungry until lunch were more likely to cheat a little.

If you skip breakfast, this study showed, you're likely to eat more, not less, than if you start the day with a meal.

> Four out of five successful dieters eat breakfast every day of the week.

Breakfast portions

To help you to assess portion sizes, we use both standard measurements and the *ChangeOne* portion-size guide. In the breakfast portions below, members of the 1600 Club can double the starch or grain serving.

Type of food	Example	Amount	*ChangeOne* guide
One starch or grain	Cornflakes	25 g (1 oz)	Cricket ball
	Porridge	115 g (4 oz)	2 golf balls
	Toast	1 slice	Tennis ball
	Roll	Small	Tennis ball
One dairy or high calcium food	Milk	250 ml (8 fl oz)	Takeaway coffee cup
	Yogurt	150 g (5½ oz)	
One piece of fruit	Orange, apple	1	1 fist
	Berries, cut fruit	115 g (4 oz)	Cupped handful
Optional	Butter, jam	1 teaspoon	Thumb tip
	Nuts	1 tablespoon	Thumb

The reason is pretty obvious when you think about it. The longer you go without eating, the hungrier you get. And the hungrier you get, the more likely you are to devour anything you can get your hands on. When you start the day with breakfast, you begin by taming the hungry beast inside and make it easier to keep cravings in check.

You'll also be starting your day with an easy success: of the three meals, a healthy, sensible breakfast is the simplest to achieve. That will help you stay on track for the day. Psychologists say that levels of two brain chemicals that give us a sense of control – cortisol and adrenaline – peak very soon after we get up. The confidence they provide may make it easier to stick to our good intentions, such as a healthier diet. These chemicals ebb later in the morning, so it can be tougher to say no to the biscuits someone brings into the office – especially if you're feeling extra hungry because you skipped breakfast.

Still not convinced? Here's a compelling argument: most successful slimmers eat breakfast. Since 1993 researchers at two universities in the US have been gathering data on people who manage to lose 14 kg (30 lb) or more and keep the weight off for at least one year. The project, called the National Weight Control Registry, is designed to learn – from the people who know best – what it takes to lose weight permanently. And guess what? Four out of five say they eat breakfast every day.

Making the change

Choose a *ChangeOne* breakfast each day this week. Mix and match the meals any way you like. The important thing is to start your day with a good breakfast and then go on with life – and the rest of your day's regular meals. Don't worry that you'll end up consuming more calories than usual. Like a lot of breakfast converts, you're likely to feel less hungry mid-morning and at lunch time.

Don't let the morning rush at your house get in the way. Putting breakfast together doesn't have to require more time than it takes to fill a bowl with

Help!

'I'm just not hungry in the morning. Do I really have to force myself to eat something if I'm not hungry?'

Give it a try. One reason you're not hungry may be that you're not used to eating so early. So try this: start off with a few bites of something that sounds appealing – toast, say, or a cereal bar – for five mornings in a row. After two or three mornings, you might start to notice your early-morning appetite increasing. Also, schedule supper a little earlier than usual if you can and eat only enough to feel satisfied without being stuffed. This will increase the chances of your appetite waking up when you do. If you're still struggling, eat just one item from a *ChangeOne* breakfast – a piece of fruit, for instance – and save the rest for a mid-morning mini meal.

ChangeOne Fast Track

Hoping to drop a size before your next school reunion? Determined to cut a slimmer figure in your swimsuit next summer? To speed your progress, choose one or more of these Fast Track changes this week:

Eat breakfast twice

Instead of having your usual lunch, make your midday meal another *ChangeOne* breakfast. Eating breakfast twice during the day isn't our idea. Recently several major cereal manufacturers have been touting it as a novel weight-loss method.

Help yourself to a bowl of their flakes for breakfast and lunch, they promise, and you can have a full supper and still shed weight. It works, especially if high-calorie lunches are your downfall.

Be more active

Add 15 minutes of extra physical activity to your schedule every day this week. Walking is fine: a quick circuit of the office complex, or up and down a few flights of stairs if they're handy.

Aim for 15 minutes of activity every day when you would otherwise have been inactive. And here's why. If you weigh 82 kg (180 lb), for instance, you burn about 2.2 kcals a minute sitting in a meeting or parked in front of the TV. If you get up and take a walk, you more than double that number, to 4.7 kcals. Quicken your pace to a brisk walk and your metabolism burns up 7.2 kcals a minute.

The benefits can add up fast. Sitting still you burn just 33 kcals every 15 minutes, but brisk walking burns 108 in the same period.

Keep a food diary

People who are asked to keep close track of what they eat during the day, researchers found, almost always begin to lose weight – even if they don't consciously go on a slimming diet. There are several reasons for this.

When you're keeping a food diary, you become more aware of what you eat. And when you know you have to write down every nibble, you think twice before you eat a Danish pastry at your mid-morning coffee break or a piece of chocolate cake for tea.

Keeping a food diary also reveals eating patterns you may not have been aware of – the fact that you snack more than you imagined, for instance, or that most of your eating occurs late in the day. Those insights can help you shape the best strategy for losing weight. You'll find a handy Food Diary form and instructions on page 309. Track your eating in it every day this week.

Speed up the programme

Although our volunteers like the week-by-week pace of *ChangeOne*, you could do the first four weeks' assignments in less time to speed your weight loss. For example, give yourself three days for breakfast, four days for lunch, three days for snacks and four days for supper.

That would get you through the first four weeks and have you dieting from breakfast to bedtime in two weeks, instead of the four we recommend. The tradeoff is that you won't have as much time to experiment with meals to find the foods that satisfy you, and you could miss out on the opportunity to discover – and solve – problems in your eating patterns. But if your goal is to look stunning for your beach holiday and you don't have a lot of time…

cereal, scatter a little fruit over it and pour on the milk. If you're really in a hurry:

■ Set the table for breakfast before going to bed. You'll save time, and the breakfast table will be a reminder when you get up.

■ Take care of one or two morning tasks the night before. Instead of deciding what to wear after you get up, for example, select the next day's outfit before you go to bed.

■ Prepare a fruit salad on Sunday so that you can quickly serve yourself some the first few mornings of the week.

■ Set your alarm clock for 10 minutes earlier than usual.

If all else fails, keep a box of cereal bars and plenty of fresh fruit to hand for an easy-to-pack breakfast.

Behind the *ChangeOne* breakfast menu

Each *ChangeOne* breakfast is designed to contain around 350 kcals or less. That's enough energy to power your morning and still get you started on losing weight.

What's more, each *ChangeOne* breakfast includes at least one food that's rich in fibre. There are several good reasons for this. The biggest shortfall in most people's diets is fibre: we should get about 25 to 30 grams a day to be at our healthiest; we average around 15.

Fibre defends us from several common health problems. It's also a key player in a healthy weight-loss diet. Because it's filling, fibre makes a meal feel more satisfying on fewer calories. One type – soluble fibre – absorbs water to form gels that slow down digestion, so fibre-rich foods stay with you longer than other foods, keeping hunger at bay. (For more on fibre-rich foods, see 'More good reasons to fill up on fibre' on page 34.)

To test the hunger-taming effects of fibre-rich foods, scientists at the University of Sydney compared two seemingly similar breakfasts: a bowl of bran flakes, which are high in fibre, and a bowl of cornflakes, which are not. Volunteers in the bran cereal group reported feeling less hungry later in the morning than

continued on page 31

Help!

'What if I can't find a pot of yogurt with only 80 kcals? Or a cereal bar that has 120 kcals? How exact do I have to be?'

Don't get too hung up on exact calorie counts. If you can come within 10 to 20 kcals of the recommended amount in the target food, you'll be fine. Remember, the *ChangeOne* programme is more about recognising healthy foods and eating reasonable servings than it is about counting calories.

Bagel delight

½ ordinary bagel, or 1 mini bagel, split in half

2 teaspoons reduced-fat cream cheese (2 thumb tips),
1 tablespoon yogurt cheese (see below) (whole thumb)
or 2 tablespoons very-low-fat fromage frais

1 teaspoon jam (thumb tip)

1 peach, sliced

150 g (5½ oz) sugar-free or plain non-fat yogurt
(tennis ball)

kcals 260, fat 4 g, saturated fat 2 g, cholesterol 6 mg, sodium 388 mg,
carbohydrate 48 g, fibre 2.5 g, protein 14 g, calcium 350 mg.

Time-saver
*Cut bagels in half when
you bring them home
from the supermarket,
then freeze them in a
resealable plastic bag.*

HOW TO MAKE YOGURT CHEESE

Line a drip-coffee basket, or small sieve, with a paper filter, and
rest the filter on a bowl or measuring jug. Put 200 g (7 oz)
plain fat-free or low-fat yogurt in the coffee filter (use a yogurt
that does not contain gelatine). Cover and refrigerate for at
least one hour. The liquid in the yogurt will drip through the
filter, allowing the yogurt to thicken into a spreadable 'cheese'.

Time-saver
Pack a breakfast in a bag the night before so you can grab it and go in the morning.

HEALTH TIP

Fresh fruit is low in calories but high in fibre: 75 g (2½ oz) blueberries contain 40 kcals and 2 g of fibre. You can swap the berries for other fruit in season: an apple has 47 kcals and 1.8 g fibre; an orange 60 kcals and 2.7 g fibre; 3 plums 31 kcals and 1.4 g fibre; and 150 g (5½ oz) of strawberries 41 kcals and 2 g fibre.

Breakfast on the go

1 cereal bar, 120 to 160 kcals

75 g (2½ oz) **blueberries** (2 golf balls)

200 g (7 oz) plain or sugar-free, fat-free or low-fat yogurt

kcals 300, fat 5 g, saturated fat 3 g, cholesterol 8 mg, sodium 200 mg, carbohydrate 40 g, fibre 4 g, protein 14 g, calcium 450 mg.

ABOUT CEREAL BARS

Cereal bars are not always as healthy and innocent as you might think – some brands contain a lot of fat and sugar. Those at about 120 to 160 kcals may be a bit harder to find than their heavyweight cousins, but with a bit of careful label reading you'll find flavours you like. Brands to try include Kellogg's Nutri-Grain, Jordan's, Alpen and Traidcraft. Look for a bar with at least 1 gram of fibre. But if you have a favourite that contains no fibre, go ahead and enjoy it – there's fibre in the fruit you eat with it.

continued from page 28
those who ate cornflakes. Similarly, researchers at the New York Obesity Research Center at St Luke's-Roosevelt Hospital recently pitted a sugary, low-fibre breakfast cereal against porridge, a high-fibre cereal. When volunteers ate the sweetened flakes, they tended to eat as much at lunch as if they'd had nothing but a glass of water at breakfast. When they sat down to a bowl of porridge, they felt fuller longer and ate up to 40 per cent less for lunch.

> Set the breakfast table the night before for easier mornings.

A fruitful choice

ChangeOne breakfasts also include at least one serving of fruit. Fruit, like whole grains, is a terrific source of fibre. One apple has 1.8 grams of fibre, which is 10 per cent of the recommended daily amount. Also, most people who hit the recommended goal of five servings of fruits and vegetables a day get at least one of those at breakfast.

When we say fruit, we mean fruit you can chew. Fruit juices are fine now and then, but many are surprisingly high in calories, especially if they've been sweetened (when they'll be called a drink or cocktail). A 250 ml (8 fl oz) glass of cranberry juice drink contains a hefty 140 kcals. Even apple juice has around the same number of calories as cola. What's more, most fruit juices don't have nearly as much fibre as the fruit they're made from. Compare 150 ml (5 fl oz) of these juices with their whole fruit:

Orange juice	An orange
Kcals: 54	Kcals: 60
Vitamin C: 59 mg	Vitamin C: 86 mg
Fibre: 0.2 g	Fibre: 2.7 g
Apple juice	An apple
Kcals: 57	Kcals: 47
Vitamin C: 21 mg	Vitamin C: 6 mg
Fibre: negligible	Fibre: 1.8 g
Grapefruit juice	A grapefruit
Kcals: 50	Kcals: 48
Vitamin C: 47 mg	Vitamin C: 58 mg
Fibre: negligible	Fibre: 2.1 g

ChangeOne encourages you to help yourself to fruit not only at breakfast but for snacking too. We stop short of

continued on page 34

The cereal story

A good bowl of cereal, cold or hot, is one of the wisest breakfast choices you can make, as long as you select wisely. Try to find cereals with lots of dietary fibre – at least 3 grams per serving. And check the ingredients for whole grains like oats or wheat. Pictured on the right are the most familiar breakfast cereals in portions that contain about 100 kcals.

A PERFECT BOWL OF CEREAL

25 g (1 oz) bran flakes (tennis ball)
2 tablespoons raisins or sultanas
   (2 thumbs)
2 teaspoons chopped nuts or
   sunflower seeds (optional, adds
   30 kcals) (2 thumb tips)
200 ml (7 fl oz) skimmed or
   semi-skimmed milk

kcals 300, fat 9 g, saturated fat 3 g, cholesterol 14 mg, sodium 360 mg, carbohydrate 51 g, fibre 4 g, protein 13 g, calcium 275 mg.

MAKE YOUR OWN MUESLI

You can create your own signature breakfast cereal by mixing oats with your favourite dried fruit and seeds. Here's a muesli that will last for days:

- 125 g (4½ oz) porridge oats
- 60 g (2¼ oz) ready-to-eat dried apricots, chopped
- 60 g (2¼ oz) banana chips
- 25 g (1 oz) pumpkin or sunflower seeds

Mix and store in an airtight container. This will make enough for 10 servings.

GREAT TOPPINGS

Staring down at the same old bowl of flakes can be daunting. Here are five toppings to liven up your cereal:

- 1 tablespoon unsweetened desiccated coconut (50 kcals)
- 1 tablespoon chopped banana chips (30 kcals)
- 2 teaspoons chopped almonds (50 kcals) or sunflower seeds (58 kcals)
- 1 teaspoon cinnamon and sugar (20 kcals)

Top row left to
right: muesli (30 g),
cornflakes (30 g),
puffed wheat (30 g).
*Middle row left to
right:* Weetabix (1½),
All Bran (40 g), bran
flakes (30 g). *Bottom
row left to right:*
grape nuts (30 g),
porridge oats (30 g),
Shreddies (30 g),
Rice Krispies (30 g)

CHOOSING MILK

Still drinking full-fat milk? Now's the time to lighten up.
Take it one change at a time: step down from full-fat to semi-
skimmed, then from semi-skimmed to skimmed. It won't take
long before lower-fat milk tastes as good as what you were
drinking before. Here's what you'll save in artery-clogging
saturated fat and calories in each 100 ml (3½ fl oz):

Type of milk	Saturated fat	Kcals
Full-fat	3.9 g	66
Semi-skimmed	1.8 g	46
Skimmed	0.1-0.3 g	33
Soya milk	0.3g	32

HOT CEREALS

If it's cold outside,
there's nothing like
a steaming bowl of
hot cereal to warm
you up. Porridge is
the classic, but you
can choose from
many others:
■ Instant oat cereal,
   eg Ready Brek
■ Weetabix with hot
   milk
■ Shredded Wheat
   or Shreddies with
   hot milk

continued from page 31
saying you can eat as much fruit as you want because most fruit contains a fair amount of sugar, which adds calories to your diet. But frankly, we've never met anyone who got fat eating too many mangoes. If the choice is between a pastry or chocolate bar and a piece of fruit, reach for the fruit.

Weight loss secrets from the dairy

Something else you'll find in *ChangeOne* breakfasts: most meal plans include milk or yogurt. Low-fat dairy products are a terrific low-calorie source of calcium, which you need for a key trio of health reasons: calcium helps to keep bones strong, it reins in blood pressure, and recent studies suggest that calcium may lower the risk of colon cancer.

continued on page 36

More good reasons to fill up on fibre

With all the attention being given to carbohydrates, protein and fat, it's easy to forget fibre. But when you're dieting, fibre could well be the part of food most worthy of focus.

Fibre, which is the indigestible part of food, gives whole grains, fruits and vegetables their snap, crunch and crispiness. And since your body can't digest fibre, it passes through without adding any calories.

The research tells the story. In a 1999 study published in the *Journal of the American Medical Association*, researchers tracked the diets of 2909 men and women over 10 years. Those who chose fibre-rich foods ended up weighing almost 4.5 kg (10 lb) less, on average, than those who consumed very little fibre.

Chances are they scored in other ways, too. Fibre-rich foods have been shown to lower LDL cholesterol, the bad stuff. University of Toronto researchers recently showed that a diet that gets more than one-third of its calories from fibre-rich foods like fruit, vegetables and nuts can lower LDL cholesterol by 33 per cent. Volunteers on a high-fibre diet saw their LDL numbers drop within the first week.

Fibre eaters are also less likely to develop diabetes as adults. In two major studies conducted by scientists at the Harvard School of Public Health, people who ate the most fibre from whole grains had the lowest risk of type 2 diabetes: high-fibre grains cut their risk of contracting the disease by 30 per cent.

And here's one more reason to reach for whole grains, fruits and vegetables: many studies show a lower risk of several kinds of cancer among people who include lots of fibre in their diet. By eating a healthier diet based on plant foods, most of us could cut our cancer risk by at least one-third, experts say.

Fibre is the perfect diet food: no calories, and very filling.

Changing time zones

'Great!' Walter Williams, 50, remembers thinking when he learned that the first step in *ChangeOne* was eating breakfast. 'At last, a diet that means I get to eat more, rather than less.'

Like a lot of people, Walter, a systems engineer, mostly skipped breakfast. By lunch time, he remembers, he was ravenous. 'I was so hungry I'd go down the cafeteria counter at work and fill my tray as high as I could manage. Soup, a main dish, chips, a big glass of sweetened fruit juice, something sweet to finish. Even after all that, at supper time, I'd eat another giant meal. And often, at around nine in the evening, I'd make a sandwich or heat up a piece of pizza. I just seemed to be hungry all day.'

At first, Walter wasn't convinced that eating breakfast would help him to get his appetite under control. Starting the day with a meal actually seemed to make him hungrier in the morning, he recalls. But he stuck with it, and after a week he noticed a change.

'At lunch, I felt less of an urge to eat everything in sight. Before long I was having a sandwich on wholemeal bread and maybe a piece of fruit. No chips. No sweet. And that was enough to keep me satisfied through the afternoon.'

Even at supper, he found, he could eat less and still feel satisfied. He was also less tempted to grab a sandwich or pizza slice before bedtime.

'Eating breakfast had the effect of changing my appetite,' he says. 'I'm hungry in the morning now, and again at noon, and then at six for supper. I'm eating earlier in the day. One effect has been to eliminate that big late-night snack I used to have. And I'm satisfied eating a much more reasonable lunch than before. All that from one simple change: eating breakfast.'

Walter lost 6.7 kg (15 lb) on *ChangeOne*. His goal? Just 4.5 kg (10 lb).

continued from page 34

Calcium also turns out to have a surprising weight-loss benefit. The evidence first showed up in a study to test whether the blood pressure of men could be lowered by adding 300 g (11 oz) of yogurt to their daily diet. The readings dropped and, as an added bonus, the men also lost weight – 5 kg (11 lb) in a year, on average.

Another study showed that dieters who ate three to four servings of dairy products daily lost 70 per cent more weight in six months than people on the same diet who were not eating dairy foods. And those in the dairy group lost more fat around their middles.

The magic ingredient in dairy products seems to be calcium. One two-year study found that university-age women who ate a low-calcium diet gained weight; women who got plenty of calcium maintained a steady weight, or even lost a bit.

Why? Experts have found that getting too little calcium triggers the release of a hormone called calcitriol, which tells the body to store rather than burn fat. When calcium levels are high, calcitriol levels stay low, and the body burns fat instead of storing it. Calcium's not quite the whole story, as subjects who took a calcium supplement pill in the diet studies didn't lose quite as much weight as people who got the mineral in their meals. This suggests that something else in dairy products may help to spur weight loss.

But what if you're allergic to dairy foods? More and more people have an intolerance to milk, which means they don't have enough of the lactase enzyme, vital for the digestion of milk sugars. But even with low lactase you may be able to digest a little milk with no discomfort thanks to sugar-processing microbes we all carry in our intestines. If you're lactose intolerant and want to find out if these microbes will help you to tolerate dairy foods in small amounts, try adding milk gradually to your diet. Start with a small glass a day.

Of course, you don't have to drink milk or eat other dairy products to be healthy or lose weight. You can substitute low-fat soya milk or rice milk and get your calcium in other ways – from a supplement or in calcium-fortified foods, for

Pop a pill

For years, researchers were divided on the value of taking a multi-vitamin. Now there's a growing consensus that taking a one-a-day-type pill is a smart move.

In 2002 a landmark article in the *Journal of the American Medical Association* recommended taking a multivitamin daily. That's especially good advice when you're trying to cut back on calories. Even the best-planned diet can fall short on essential vitamins and minerals. A multi-vitamin will fill in any gaps.

example. The *ChangeOne* menu includes several foods with added calcium to help you to reach the recommended level. Other non-dairy sources rich in calcium include tofu, baked beans, white bread, oranges, almonds and canned fish (such as sardines) that are eaten with their bones.

Changes ahead: lunch

This week, while you focus on breakfast, keep an eye on what you eat for lunch. Don't change your lunch menu; we'll get to that next week. Eat the way you usually do for the rest of the day. Just note where you have lunch and what you eat. Be aware of the choices you have: eat out? at your desk? in a pub? And be alert to how you feel. Do you jam lunch into the middle of a frantic day, or is it a relaxed time? On at least one day – each day of the week if you have time – write down what you eat for lunch and estimate the serving sizes.

More breakfast choices

Can't find something you like from among the five suggested breakfasts? Starting on page 252, you'll find more quick and delicious *ChangeOne* breakfast ideas. Here's a sampler:

Glazed blueberry muffins
page 252

Dried cranberry scones with orange glaze page 253

Tropical smoothie
page 254

Vegetable frittata
page 255

Peach and yogurt loaf
page 256

Cottage cheese melba
page 258

WEEK **2**

Lunch

Contrary to what you've heard, the single biggest problem any slimmer faces in the battle of the bulge isn't what they eat, it's how much. We now annually consume more food per person, on average, than we did in 1990. How is that possible? Take a look at lunch.

Double cheeseburgers with two rashers of bacon, extra-large soft drinks, super-size chips – runaway inflation has hit the lunch counter.

This week sanity prevails. You'll eat delicious lunches that satisfy without crazy excess.

For many people lunch presents the biggest challenge of the day. We grab our midday meals in the middle of crowded schedules, work, errands and distractions. And because lunch is the meal we're least likely to eat at home, we typically have less control over what's on the menu.

But that's all the more reason for you to learn ways to make lunch a great-tasting, sensible meal. With some advance planning, and by using the lunches in this chapter and on pages 259 to 267, you'll be able to keep your calories in line and still enjoy your midday meal.

Pizza and salad

Pitta pizza:

1 mini or picnic pitta bread (55 g/2 oz)
2 tablespoons tomato sauce (2 thumbs)
25 g (1 oz) reduced-fat mozzarella, grated (surface of palm)
Grilled vegetables

1 green salad with 2 tablespoons fat-free dressing
(2 salad-dressing caps)
or 2 teaspoons vinaigrette (2 thumb tips)

1 apple

To prepare pizza:
Spread sauce on pitta bread, sprinkle with cheese, top with grilled vegetables and bake at 180ºC (350ºF, gas mark 4) for 5 minutes until cheese bubbles. For ham or pepperoni pizza, use half the amount of cheese and top with 2 thin slices of meat.

kcals 320, fat 8 g, saturated fat 4 g, cholesterol 18 mg, sodium 720 mg, carbohydrate 50 g, fibre 4 g, protein 15 g, calcium 250 mg.

TIPS FOR TOPPINGS

As most vegetables in *ChangeOne* are unlimited, you can pile on as many as you like:
- Artichokes, canned in water
- Broccoli
- Courgette, grilled
- Mushrooms, fresh or grilled
- Onion, chopped
- Pepper, chopped
- Pepper, roasted
- Rocket
- Spinach
- Sweetcorn
- Tomato, sliced

Soup and salad

300 ml (10 fl oz) fresh vegetable soup (bowl)

3 breadsticks, small

1 green salad unlimited topped with:

55 g (2 oz) grilled chicken (half your palm)
2 tablespoons olives (two thumbs),
 or 1 tablespoon chopped nuts (1 salad-dressing cap),
 or 1 tablespoon grated cheese (1 salad-dressing cap)
2 tablespoons fat-free dressing (2 salad-dressing caps)
 or 2 teaspoons vinaigrette (2 thumb tips)

75 g (2½ oz) grapes (cupped handful)

kcals 350, fat 8 g, saturated fat 2 g, cholesterol 43 mg, sodium 2193 mg, carbohydrate 49 g, fibre 6 g, protein 21 g, calcium 125 mg.

ABOUT SOUP

Soup is great for staving off hunger. Researchers at an American university found that chicken and rice soup was more filling than the same amount of chicken and rice with a glass of water. Why? Soup is satisfying because it brings out all the flavours of its ingredients. Also, soup may linger in your stomach, which will keep you feeling full.

Instead of	Try
Vegetable soup	Gazpacho (55 kcals)
(300 ml/10 fl oz, 110 kcals)	Mushroom (150 kcals)
	Spinach (150 kcals)
	Carrot and coriander (105 kcals)
	Lentil (250 kcals)
	Minestrone (135 kcals)
	Tomato (108 kcals)

Don't let lunch send you off course

Let's face it: food purveyors have our number. Super-size it! Two for the price of one! Twenty-five per cent extra free!

We're conditioned to look for a bargain, and more food for less money sounds about as good as it gets. 'For only a little bit more I can get large fries and a large cola with that double beefburger with bacon? Yes, please.'

But consider the numbers. A double beefburger with cheese and bacon provides a massive 600 kcals. Add on the large fries and get another 500 kcals. With a small drink – or what passes for small these days – you're up to about 1300 kcals. That's the basic *ChangeOne* calorie target for a whole day, all in one meal!

Of course, most slimmers know better than to order a double beefburger with cheese and bacon. But even healthy sounding lunch selections can hide a surprising number of calories. 'I always thought chicken was the healthiest choice,' one of our volunteers told us. Then she learned that at one leading restaurant chain, a single serving of crispy chicken with dips packs 550 kcals. An individual-size pizza? Throw on lots of high-fat toppings like sausage, salami or cheese and the kcals can exceed 800. The same is true of innocent-sounding veggie burgers and seemingly healthy salads smothered with high-fat dressings.

Lunch portions

These meal plans use both standard measurements and the *ChangeOne* portion-size guide. Here's what a standard serving looks like:

Type of food	Example	Amount	*ChangeOne* guide
One starch or grain	Potato	Medium	Tennis ball
	Bread roll	55 g (2 oz)	Tennis ball
	Rice, pasta	140 g (5 oz)	Tennis ball
One protein	Cheese, grated	25 g (1 oz)	Covers surface of palm
	Lean beefburger	55 g (2 oz)	1 cm (½ in) thick coaster
	Cooked ham	85 g (3 oz)	3 CDs
One fruit	Orange, apple	1	1 fist
	Berries, cut fruit	75 g (2½ oz)	Cupped handful
Vegetables		Unlimited	

You get the point? Unless you know what to select – and make sure that you can get it – you could find yourself having to choose between going hungry or going overboard on calories.

Check-in

Over the past week you began to take control of breakfast. If you weren't a breakfast eater before, you've become one. If you were already sitting down to the breakfast table, you've started helping yourself to healthier choices or more sensible portions. Don't fret if you missed a day or two. Don't worry if you ended up grabbing a Danish pastry one morning on the way into work. The important thing is not to fall into the trap of thinking you failed just because you had a mishap or two. What matters is that you're finding time to sit down first thing in the morning to a breakfast that starts your new healthy diet off on the right track.

If you're not quite there yet, consider taking another week to get breakfast under control. With the confidence that comes with making just one change for the better, you'll find it easier to move on to the next. If you feel happy with breakfast, you're ready to move on to lunch.

Making the change

This week, while you keep up the good work at breakfast, help yourself to your choice of the *ChangeOne* lunches pictured in this chapter. *ChangeOne* lunches contain about 350 kcals. That includes everything – food and drink. Compare that with the calories in most fast-food and pub meals and you'll see why sticking to the *ChangeOne* menu will speed your weight loss.

The meal plans you'll find here include lunches you can make at home, lunches you can pack, lunches you can order at a good sandwich shop that's willing to do it your way, and even a fast-food meal that will work for you. Mix and match them any way you like. If you prefer to have pretty much the same lunch every day, that's fine. If variety is the spice of your life, help yourself. What matters is sticking as closely as you can to the *ChangeOne* lunch meal plan every day this coming week.

As much as possible, decide in advance what and where you're going to eat. In one step you're in control. No more searching the vending machine for something, anything, that looks halfway healthy. No more raiding that bag of tortilla chips or devouring a chocolate bar because you're famished and it's the only edible item in your desk drawer.

Instead, consider some other options.

If you eat most of your lunches out: Make a list of the *ChangeOne* lunches that you'll be able to order at your favourite lunch spot or company cafeteria. Try to choose a

continued on page 45

Change One Fast Track

If you're anxious to speed your progress, choose one or two of the following Fast Track changes and you're likely to see pounds melt away faster:

Turn off the TV

At least three times this week, turn off the television and walk for half an hour when you would otherwise have sat in front of the TV. It doesn't take a genius to figure out that sitting around watching television is bad for anyone's waistline. Yet even researchers have been surprised by the link between TV viewing and tubbiness.

Women who watch three hours of television a day have an average body mass index (BMI) that is 1.8 points higher than those who watch just one hour a day, according to a recent study by University of Utah researchers. For a 5 ft 7 in woman, that's an extra 12 pounds. (To calculate your BMI, look at page 313.)

Hate to miss your favourite shows? Tape the ones you really want to see. By fast-forwarding through the advertisements you'll save at least eight minutes per half-hour show – extra minutes you can grab to do something active and keep off the couch.

Put down your fork

When you eat too fast, you deny your body the time it needs to signal that you're full. It takes about 20 minutes from the time you start eating for your stomach and brain to coordinate on these so-called satiety signals.

This week lay down your knife and fork between each bite. Take notice of what happens when you slow down. Savour what you're eating. And try another tactic: the minute you feel satisfied, get up from the table. Stop eating, even if there's still food on your plate.

Pour it on

This week carry a bottle of water with you and take a swig whenever you feel thirsty. That way you'll be less tempted to grab a sugary, calorie-filled drink. And drink one glass of water with lunch and dinner. When you include a glass of water with your meal, you get some calorie-free help on quenching your hunger along with your thirst.

Use the 50 per cent solution

Supper portions, like lunch, are often bigger than most of us want or need. And since supper is usually the biggest meal of the day, giant portions can really pile on the calories. This week downsize your main courses. Serve up half of what you normally would eat. After you're done take a few minutes to relax and savour the meal. If you're still hungry, help yourself to half of what's left over. Otherwise, get up from the table.

Create a diversion

Identify one time of the day when you're eating for no other reason than because that's when you typically eat. This would not be a regular mealtime, but perhaps a mid-morning coffee break, afternoon snack, or late-evening splurge.

Now instead of eating at that time, do something else – something that really appeals to you. Read the paper, take a brief stroll, pursue a hobby, call a friend – anything that gets you through that period. You may find that the reason you ate at that time was habit, not hunger. Develop a habit that doesn't involve food and you could cut more than 100 calories a day.

Chef's salad

Time-saver

Buy 115 g (4 oz) at a time of different wafer-thin cooked meats. Roll up each slice and cut across into quarters. When making your salad, top it with one piece each of three different meats.

Green salad topped with:

25 g (1 oz) roast turkey breast (1 CD)
25 g (1 oz) cooked ham (1 CD)
25 g (1 oz) cheese (1 CD)
2 tablespoons fat-free dressing (2 salad-dressing caps)
    or 2 teaspoons Italian dressing (2 thumb tips)

1 medium wholegrain roll (55 g/2 oz) (tennis ball)

85 g (3 oz) diced melon (cupped handful)

kcals 330, fat 13 g, saturated fat 6 g, cholesterol 62 mg, sodium 976 mg, carbohydrate 30 g, fibre 4 g, protein 26 g, calcium 240 mg.

TIPS FOR TOPPING YOUR SALAD

Combine any three of these to top your salad. Serving size for each is 25 g (1 oz) (the size of a CD, or as indicated), slightly less for cheese, unless otherwise noted.

- Turkey breast
- Chicken breast
- Lean roast beef
- Shredded chicken
- Cooked ham

- Canned tuna (in water)
- Gruyère cheese
- Cheddar cheese
- Edam cheese
- Grated Parmesan cheese
  (surface of your palm)

- Tofu cubes
  (1 thumb)
- Kidney or other beans,
  2 tablespoons (2 thumbs)
- Chopped nuts,
  1 tablespoon (1 thumb)

continued from page 42

place that will do it your way, including keeping portion sizes under control. When in doubt, check the serving sizes in this chapter for a rough idea of what a *ChangeOne* lunch should look like, and keep the handy visual equivalents in mind. Before you dig into lunch, make sure that what's on your plate matches up. At some lunch places, you may eat just half of what you're served. If possible, ask for a take-away container when giving your order, and enjoy the extra tomorrow. Think of it as two meals for the price of one. Now that's a bargain.

If you usually eat at home: Choose the meals you think you'll like the best from the *ChangeOne* lunch suggestions. Or each day this week, try a different one. You may find that something you wouldn't normally eat tastes great and really fills you up. Remember, there's little risk. If you feel ravenous by mid afternoon, you can have a snack and your usual supper later. Eventually you may want to stick to one or two particular meals (see 'Keep it simple', below). If you end up selecting a wide variety, consider writing each day's lunch menu on your calendar. When you begin to feel hungry as midday approaches, you'll know exactly what's coming.

If you plan to pack a lunch: Make up your shopping list and buy what you'll need at the beginning of the week. Don't forget lunch bags and storage containers. If your early mornings are a mad rush, do as much preparation as you can the night before – until you get in the swing of packing your lunch, it's easy to rush out the door empty-handed. Write 'Lunch?' on a Post-it and stick it on the refrigerator or front door to make sure you won't forget.

Keep it simple

Many people prefer not to have to decide every day what they're going to eat. They find it comforting to open up the lunch box to the same Cheddar and pickle sandwich with an apple and an oat and raisin biscuit. And talk about being in control: if you eat the same lunch every day, you never have to wonder about how many calories you're consuming.

Help!

'I don't have a refrigerator at work to store my packed lunch. Should I worry about food going off?'

No. The packable lunches on the *ChangeOne* menu will keep just fine for five hours in a coolish spot on a shelf or in a desk drawer. To be on the safe side, try a few simple preparation tips:

- Freeze a small plastic bottle of water or carton of fruit juice to use as a sandwich chiller, then as a drink.
- Use a refreezable ice pack.
- Buy an insulated lunch box.
- Peel eggshells only when you're ready to eat the hard-boiled eggs.

Some slimming experts even recommend the eating of monotonous meals. In one study volunteers who were offered a four-course meal consumed 44 per cent more calories than those offered just one course.

Still, not everyone wants to sit down to the same thing every day. And there's a virtue to variety. By trying out several *ChangeOne* lunch options, you'll find the ones that work best for you. All that really matters is arriving at a plan for lunch that you can stick with.

Behind the *ChangeOne* lunch menu

Some of the choices found on the *ChangeOne* lunch menu may surprise you. Like avocado slices. Peanut butter. Cheese. Nuts. None of these would make its way into a low-fat diet. Yet we've included them in *ChangeOne* for a good reason. The latest evidence shows that you don't have to cut way back on fat to lose weight. New data shows that most people shed weight more successfully on diets containing moderate amounts of fat than they do on very low-fat regimens.

Surprised? No wonder. For years nutritionists have told us to cut back on fat. All fat. Too much fat on the menu makes people fat, they said. Gram for gram, fat contains twice as many calories as protein or carbohydrates. And just as bad, it puts our hearts and arteries at risk by increasing cholesterol. Or so they said.

And we listened. Over the past three decades, the total number of calories from fat in the average diet has fallen considerably and is still falling.

But now, in a stunning reversal, the experts are offering very different advice. Some fats are actually good for our hearts, they say. What's more, slashing fat from your diet, rather than helping you to lose weight, may actually make it harder to maintain a healthy weight. Very low-fat diets could even be unhealthy.

Good fat, bad fat

The truth is, experts have long known that there are various kinds of fat. The two main categories are saturated fat and unsaturated fat. Saturated fat comes mainly from animals,

continued on page 49

Ready for lunch?

Thinking over the food choices you made last week will help you to find the best ways to master the midday meal this week. Complete these nine questions by circling the number to the right of the appropriate answer.

1. **Last week how often did you know in the morning what you'd have for lunch?**

Never	1
A few days	2
Most days	3
Every day	4

2. **How often did you know at least where you would have lunch?**

Never	1
A few days	2
Most days	3
Every day	4

3. **How often did you grab whatever happened to be handy?**

Most days	1
Several days	2
Rarely or never	3

4. **Which phrase best describes the choices available to you at lunch?**

Very little choice	1
Some choice – same three or four things	2
Ample choice – varied and interesting	3

5. **How would you rate your typical lunch?**

Not very healthy	1
Healthy enough	2
Very healthy	3

6. **How many servings of vegetables did you typically eat at lunch? (Chips don't count.)**

None	1
1	2
2 or more	3

7. **What was your usual choice for a sandwich bread?**

White or French roll	1
Wholemeal, rye or other dark brown bread	2
Multi-grain or other wholegrain bread	3

8. **How often did you eat lunch at home this past week or bring lunch to work?**

Never	1
1-2 times	2
3-4 times	3
5-7 times	4

9. **What was your usual drink at lunch?**

Regular soft drink	1
Sweetened fruit drink	2
Milk	3
Sugar-free soft drink or water	3

Turn to next page to total your score.

Quiz score

Add up the numbers you've circled in the right-hand column.

A score of 24–30: You're already well on your way to eating a good lunch.

A score of 19–23: A few simple strategies could help to make the switch to a *ChangeOne* lunch easier.

A score of 9–18: Okay, you've got serious work to do. By improving your lunches, you can take a giant step towards trimming calories and slimming your waist-line. Put ticks beside questions that scored a 1 or 2. Then look for the corresponding answers in the key below for tips that will help you this coming week.

1, 2, 3. If you have no idea where you'll have lunch – or what you'll choose – you're at risk of eating whatever's handy when lunch time rolls around. That could spell trouble for your diet. On pages 42 and 45 you'll find tips on how to master lunch by planning ahead.

Of course not all of us always know ahead of time where we'll eat lunch. If that sounds like you, then it's time to keep a very close watch on portion sizes, wherever the lunch hour finds you.

4. Not much choice available? Your best option may be to bring lunch with you. You'll find several tasty packable lunches in the *ChangeOne* menus. If you're pressed for time in the morning, put your lunch together the night before.

5. Is your lunch falling short on good nutrition? Most of what's available at fast-food restaurants and other lunch cafés is high in fat and sugar and low in fibre and nutrients. If your typical lunch rarely sees a green vegetable, it needs work. If there's a big juicy cheeseburger on your plate – well, you already know there's work to do. If the lunch venues available don't offer much choice, your best bet is to pack your lunch.

6. What, no vegetables? You're missing out on one of the best healthy slimming foods around. Follow the *ChangeOne* menu this week and you'll get at least one serving at lunch, usually two.

7. White bread? You'll get more nutrients – and feel fuller for longer – when you eat breads that are made from wholemeal or rye flour. You'll get even more fibre, as well as healthful vitamins and minerals, from breads that contain whole grains like oats.

8. Not the lunch box type? Don't dismiss the idea out of hand. This week give it a try for a day or two. There's no better way to control exactly what and how much you eat. Many people find that packing a lunch relieves them of the pressure of having to choose the food they'll have when they're hungry.

9. Sugary soft drinks pack a load of calories (about 130 kcals in a 330 ml can). Some experts place much of the blame for the country's growing weight problems on the popularity of sugary drinks.

That's an awful lot of calories from foods that don't supply much else in the way of nutrition. Switch to a sugar-free drink or have a glass of still or sparkling water, and you'll shave 130 kcals from your diet, just like that. A small glass of fruit juice will provide vitamin C, which will facilitate the absorption of iron from your meal. For a longer drink, why not mix fruit juice and sparkling water?

Skimmed or semi-skimmed milk, a great source of calcium, is another smart beverage choice. Yes, milk contains calories. But it's also loaded with protein and calcium, which is essential for healthy bones. And, as you discovered last week, there's new evidence that it also helps to speed weight loss by encouraging your body to burn more fat.

continued from page 46

either in the form of meat or the fat in cheese, milk and other dairy foods. Unsaturated fat comes mainly from plants and fish. One of the biggest sources in our diets is vegetable oils such as corn, sunflower, olive and groundnut.

The culprit, when it comes to heart disease, is saturated fat. Because of its chemical makeup, saturated fat causes the body to churn out extra artery-clogging LDL cholesterol. The saturated fat in cheese, butter and other dairy products has the strongest effect on LDL. The form in meat isn't quite as dangerous when it comes to boosting LDL levels.

Unsaturated fat, in contrast, has been shown to lower LDL. It can also raise HDL cholesterol, the friendly form that removes dangerous cholesterol from the body. The result: getting plenty of unsaturated fat protects your arteries from hardening. Global studies bear it out: the less saturated fat and more unsat-urated fat people eat, the lower their risk of heart disease.

So why did so many nutritionists recommend cutting back on all fat? Because some of them thought the good fat/bad fat message was too complicated for people to understand. By telling people to cut back on all fat, the thinking went, saturated fat levels would fall. And with the country's waistline expanding, cutting back on total fat didn't seem like such a bad idea.

> Plan on eating half of your restaurant lunch and taking home the rest.

Carbohydrates aren't so simple

Now it does. When we dutifully cut back on fat, we replaced it largely with carbohydrates, mostly the simple kind found in chips, white bread, biscuits and sugar. That's bad news for two reasons. First, it turns out that a high-carbohydrate, low-fat diet of this kind increases levels of triglycerides, a form of fat in the blood. Higher triglyceride levels are strongly linked to a greater danger of heart disease.

Second, a diet low in fat and high in simple carbohydrates may actually make it harder, rather than easier, to lose weight. Simple carbohydrates, because they are so easy for the body to digest, send blood sugar levels spiking up. The surge in blood sugar triggers a surge in insulin from the pancreas. That's normal. One of insulin's jobs is to move blood sugar into muscles, where it provides fuel for movement. But another of its roles is to prompt the body

Friendly fast food

1 regular (55 g/2 oz) hamburger (1 cm/½ in thick coaster) on a bun with lettuce, tomato, ketchup or mustard, pickle

1 green salad topped with chopped vegetables (tomato, red cabbage, green pepper) (unlimited)

2 tablespoons fat-free dressing (2 salad-dressing caps)

kcals 325, fat 13 g, saturated fat 6 g, cholesterol 53 mg, sodium 720 mg, carbohydrate 40 g, fibre 0.5 g, protein 13 g, calcium 95 mg.

TIPS FOR ORDERING

Even favourite fast-food chains offer some lower-calorie choices. Ask them where they've posted their nutrition information, and check out these possibilities:

Burger King – Hamburger

McDonald's – Hamburger, cheeseburger, any salad (fat-free dressing)

Wimpy – Hamburger, cheeseburger, bacon in a bun, chicken wrap

Pizza Hut – 1 slice of a 30 cm (12 in) Hawaiian, ham and mushroom, or margherita pizza

to store excess energy as fat. That's normal too. But if blood sugar and insulin levels continually surge and plummet, it can spell trouble. And that's what seems to happen when you eat a lot of simple, easy-to-digest carbohydrates. Blood sugar soars and then plummets. Slumping blood sugar causes hunger pangs. Naturally, we reach for something to eat. If that something is another simple carbohydrate, up go blood sugar levels. Researchers are beginning to think that the resulting roller-coaster makes people hungry more often during the day, and that the surges of insulin prime the body to store fat.

There's still much left unresolved about carbohydrates, the role of insulin and the effect of blood sugar levels. But one thing is clear: cutting back on fat and filling up with simple carbohydrates like low-fat biscuits and cakes hasn't made us thinner. We're fatter than ever. And evidence is accumulating that a diet with moderate amounts of fat may make it easier to shed excess weight.

Eat fat, get slim

Consider the surprising results of an experiment conducted at Brigham and Women's Hospital in Boston, USA. Thirty overweight people followed a low-fat diet. Another group of 31 people followed a diet with a moderate amount of fat – very much like the *ChangeOne* diet. Six months later volunteers in both groups had lost the same amount of weight. But after 18 months a tell-tale difference surfaced. By then, only 20 per cent of the people in the low-fat group were still on their diet, compared with 54 per cent of those in the moderate-fat group. What's more, the moderate-fat slimmers, as a group, had lost more body fat and reduced their waistlines more than the low-fat dieters.

continued on page 54

Help!

'Last week I was so hungry by the middle of the morning that I felt almost light-headed. Is that normal?'

Well, the light-headed part is. Hunger can make you feel woozy. It can also make you feel distracted or grumpy. If you get that hungry, however – at any time of the day – it's time to eat something. If you're especially heavy or active, you may need more calories. Your body is burning more to keep you moving.

We're not talking about devouring jam doughnuts. In a reduced-calorie diet like *ChangeOne*, it's important to make every calorie count for nourishment. Choose snacks that do what they're supposed to do: take the edge off hunger. Next week we'll take a closer look at snacks. For now, consider helping yourself to one of the following if hunger threatens:

- A piece of fruit
- A handful of nuts (about 25 g/1 oz)
- All the celery or carrot sticks you like
- A big glass of tomato or vegetable juice
- A mug of clear chicken or miso soup
- A glass of skimmed or semi-skimmed milk, or a small pot of low-fat yogurt

Don't be afraid to reach for a snack. One recent survey found that snacking wasn't the downfall of most failed slimmers; what got most into trouble was eating too much at one of the three big meals of the day. Tame your hunger and you'll stay in control.

Build a better sandwich

A deli can be a dieter's best friend, believe it or not. The options are endless, and if you're vigilant, you can craft a satisfying and sensible sandwich.

But whether you're ordering over the counter or making your own, keep an eye on what's in even the supposed lightweight choice – turkey, tuna, even meatless options. You can easily overstuff a sandwich with 140–225 g (5–8 oz) of meat – twice as much as it's smart to swallow in a meal – or smothered with mayonnaise (as much as 700 kcals worth in a tuna sandwich).

What you get, the experts point out, can be a day's worth of calories between two slices of bread. Not only will that blow your diet, it will also slow down your progress.

What you want is what you see here. Check out these *ChangeOne* tips for building a better sandwich.

Bread
- Wholegrain roll (tennis ball)
- Rye bread, 2 slices
- Pumpernickel bread, 2 slices
- Flour tortilla (wrap), medium (dessert plate)
- French, ciabatta or sourdough bread (2 mobile phones)
- Soft finger roll, 7.5 cm (3 in) (length of longest finger)

Meats or alternatives
- Cooked ham, 55 g (2 oz) (2 CDs)
- Tuna salad (made with reduced-fat mayonnaise), 85 g (3 oz) (2 golf balls)
- Lean roast beef, 55 g (2 oz) (2 CDs)
- Corned beef, 35 g (1¼ oz) (2 CDs)

Cheese or alternatives
- Reduced-fat Cheddar, 25 g (1 oz) (credit card)
- Additional meat or tuna, 25 g (1 oz) (CD or table tennis ball)
- 2 tablespoons peanut butter (2 thumbs)
- 2 tablespoons hummus (2 thumbs)

THE PERFECT DELI SANDWICH

Turkey with Gruyère cheese:

2 slices white or wholemeal bread
55 g (2 oz) roast turkey breast (2 CDs)
20 g (³/₄ oz) Gruyère cheese (credit card)
Sliced tomato, mustard

55 g (2 oz) shredded lettuce, carrot, cabbage, red onion (cupped handful)

85 g (3 oz) melon salad (cupped handful)

kcals 340, fat 10 g, saturated fat 5 g, cholesterol 63 mg, sodium 570 mg, carbohydrate 35 g, fibre 3 g, protein 28 g, calcium 214 mg.

Deli delights

You can enjoy your deli favourites if you keep to a modest 55 g (2 oz) of filling (the equivalent of a couple of CDs). That said, here are popular cooked, cured and processed meats ranked from best to 'wurst' based on calories and artery-clogging fat. There's no harm in enjoying them once in a while, but keep in mind that they're all higher in calories than leaner fillings like smoked chicken and turkey breast.

- Parma ham (all fat removed)
- Corned beef
- Cooked beef/pork
- Salami
- Liver sausage

- Pastrami
- Chorizo
- Salt beef
- Bresaola
- Garlic sausage

Veggies
- Lettuce and tomato
- Grilled vegetables (unlimited)
- Spinach leaves (unlimited)
- Rocket or watercress (unlimited)
- Thinly sliced apple, 3 slices
- ¼ avocado, sliced

Dressings
- Dijon or English mustard (unlimited)
- Reduced-fat mayonnaise, 1 tablespoon (thumb)
- Honey mustard, 2 teaspoons (2 thumb tips)
- Fat-free salad dressing, (2 salad dressing caps)

continued from page 51

Why? One reason, researchers say, is that a diet with moderate amounts of fat is simply more satisfying than a harsh low-fat regimen. It's a healthy diet people can live with. And that's the only kind of diet that really works over the long term. Another reason may be that people eating moderate amounts of fat are less likely to overdo simple carbohydrates, and keep their hunger in check more easily.

The new advice is the same whether you hope to protect your heart or shed excess weight. Replace saturated fat with unsaturated fat wherever you can – by switching from butter to olive oil, for instance, and by eating less meat and more fish. (Fish is abundant in polyunsaturated fats, particularly a form that contains omega-3 fatty acids, which have been shown to protect the heart.) Keep portion sizes under control so you don't overdo calories. And steer your diet away from simple carbohydrates like sugar and white bread and towards more complex carbohydrates like those in wholegrain breads and cereals. These recommendations are the basis of the *ChangeOne* menu because they are the surest strategy for slimming down and keeping weight off.

The perfect slimming food

Something else you'll notice about the *ChangeOne* lunch menu: it features plenty of vegetables. Every meal includes at least one serving, often two. No other food fills you up on fewer calories while delivering more nutrients. Vegetables are rich not only in fibre but also in disease-fighting antioxidants and phyto-chemicals. They're mostly complex carbohydrates, the kind that keep blood sugar levels from soaring too fast and then plummeting too quickly. Vegetables are so good in so many ways that they're free on *ChangeOne* – with the exception of potatoes, which are high in simple carbohydrates.

And as any chef will tell you, nothing brightens up a plate like dark leafy greens, red or yellow peppers, a luscious ripe tomato or rich orange carrot slices. On the *ChangeOne* lunch

continued on page 57

A BIT ON THE SIDE

Faced with a choice among side salads, choose one of these – and keep in mind that pickles are freebies.

- Green salad topped with chopped veggies (tomato, cucumber, peppers, broccoli, etc) (unlimited), 2 table-spoons sliced olives, a couple of shakes of olive oil, and vinegar
- 'Clear' coleslaw made with vinegar and a touch of sugar rather than mayonnaise (cupped handful)
- Three-bean salad with low-fat dressing (cupped handful)
- Italian-style pickled vegetables (unlimited)
- Grilled vegetables (if not too oily) (unlimited)
- Sliced or diced tomato (unlimited)

Tex-Mex wrap

1 flour tortilla (18–20 cm/7–8 in), filled with:

55 g (2 oz) grilled chicken (half your palm)
1 tablespoon canned refried beans or kidney beans (1 thumb)
1 tablespoon guacamole (1 thumb)
1 tablespoon grated cheese (1 thumb)
Salsa (unlimited)
Shredded lettuce and diced tomato (unlimited)

1 orange

To prepare the wrap:
Place chicken, beans and cheese on tortilla. Microwave for 30 seconds or until the filling is warm. Add the remaining ingredients, roll up and eat.

kcals 370, fat 8 g, saturated fat 3 g, cholesterol 55 mg, sodium 392 mg, carbohydrate 53 g, fibre 5 g, protein 23 g, calcium 212 mg.

Time-saver
Buy cheese that is already grated, possibly seasoned, and sold in a resealable plastic bag.

ABOUT TORTILLAS

Choose a small or medium-sized tortilla to keep calories in check. A large flour tortilla contains as many calories as four slices of bread.

Change One First Person

In the groove

'It's become a joke in our house,' says Sue Licher, a university administrator. 'Every day my husband fixes the same sandwich. Turkey on wholemeal bread. An apple. Carrot sticks. Reduced-fat crisps. Every day.

'I try to add a little variety myself. A different sandwich. A salad. A yogurt. For both of us, packing a lunch has made a big difference. Before that, we ate whatever happened to be around at work.'

Mark Licher had never tried to lose weight before starting *ChangeOne*. 'When we went shopping for the breakfast week, I remember saying in jest, "My life as I knew it is over". All I could think of were the foods I used to eat that weren't on the menu.

'But it's funny the way it works. I didn't eat breakfast before we started *ChangeOne*, except a croissant sometimes. Now I eat melon and a piece of toast, and I'm not tempted to eat the biscuits people bring into the office. I'm just not hungry for them. And now that I'm packing a lunch, I'm fine through the afternoon. Sure, it's the same lunch every day. But the truth is, I was always eating exactly the same lunch every day before I started *ChangeOne*. It just happened to be a fast-food cheeseburger with fries. I guess I like the routine. My lunch now is a lot healthier than it was before. And I look forward to it a whole lot more than I used to.'

What his wife Sue likes best is feeling in control. 'Breakfast and lunch are the easiest for me. It's easy to get into a routine during the weekdays. Since both of us have our work routines, fitting *ChangeOne* in was no problem. And once you've got the first two meals of the day under control, the rest of the day begins to feel manageable.'

Five weeks into the programme, Sue has lost 7 kg (15 lb). Mark 5 kg (11 lb). He says, 'I'm really in the groove now. It's strange to say, but I actually find myself thinking about and enjoying food much more than I did before we started. And I'm still losing weight!'

continued from page 54
menu, you'll find many clever ways to add a serving or two of vegetables to your sandwiches and soups to make them more filling and more flavourful, without piling on calories.

Changes ahead: snacks

While you're settling on your *ChangeOne* meals for breakfast and lunch, be aware of times during the day when you have a snack attack – and what you typically do about it. Don't feel that you have to change your snacks just yet. But be aware of how you feel, the choices you've given yourself, and what you usually do to satisfy your cravings. If you have time, keep track of all the snacks you eat, and about how much of each you eat. In the next chapter we'll take a closer look at hunger and the best way to satisfy it.

More lunch choices

Can't find something you like from the lunches suggested in this chapter? Starting on page 259, you'll find more quick and delicious *ChangeOne* lunch ideas. Here's a sampler:

Hearty split pea soup
page 260

Cream of asparagus soup
page 261

Grilled turkey caesar salad
page 263

Vegetable chilli page 265

Roast vegetable wraps with chive sauce page 266

Russian salad page 267

WEEK **3**

Snacks

An entire chapter on snacks? In a book about losing weight? Are we serious? Of course we are.

Over the next few days, you'll learn how to use two snacks a day to take the edge off hunger and make losing weight *easier*.

We think you'll be surprised at what you learn. In fact, one of the dieters in our *ChangeOne* pilot group asked to repeat the snacks week. 'It wasn't until I filled in a food diary that I realised how often I snacked during the day', he explained. 'And it wasn't until we tackled snacks that I saw how often I ate something when I wasn't even all that hungry.' After two weeks of focusing on snacks, he really began to drop the weight.

You may too. For years nutritionists – and our mothers – told us not to eat between meals. Snacks seemed like they were the enemy. But now a new way of thinking about snacks has emerged. The two snacks a day recommended in *ChangeOne* will help you to stay on track. Eating something between meals, many experts say, can be one of a dieter's smartest strategies.

58

Nuts & seeds

Nuts and seeds are filled with proteins and healthy fats, which makes them nutritious but dense in calories. They are also filling, so if you eat them slowly, it won't take many to reduce hunger. Here is a selection to eat to equal a 100-kcal snack (the size that *ChangeOne* recommends).

- **Peanuts** in shells, 10 (handful)
- **Pistachios**, in shells, 30 (handful)
- **Sunflower seeds**, in shells, 25 g (1 oz) (palmful)
- **Almonds**, 16 to 20 (palmful)
- **Pumpkin seeds**, in shells (handful)
- **Peanut butter**, 1 tablespoon (thumb)

HEALTH TIP

Try to buy your nuts with their shell still on. Opening them takes time, so you're less likely to eat too many. And for many people, the cracking, splitting, picking and sorting are as satisfying as eating the nuts themselves.

ABOUT PEANUTS

Peanuts – actually a legume rather than a true nut – and peanut butter have become diet darlings of late. At Harvard University, a study showed that slimmers eating peanuts and peanut butter found it easier to stick to their diets. More good news: they're filling, they keep hunger at bay and they may also be good for your heart.

From top: pistachios, pumpkin seeds, peanuts, almonds (left), and sunflower seeds.

Savoury surprises

Break out of snacking boredom with change-of-pace foods like these. All provide 100 kcals or less.

- **Soup:** minestrone, vegetable, tomato, 250 ml (8 fl oz) (takeaway coffee cup)
- **V-8 juice,** 250 ml (8 fl oz) or more (drinking glass)
- **Wholemeal toast,** 1 small slice, spread sparingly with butter and Marmite
- **Reduced-fat, mature Cheddar cheese,** 40 g (1½ oz) (small matchbox)
- **Peanut butter,** 1 tablespoon (thumb), on a normal-size rice cake

Clockwise from top left: wholemeal toast with Marmite, reduced fat Cheddar cheese, crudités, minestrone soup and muffin pizza.

- **Hard-boiled egg**
- **Rye crispbread,** spread with 2 table-spoons reduced-fat hummus
- **Muffin pizza:** half English muffin, topped with 1 tablespoon pasta sauce and 2 tablespoons grated cheese, then grilled until cheese bubbles
- **Breadsticks,** 3, with 3 tablespoons tomato salsa
- **Oatcake,** spread with 30 g (1¼ oz) low-fat cottage cheese, plain or flavoured
- **Crudités** (unlimited), with 3 tablespoons tsatsiki or another yogurt-based dip

Make snacks work for you

When we asked the *ChangeOne* volunteers to describe the single biggest fear they faced in dieting, many of them listed 'hunger'. That's not surprising. Dieters often think they have to resist hunger in order to lose weight. This week, we want you to pay close attention to hunger cues. And instead of resisting them, we want you to feed them – with a healthy snack. Here's why.

Hunger is an extremely powerful force. Getting enough fuel for our bodies is essential to survival. It is a matter of life and death, literally, so the body has a variety of internal signals that alert it when its energy stores are dipping low. Some come from the stomach. Some originate in the brain.

The longer we go without eating, the more powerful those signals become. It doesn't take long before they're so urgent that almost all we can think about is food. As hunger intensifies, will-power weakens. If you get hungry enough, you'll reach for anything.

That's where smart snacking comes in. Help yourself to something sensible when you feel hungry, and you'll help to ensure that hunger pangs don't rise up and destroy your determination to lose weight.

Concerned that snacking will make it harder to lose weight? Don't worry. Surprisingly, several large studies have found no link at all between the number of snacks people eat and how much they weigh. Even people who snack before bedtime – once considered a big diet taboo – don't seem to be any more likely to be overweight than people who don't.

Eating more often than just three times a day might even have advantages over the three-meals-a-day pattern when it comes to health. In a study at St Michael's Hospital at the University of Toronto, researchers tested two nutritionally identical diets. One group of volunteers ate their allotted food in three main meals. The others ate the same food in the same amounts

Check-in

Last week you added lunch to your *ChangeOne* menu. If you went off the plan for a day or two, don't worry. Change takes time. People sometimes take two steps forward and one step back. That's no reason to get discouraged. Take a deep breath, remind yourself of what matters most to you, then resolve to take two more steps forward starting tomorrow. This is an approach to eating that will last your entire life, so messing up a day or two is no big deal over the long run. If you feel frustrated because you don't have breakfast and lunch under control yet, consider taking another week to master them before moving on.

but divided it into 17 snacks. Compared to the three-meals-a-day group, the snackers actually saw their cholesterol levels drop. The experts concluded that eating smaller meals more frequently kept blood sugar and insulin levels down, which in turn reduced the body's output of cholesterol. That's good, of course, and for anyone who wants to lose weight those results hint at even more good news: holding blood sugar and insulin levels steady can also keep hunger in check.

Naturally, 17 snacks a day might be overdoing it a little. But one or two during the day – that's a proven key to dieting success. Just ask the successful slimmers who are part of the American National Weight Control Registry. A majority report that they eat five times a day: three small main meals and two snacks.

This week, help yourself to a snack when you feel hungry. But before you reach for it, we're going to ask you to do one simple thing: make sure you're really hungry.

How we snack

Almost everyone has at least one snack a day. Half of the people in a survey conducted by Columbia University in New York snacked two to four times a day. Afternoons were their favourite snack time, when they were most likely to reach for something salty. The next favourite was before bedtime, when many people's taste buds yearn for something sweet, like chocolate or ice cream.

Learn to spot hunger cues

In this chapter, we've grouped snacks and desserts together. One of our reasons is that the same foods often serve either function – frozen yogurt, fruit, a piece of chocolate, a biscuit – depending on when we eat them. Another is that most of us think of snacks and desserts as optional foods, a treat that's not part of our basic diet. On *ChangeOne* you can help yourself to sensible portions of snacks and desserts. All we ask is that you reach for them to satisfy genuine hunger.

Isn't that the reason most of us eat in the first place? Surprisingly, the answer is no. Weight loss experts say we typically eat for reasons that have nothing to do with genuine physical hunger. We take a box of buttered popcorn or a packet of chocolate-covered raisins to our seat in the cinema simply because that's what we've always done. We eat because someone just brought a birthday cake into the office, and who can resist? Often we take up our knives and forks simply because it's meal time. Or because everyone else is eating.

continued on page 66

Change One Fast Track

To speed your progress, choose one or two of the following optional Fast Track changes this week.

Downsize your dishes

Portion sizes aren't the only things that have grown bigger in recent years. So have the plates and bowls on which they're served. If you have a tendency to pile your plate high and finish it all, try switching to smaller dishes.

Use a side plate instead of a dinner plate for your main dish. Ignore the giant pasta bowls and use a smaller cereal bowl to serve spaghetti. If the plates you already have won't do, buy an inexpensive set of 'downsized' plates and bowls for everyday use. Another clever way to make a little less food seem like more: use a dessert fork instead of a regular fork and a teaspoon for your soup and cereal.

Slim your sips

Plenty of people look to a cola for a pick-me-up in the mid-afternoon. If you're still reaching for soft drinks or other beverages sweetened with sugar, you're drinking a lot of calories that aren't doing much to satisfy hunger.

Studies show that these drinks slip down without triggering satiety signals. If you drink a 330 g can of cola you'll consume 130 kcals or more before you know it. This week, switch to sugar-free versions of your favourite drinks. Or try something new and add a squeeze of lemon or lime juice to a glass of sparkling water.

Go for the gold

If you're a walker, increase your pace this week. On Day One, walk at your normal pace and keep track of how long it takes you to do your normal circuit. On Day Two, try shaving a minute off your time. Be aware of how you feel. A good brisk walk should leave you feeling winded but not gasping for air.

The quicker your pace, the more calories you burn each minute. An 82 kg (180 lb) person burns 4.7 kcals per minute walking at a leisurely 20-minute-mile pace (three miles an hour). Speeding up to a 15-minute mile (four miles an hour, about as fast as most people can walk comfortably) increases the number of calories burned to 7.2 per minute. You'll also increase your fitness level, which will translate into more stamina and energy.

If you swim, jog, bicycle, exercise at a gym or do another kind of activity, nudge your workout a bit this week by putting in a little more time or pushing the intensity a little harder.

Skip the butter

Accustomed to smothering bread or rolls with butter? One small knob of butter – 8 mm x 2.5 cm ($\frac{1}{3}$ x 1 in) – contains a massive 36 kcals and 4 g of fat, most of it saturated. If you smear a lot of butter on bread, you can easily total 120 or more kcals on butter alone.

This week, enjoy the unadulterated flavour of bread without all those extra fat-laden calories. Choose wholegrain varieties of bread and rolls. The extra fibre they contain will slow digestion and make you feel fuller, and you'll get so much extra flavour that you may not even miss that butter. Or at least not terribly.

Salty snacks

Do you have a craving for crisps?
Then go ahead and have some – just
not too many. The following lists show
you gram weights and/or quantities of
each snack food that equal 100 kcals
or less.

Crisps

- **Crisps**, 20 g (cupped handful)
- **Reduced-fat crisps**, 22 g (cupped handful)
- **Vegetable crisps**, 21 g (cupped handful)
- **Thick-cut crisps (such as Pringles)**, about 10 (18 g)
- **Reduced-fat Pringles**, about 15 (22 g)
- **Tortilla chips**, about 12 (22 g)
- **Prawn crackers**, about 32 (30 g)
- **Bagel chips**, about 8 (20 g)

Savoury biscuits

- **Rye crispbread (such as Ryvita)**, 3
- **Ritz**, 6
- **Tuc**, 4
- **Rice cakes, regular thick**, 3
- **Rice cakes, mini**, about 16 (25 g)
- **Oatcakes**, 2
- **Breadsticks**, 4
- **Poppadoms, mini**, 26 g (2 cupped handfuls)
- **Crisp cracked wheat toasts**, 2½
- **Pretzels**, 26 g (about 1 handful)

Popcorn

- **Popcorn, popped in a pot** (about 3 handfuls)
- **Microwave popcorn, butter flavour** (about 1 handful)

TIPS FOR CHOOSING SAVOURY BISCUITS

Looking for great taste and plenty of benefits
from fibre? Try Scandinavian crispbreads.
They're made with rye, which is the most
filling cereal grain, and they contain very
little fat. Another low-fat option is Middle
Eastern breads like lavosh, made from whole
wheat. Enjoy both of these plain or topped
with low-fat hummus, roasted pepper dip,
peanut butter or reduced-fat soft cheese.

Clockwise from far left:
Reduced-fat crisps, mini poppadoms, microwave butter popcorn, reduced fat Pringles, vegetable crisps, Ritz crackers, regular thick rice cakes, tortilla chips and prawn crackers (centre)

BAKED OR FRIED?

Many brands of savoury biscuits and crisps boast that they're 'baked, not fried'. The implication, of course, is fewer calories. But the difference isn't always that great. To achieve the flavour and texture, manufacturers still have to use plenty of fat, which means calories mount up quickly. So don't be fooled by the claim, and instead look for brands that supply at least 1 g of fibre and less than 3 g fat per serving.

SPICING UP POPCORN

First, put it into a large, covered pan, adding a couple of tablespoons of vegetable oil to help to heat up the kernels and prevent them from burning. Most of the oil stays behind in the pan, but enough gets onto the kernels to help salt and other seasonings to stick. Next, sprinkle lightly with salt, if liked, and your choice of seasonings. Try freshly ground black pepper, mild chilli powder, herbes de Provence or Italian seasoning herbs, or a sprinkling of freshly grated Parmesan cheese.
Or create your own flavouring combinations with spices and dried herbs. One *ChangeOne* fan likes a light sprinkling of tamari (soy) sauce.

continued from page 62

The experts call these reasons for eating, environmental cues. Something in our surroundings triggers the urge to eat. You may not be hungry in the sense that your body is running short of fuel. In fact, you may have just finished a big, filling meal. But the sight or smell or memory of past occasions prompts the urge to eat and you help yourself, often without thinking.

Emotional eating

Environmental cues aren't the only reasons we eat when we're not really hungry. Many of us eat for emotional reasons, too. After all, food can be comforting. It's part of being sociable. Getting together over a meal with friends or family can be a pleasant way to relax and enjoy each other's company after a long and busy day. And of course, food simply tastes good.

The pleasure we get from food has a biochemical basis, researchers say. When we eat something delicious, the experience triggers the release of endorphins in the brain, the same 'feel-good' chemicals that have been associated with 'jogger's high'. Certain foods may have their own mood-enhancing effects. Carbohydrates are thought to increase the absorption of an amino acid called tryptophan, which in turn boosts levels of serotonin, another biochemical associated with mental well-being.

Food provides comfort, calm and consolation. Unfortunately, none of these has anything to do with nutrition.

There are other reasons why eating is linked to emotions. If your parents comforted you or rewarded you with food, for instance, you may tend to reach for something to eat when you're feeling low or want to give yourself a reward for a job well done. If you get into the habit of eating something when you're feeling bored, you'll find yourself feeling hungry every time boredom strikes.

The same can be true for feeling lonely. 'I'd get home from work at the end of a long day, which was a hard time for me after being divorced', one *ChangeOne* volunteer recalled. 'I'd have supper. And then, maybe because I was feeling lonely, I'd just go on eating and eating. Sweets. Biscuits. I wasn't hungry. Somehow it just seemed to make me feel better. Recognising that pattern made a big difference for me.'

The problem with environmental and emotional eating is obvious. If you eat when you're not genuinely hungry, you'll

The hungry me

Tick only the boxes with the statements that apply to you. Tell yourself the truth; nobody but you needs to see your answers. Then, add up your score.

○ When I go to the cinema, I almost always get popcorn, sweets or some other treat.

☐ When I'm very busy, I sometimes don't even notice that I'm hungry.

◇ On stressful days, I often find it relaxing to eat something.

◇ If I'm bored and there's food around, I'll eat it.

☐ It's no big deal for me to say no to treats if I'm not really hungry.

◇ There are certain foods I really crave, like chocolate or salty snacks.

☐ I like the feeling of being really hungry when I sit down to a meal.

○ I have a tendency to eat everything on my plate even if I'm not really that hungry.

◇ If I'm feeling a little down or blue, eating something can really help.

○ If there's a plateful of biscuits or crisps in front of me, I won't be able to resist taking some.

○ I have to be careful about having junk food around the house. If it's there, I'll eat it.

☐ My way of dealing with stress is to get up and do something.

☐ As long as I know I'll be sitting down to a meal soon, I can deal with feeling hungry.

○ Supper just doesn't seem to be supper without a pudding.

◇ I definitely don't like the feeling of being hungry.

Turn to next page to add up your score.

almost certainly consume more calories than your body needs. There are healthier ways than overeating to deal with stress, boredom or loneliness. Simply distracting yourself by doing something else you enjoy – listening to music, phoning a friend, reading a book, watching a film, going for a walk, or doing a crossword puzzle – often works. How do you know if environmental or emotional cues are controlling when and how much you eat? The first step is paying attention to what genuine hunger feels like.

Last week, you began to be more aware of times during the day when you felt hungry between meals – and what you did about it. Using what you learned then, take 'The hungry me' quiz on this page.

Quiz score

Add up the number of boxes you ticked according to colour.

☐ green _____
◯ red _____
◇ yellow _____

What your score means

☐ If you ticked mostly green boxes, at least you're not snacking because you're bored or stressed. This week, choose your snacks from among the recommended *ChangeOne* snacks and you'll keep calories under control.

◯ If you ticked mostly red boxes, you tend to be an 'on cue' snacker. You reach for a snack not necessarily because you're hungry but because of cues in the environment around you. Recognising those cues – and asking yourself if you're really hungry –

could help you to avoid taking in calories you don't really want.

◇ If most of the boxes you ticked are yellow, you tend to be an 'emotional' snacker. You have the urge to eat something when you're feeling anxious, or sad or lonely, or under stress. Many people do. Recognising what real hunger feels like – and finding ways other than eating to deal with your emotions – will help you to control calories and also eat more healthfully.

If your score was divided evenly among greens, reds and yellows, you're half way to becoming a smart snacker. The tips in this chapter will guide you the rest of the way there.

Knowing when you're genuinely hungry

One day early this week, try a simple experiment. If you typically have either a mid-morning or mid-afternoon snack, skip it. Delay the next meal to about an hour later than usual. Then pay attention to how you feel. After you've gone four or five hours without eating anything, your body will begin to send out physical hunger cues. Some of these come from a part of the brain called the hypothalamus. When blood sugar levels fall, the hypothalamus senses an impending energy crisis and begins to issue 'feed me' orders by way of the central nervous system. Your tummy growls. Your thoughts focus on food. You may find yourself getting a bit irritable.

This physical hunger is different from the emotional or environmental kind, and it is not the same as a food craving. Food cravings focus on specific foods. You may crave chocolate when you're feeling lonely, or a fast-food hamburger when you're travelling in the car. Cravings are almost always responses to emotional or environmental cues.

Physical hunger isn't so specific. When your body needs more energy in the form of food, you don't focus on the taste of a particular food. You want any food that will fill you up.

Two key questions

As part of your hunger test this week, try another experiment. When you finally sit down to eat, make a point of slowing down and paying attention to how you feel as you eat. Notice what it feels like as your sensation of hunger gives way to the feeling that you're satisfied.

During the rest of this week, each time you feel the urge to have a snack between meals, pause for as long as it takes to ask yourself these two simple questions: am I really hungry? Can I wait until my next meal to eat?

If the answers are a resounding Yes! and No! help yourself to a snack. But if your answer is lukewarm, wait a bit. Get up and change what you're doing. Here are some options:

■ Take a quick walk
■ Drink a big glass of water
■ Make a phone call
■ Do a necessary chore such as dusting, tidying up or organising papers
■ Wash your face or hands
■ Brush your teeth
■ Practise a relaxation technique like deep breathing
■ Fill in three words on a crossword puzzle
■ Flick through a magazine or newspaper

continued on page 73

Calcium choices

Not only does calcium build strong bones, new research shows it also helps the body to burn fat. Calcium-rich snacks in 100 kcal portions include:

■ Low-fat or fat-free yogurt, plain or sugar-free and with fruit (200 g/7 oz)
■ Yogurt smoothie: in a blender, mix 115 g (4 oz) plain fat-free yogurt, 125 ml (4 fl oz) semi-skimmed or skimmed milk and 255 g (8½ oz) frozen unsweetened strawberries
■ Semi-skimmed or skimmed milk (250 ml/8 fl oz), plain or flavoured with syrup or used to make cocoa
■ Laughing Cow Light cheese (1 packaged wedge)
■ Reduced-fat soft cheese (25 g/ 1 oz) with celery sticks
■ Calcium-fortified orange juice (250 ml/8 fl oz)
■ Ice lolly made with calcium-fortified juice
■ Sugar-free rice pudding or custard made with skimmed or semi-skimmed milk (250 ml/8 fl oz)

Sweet snacks

As long as you trust your will-power enough to stick to our portion sizes, then *ChangeOne* has some sweets for you. Here are 100 kcal helpings of some favourites.

Sweets

- **M&M's**, 30 (half a handful)
- **Chocolate buttons**, 1 bag treat size
- **Maltesers**, 1 packet fun size
- **Caramel-peanut chocolate bar**, 1 fun size
- **Chocolate and wafer bar**, 0.35 oz, 2
- **Wispa bar**, 1 treat size
- **Milky Way bar**, 1 treat size
- **Fudge**, 1 regular
- **Chocolate mint thins**, 3
- **Jelly beans**, about 16 (30 g)
- **Marshmallows**, large, 5
- **Wine gums**, 5
- **Rolos**, 4
- **Boiled sweets**, 4
- **Mini rice cakes (sweet)**, about 13 (25 g)

Fruit

There's no denying that fruit is good for you, but the calories in fruit can add up. We recommend buying medium-sized fruit when possible, but having a portion that's a little larger won't undo your *ChangeOne* plan.

- **Dried apricots**, 40 g (1¼ oz) (half a handful)
- **Raisins**, 3 tablespoons (three thumbs)
- **Grapes**, 120 g (4¼ oz) (tennis ball)
- **Apple**, 1
- **Orange**, 1

- **Banana**, 1
- **Melon balls**, 160 g (5¾ oz) (cricket ball)
- **Pineapple chunks, fresh**, 75 g (2½ oz) (2 golf balls)
- **Fresh dates**, 4
- **Kiwi fruit**, 3
- **Banana chips**, 20 g (handful)

Clockwise from far left: M&M's, dried apricots, Maltesers, raisins, jelly beans, Milky Way bar, fresh dates, Kiwi fruit and chocolate mint thins (centre)

WHY CAN'T FRUIT BE UNLIMITED?

It's good and good for you, so why can't you eat as much fruit as you want? Because the natural sugar content of fruit gives it more calories than are in most vegetables. *ChangeOne* suggests two servings of fruit, one at breakfast and one at lunch, plus the option of a third for a snack. Eating more than that is all to the good from the viewpoint of general nutrition, but keep in mind that the extra calories could slow down your weight-loss efforts.

SWEET STRATEGIES

When nothing but sweets will do:

Minis are in. Buy the smallest pieces you can find. From the label, calculate how many pieces add up to 80 to 100 kcals (you'll probably need a calculator to do this!). Eat them one by one, taking time between bites to savour them completely.

Hide and seek. Packets of fun- and bite-size sweets and bars are easy to find in supermarkets. A portion is one or two pieces. Put them in an out-of-the-way spot – say, high in a cupboard behind the wine glasses – and then go there only to take out what you'll eat for the day. If you have to pull out some wine glasses before you can get a treat, you'll have time to reconsider your need.

Buy high-quality sweets that you really like. When the flavour is intense or when you're eating a favourite, you'll be satisfied with less.

Baked desserts

Cakes, pies, baked custards and hot fruit puddings are deservedly popular. Here are portions for some well-loved desserts that provide about 100 kcals.

- **Angel cake**, 1 slice (about ¹/₁₂ of the cake)
- **Fruit pie** (apple, berry, etc) (as thin as you can slice it and still see it, about 4 forkfuls)
- **Brownie**, 5 cm (2 in) square (half a business card)
- **Chocolate gâteau**, 1 slice about 1 cm (½ in) thick (lip-balm width)
- **Fairy cake with icing**, 1 (50 pence piece-size across)
- **Crème caramel, low-fat**, 140 g (5 oz) (small yogurt pot)

Clockwise from top left: spiced pineapple, fairy cake with icing and chocolate gâteau.

Baked apple

Core a small Bramley apple. Sprinkle inside with cinnamon and sugar. Cover and microwave for 3 minutes or until soft.

Spiced pineapple

Sprinkle 2 slices of fresh pineapple, about 100 g (3½ oz), with 2 teaspoons muscovado sugar mixed with a pinch of ground ginger. Cover and microwave for 2 minutes, then top with 1 tablespoon low-fat fromage frais.

Glazed bananas

Slice a small banana into 2.5 cm (1 in) pieces. Sprinkle with ½ teaspoon soft brown sugar and dot with ½ teaspoon butter. Microwave for about 1 minute until bubbly.

continued from page 69

With any luck you'll be distracted enough that, if you weren't hungry, you'll forget about snacking. Food cravings typically disappear as quickly as they come, and hunger from environmental or emotional cues lasts only as long as the cues are right in front of you.

But if, after five minutes or so, you're still hungry, then it's time for a snack.

Reach for a snack that satisfies

Snacks seem to be everywhere these days. Vending machines are crammed with them. Supermarkets have entire aisles devoted to them. There are snacks at the check-out, as well as snacks at the cinema, snacks at the petrol station and snacks at the newsagents.

And like so much else on the food landscape, many of these so-called snacks are oversized, fat-laden, calorie extravaganzas. The biscuits on sale at deli counters these days are often the size of saucers. Family-size bags of crisps or tortilla chips look big enough to feed hundreds. Even cookery books have felt the pressure: in 1967 one cookery book's recipe for brownies made 36; in the latest edition the exact same recipe makes 16 brownies. The fact is, even what passes for an individual-sized serving these days can spell big trouble when you're trying to lose weight. A 200 g (7 oz) bag of tortilla chips can easily contain almost 1000 kcals. Of course, you could stop eating when you start feeling satisfied. But who among us is able to do that with these nutritional booby traps?

Nibblers can take heart, however. We've put together a wide selection of good-tasting, low-calorie snacks that will tame your hunger without scuttling your diet. Of course you'll find carrot and celery sticks on the list, simply

continued on page 77

Help!

'My husband lost 2.2 kg (5 lb) in two weeks. I've barely lost anything. And we seem to be eating the same amount of food. What's going on?'

You're different people. Some people can eliminate one thing from their diet – sugary fizzy drinks, for instance – and begin losing weight immediately. Others have to watch everything they eat, and still their progress seems slow. There are many reasons. Some people's metabolic rates are higher than most, so they burn more calories even when they're just sitting around. Some people do a lot of fidgeting during the day, which also burns calories. One study found that fidgeters can burn more than 500 kcals a day jiggling their legs or pacing about.

If you're feeling frustrated by the slow speed of your weight loss, consider making an additional Fast Track change. (You'll find Fast Track suggestions on page 63.) And don't give up. Remember the tortoise and the hare. Even with weight loss, slow starters can be the first ones across the finishing line.

Frozen treats

In summer, or at any time, everyone loves a frozen dessert. Here are lots with fewer than 100 kcals. The trick is to indulge and enjoy, without going over the top. Remember, they're a treat.

Iced treats

- **Frozen yogurt,** 60 g (2¼ oz) (1 scoop), 80 kcals
- **Reduced-fat ice cream,** 60 g (2¼ oz) (1 scoop), 90 kcals
- **Weight Watchers toffee iced dessert,** 100 ml pot, 93 kcals
- **Super premium chocolate ice cream,** 4 tablespoons (golf ball)
- **Sorbet,** 60 g (2¼ oz) (1 scoop), 60 kcals
- **Orange and lemon Fruitice,** 73 ml lolly, 92 kcals
- **Home-made sorbet,** see below (2 golf balls)

Frozen fruits

- **Frozen grapes,** 175 g (6 oz) (tennis ball)
- **Frozen banana.** 1
- **Frozen strawberries,** 250 g (8½ oz) (baseball)

Easy sorbet:

1. Freeze a can of fruit in heavy syrup.

2. Take out of the freezer 30 minutes ahead of serving time and place on the work surface. Open the can at both ends and push out the contents into a food processor. Add 125 ml (4 fl oz) apple juice and process until smooth.

3. Serve soft, or refreeze.

TIPS ON TOPPINGS

If you could have just 1 tablespoon of topping on your ice cream, what would you choose? Here are some favourites rated from lowest to highest in kcals per tablespoon. Remember that those over 50 kcals may have to stand in for your second snack of the day.

	kcals
Raisins	27
Crunchy cereal	28
Chocolate sauce	41
Chopped almonds	47
Butterscotch topping	52
Chocolate chips	52
Strawberry coulis	53
Hot fudge sauce	70
M&M's	71
Chocolate vermicelli	72

CHOOSING FLAVOURS

Fruit flavours, for example strawberry and peach, are lowest in calories because the fruit takes the place of higher-calorie, higher-fat ingredients such as full-fat milk and cream. Highest-calorie ice creams are vanilla and those varieties with added bits such as cookie dough pieces, toffee or nuts.

ABOUT FREEZING FRUIT

Fruit is easy to freeze and refreshing to eat. Start with your choice of ripe fruit – grapes, bananas, berries, melons, peaches, pineapple, plums, mangoes, nectarines – whatever you like.
Cut whole fruit into bite-size pieces. Place on a baking tray and freeze until firm. Remove from the tray and place in a resealable plastic bag or container. Store in the freezer until needed.

Biscuits

Biscuits and cookies are a special treat, whether home-made or bought. Here is a list of how many you can eat for a snack or sweet that will be 100 kcals or less.

- **Butter crunch**, 2
- **Chocolate chip**, 5 cm (2 in), 2
- **Oat and raisin**, 5 cm (2 in), 2
- **Ginger nut**, 5 cm (2 in), 2
- **Rich tea**, 2
- **Jaffa cake**, 2
- **Garibaldi**, 2
- **Cream-filled plain or chocolate sandwich**, 1½
- **Fig rolls**, 1½
- **Biscotti**, 1
- **Digestive, plain or with milk chocolate**, 1

Clockwise from top left: cream-filled chocolate sandwich, ginger nut, milk chocolate digestive, Garibaldi, fig roll, oat and raisin cookie, Jaffa cake, chocolate chip cookie.

TIPS FOR BUYING BISCUITS

Don't rush to buy lower-fat versions of regular biscuits: they just don't taste as good, they tend to cost more and most shave off few if any calories. And be careful of portion sizes when it comes to biscuits bought at the deli – not only are they huge in circumference, but they can be thicker than a normal biscuit. Often, one-third of a large biscuit is all you need; save the rest or share.

continued from page 73
because they make excellent munchies. But you'll also find some surprises, like Jaffa cakes, pistachios, tortilla chips and even chocolate buttons.

Behind *ChangeOne* snacks

Every *ChangeOne* snack contains about 100 kcals – enough to ease hunger pangs and still keep you within your calorie guidelines. We've chosen snacks that offer plenty of flavour. It may be obvious, but it's worth repeating: if something doesn't taste good, don't eat it. Why waste calories on a low-fat biscuit that tastes like sawdust when you can help yourself to a handful of rich-tasting nuts or a piece of pitta with sizzling salsa?

Beyond good taste, a snack worth its calories should also be satisfying in other ways. If it's hot and humid, you want something cool and refreshing, like a real fruit sorbet. If you're indoors on a cold, rainy day, you want something delicious like hot chocolate that will warm you up. Naturally, a snack should also satisfy your hunger long enough to tide you over until the next meal. Research shows that snacks that take up a lot of volume per calorie – popcorn, or fruit and yogurt smoothies blended with ice, for instance – tend to make people feel fuller on fewer calories.

Snacks that pack a lot of nutrition also turn out to be more satisfying and filling than those with a lot of empty calories. Remember the handful of nuts we mentioned? One recent study found that snacking on them may actually help people to keep their weight down. The reason: nuts are loaded with protein, vitamins and, yes, fat. With all that, it doesn't take many to satisfy your appetite. Munch on low-fat biscuits, which are made up mostly of simple carbohydrates, and you can go on eating and eating, hoping you'll find some flavour in the next bite, piling on calories before you begin to feel satisfied. A few nuts, on the other hand, can give you that satisfaction.

Choosing a nutritious snack is important for another reason: when you're on a low-calorie diet, it's just good sense

Unlimited snacks

Some foods are so low in calories that you can help yourself to as much as you want. Here are a few:
- Sugar-free ice lolly
- Raw pepper slices
- Cherry tomatoes
- Carrots and celery sticks
- Sugar-free fruit jelly

to make those calories count. As we've said, a lot of us tend to think of snacks as a little something extra – a treat we allow ourselves that isn't really part of our slimming diet. We're kidding ourselves. In fact, treats are a surprisingly big part of what we eat during the day. According to one survey, about 20 per cent of our total calories on average come from snacks – all the more reason to make sure those calories deliver essential nutrients as well as good taste.

On *ChangeOne*, snacks will make up about 15 per cent of your total calories. Naturally, since no one expects a snack to be a balanced meal in itself, we're including some less nutritious favourites just because they taste good. After all, it's not about never eating sweets, biscuits and other treats again. It's more about eating them less often and in reasonable portions, and enjoying them more.

Fitting a snack into your *ChangeOne* programme

You can choose two snacks, or a snack and a dessert, or two desserts during the day. You can also serve up slightly larger portions of food at your meals, especially if you find yourself getting too hungry. As often as possible, try to make sure that one selection comes from the Calcium choices on page 69. You already know the evidence linking calcium to weight loss. And getting enough calcium is important for strong bones.

Use snacks this week to help you to manage your hunger. If you get ravenous in the morning, eat something. If your appetite roars to life in the afternoon, grab a snack. Before you do, remember to take the hunger test. Ask yourself: Am I really hungry? Can I wait until my next meal?

Eight tips for controlling hunger cues

1. Instead of buying snacks at the cinema, a match or other event, chew a stick of sugar-free gum. Soon you'll associate the taste of gum, rather than high-calorie food, with that setting.
2. At parties, stand as far away as you can from the bowls of snacks.
3. On car trips, plan ahead and take a few *ChangeOne* snacks. If you have a tendency to munch in the car, bring just a single serving, not the whole box. Put the rest in the boot.
4. Buy snacks in small packs. If you buy the giant size to economise, divide it into single-serving-size sealable plastic bags or containers as soon as you get home.
5. Put the healthiest snacks where you'll see them when you first open a kitchen cupboard or the fridge. Hide the others behind them.
6. Don't snack in your office. (And definitely don't keep bags of crisps in your desk drawer.) Go somewhere else – kitchen, cafeteria, coffee area or outside. That way you won't associate your office with food.
7. At home, enjoy your snacks in the kitchen and nowhere else.
8. Don't eat to relax. Relax, then eat. Stress is such a big factor in diet that we've devoted a whole chapter to it. Look ahead to Week 9, which begins on page 180, for stress-busting tips.

No more open-ended snacking

'I realise now that I was simply setting myself up for trouble', says Michael Krauss, an Internet designer. 'I had all kinds of snacks around the house. I'd open a bag of crisps and just start on them without even thinking about what they tasted like. I never took time to think about whether I was hungry. It was a habit I picked up at college, I think.

'On *ChangeOne*, it didn't take me long to realise that snacking was my biggest problem. That was really where the calories were coming from. I ended up putting off the supper week and taking two weeks to get snacks under control. But once I did, I started to see results on the scales right away.'

One of the first improvements Michael made was to do away with what he calls open-ended snacking: that usually meant digging into a big bag of crisps and eating with no end in sight. 'Now when I get hungry for a snack, I decide how much I want, and I put that amount out and seal up the rest. Instead of digging into a bag of pretzels, I take two or three. It sounds simple, but it's made a huge difference for me.'

Another change that helped was slowing down to taste what he was eating. 'As soon as I began paying attention to flavour and texture, I began to make a kind of cost/benefit analysis. I'd think, "Okay, do I really like this well enough to justify the calories?" And for the first time, I found myself thinking, "These crisps taste rather greasy. Or, these biscuits aren't really that good. Certainly not good enough to waste 200 kcals on".'

Before long, Michael found himself snacking less often, but enjoying it more. He also started seeing the weight fall off fast. Week 4: a weight loss of 6 kg (13 lb).

More snack choices

Can't find something you like from among the five suggested snacks? Starting on page 284, you'll find more quick and delicious *ChangeOne* snack ideas. Here's a sample:

Chocolate snacking cake
page 284

Brownie bites page 285

Chocolate chip and oat cookies page 286

Crisp pecan biscuits
page 287

Cocoa walnut meringues
page 287

Curry-spiced fruits, nuts and seeds page 288

Roasted pepper pinwheels
page 288

Sesame pitta crisps
page 289

Tortilla chips page 289

Melon salad with raspberry vinaigrette page 290

Blueberry mousse
page 291

Fruit boats with orange and balsamic glaze page 292

Changes ahead: supper

This week, while you focus on snacking, start paying attention to what you have for supper. Don't change what you eat. Just notice what it is. Also be aware of how much time you spend eating supper. Record how many nights you eat in and how many nights you eat out at restaurants or friends' houses. If you have time, keep a food diary of your suppers for the week, listing the foods in them and approximately how much you ate (you'll find an easy-to-use form on page 309). Pay attention to the way you experience hunger and fullness too. Those sensations can be a useful guide when it comes to eating sensible-sized portions.

Supper

Pull up a chair, it's supper time.

For most of us supper comes at the end of a long day of work or errands. It's the time when we relax and reward ourselves. If you've been following *ChangeOne* week by week, this chapter will complete a month of determination and healthy changes. Well done! You've taken control of breakfast, lunch and snacks.

This week we want you to enjoy flavourful meals each evening, and to slow down and enjoy the company. By doing so, you'll actually eat less.

Suppers are typically the biggest meal of the day, as well as the source of the most calories. That's why taking charge of supper can have the biggest payoff when it comes to losing weight. Many of our *ChangeOne* volunteers saw their weight loss accelerate when they got supper into shape. By being sensible about portions, and using the meals in this chapter and on pages 268 to 283 as a guide, you'll discover that you, too, can enjoy delicious suppers and keep melting the weight away.

Slow down, relax and enjoy supper

On the following pages you'll find a tantalising selection of *ChangeOne* supper suggestions, with plenty of ways to tailor them to your own tastes. We've made the menus as varied as possible to take advantage of the extraordinary culinary diversity available to us – from Chinese stir-fries to Italian pasta dishes to beefburgers on a bun. Of all the meals of the day, after all, supper is the one that most reflects our family history, culture and special tastes.

(If you eat a lot of dinners out, you may want to glance at the next chapter, in which we take a look at strategies you can use to eat smart at restaurants. But first take a few minutes to look over the supper meal plans on these pages. They'll give you a good idea of what a *ChangeOne* supper contains and what sensible portion sizes look like.)

When you sit down to supper this week, there's one simple change you'll want to make, no matter what's on the table: slow down and savour the meal. Too often these days we're doing a mad dash from here to there, devouring meals without really taking the time to taste what's in front of us.

Supper portions

These meal plans use both metric and imperial weights and those from the *ChangeOne* portion-size guide:

Type of food	Example	Amount	*ChangeOne* portion
One starch	Rice, pasta, noodles	140 g (5 oz)	Tennis ball, cricket ball
or one grain	Bread roll	Medium	Tennis ball
One protein	Chicken, beef	115 g (4 oz)	Pack of cards
	Tofu	85-115 g (3-4 oz)	Pack of cards
	White fish	170 g (6 oz)	Chequebook
	Oily fish such as salmon or mackerel	85 g (3 oz)	Pack of cards
Vegetables	Any vegetable, except potato	Unlimited	

And eating too quickly is one reason so many of us find ourselves struggling with weight.

So this week, give supper your attention. Set aside enough time to be sure that you don't feel rushed. You may not be able to treat yourself to a leisurely supper every night, but if you can guarantee that you enjoy an unhurried supper at least three times during the coming week, you'll begin to see why savouring a meal is one of the simplest and smartest slimming strategies.

Here's why: research shows that just as the body sends hunger signals to the brain, it also communicates when it's had enough food. Those cues, called satiety signals, are the body's way of balancing calories we consume with calories we burn. They work effectively as long as we take time to notice them.

If you've ever got up from a Christmas dinner feeling as if you're as stuffed as the turkey, you'll know how easy it is to eat more than you need – sometimes a lot more. Studies show that it takes up to 20 minutes after food reaches your stomach for satiety signals to kick in.

It takes up to 20 minutes after food reaches your stomach for satiety signals to kick in.

Hence the problem with fast food, and fast eating in general, regardless of what's on the menu. Gulp down food in a big hurry and you don't give your body time to tell you, 'Stop, I've had enough!' You can end up consuming far more calories than you need or even want.

'I realise now I was like a feeding machine', one of our volunteers told us. 'Hand to mouth, hand to mouth – I never paused. I just ploughed through whatever was in front of me. I never stopped to think about what it tasted like. Or how I felt. The change that made the biggest difference for me was learning to put my fork down every few bites and just stop for a minute.' As she learned, a leisurely meal gives your body and brain time to catch up with your fork. Slow down and you'll feel satisfied on far fewer calories than if you rushed through supper.

Making the change

Given how busy life is for many of us, taking time for supper isn't always easy. You may have to rearrange your schedule a little. You may need to watch that episode of *EastEnders* later. You may have to reorganise an appointment or two.

Even so, give it a try. Make it a goal that everyone in your house who plans to eat supper sits down together. You'll find it's worth the effort, not only for the opportunity to relax and savour the meal but also for the new chance to spend time with your friends and family. If you're used to an eat-and-run approach to supper, you can rediscover its pleasures – and make yourself a smarter eater – with these seven simple changes:

1. Arrange your schedule so you have at least 30 quiet minutes for supper.

2. When you have supper at home, always have it in your dining area. That way you won't associate food with other parts of the house – the sofa in front of the television, for instance.

3. If the menu allows, divide your meal into courses – for instance, a main dish and vegetables, salad and pudding. Choose the order that works best for you.

4. Make the meal the focus of supper time. Turn off the television. Put away the newspaper. Let the answering machine take your calls. A little quiet music is fine, as long as it doesn't distract you from the meal.

5. Serve a glass (250 ml/8 fl oz) of water with the meal. Between each bite, put down your fork and take a small sip of water. Sipping water forces you to slow down. Water with supper also makes a meal more filling without adding calories. Many people also find that it helps them to clear their palate and more fully experience the flavours in a meal.

6. Pay attention to how the food tastes. Notice how the flavours complement or contrast with one another. Take small bites and let them linger in your mouth so that the full flavour is released.

7. After a course, take a minute or two to relax, chat and savour what you've just eaten. It may sound paradoxical, but lingering over supper could be an important key to maintaining a healthy weight.

Check-in

Last week you added snacks to your *ChangeOne* menu. You'll find that low-cal snacks help you to manage hunger and stay in control of what you eat. Still mastering the art of snacking? Struggling with breakfast or lunch? Then by all means take another week to get them under control. If you find you are too rushed in the morning to put together a *ChangeOne* breakfast, look back at Week 1 for some time-saving tips. If you're having trouble controlling portion sizes when you go out to lunch, try packing a lunch a few times this week. Still grabbing a chocolate bar from the vending machine when you suffer a mid-afternoon snack attack? Select a smarter snack from the *ChangeOne* suggestions in Week 3 or from the additional ideas on pages 284 to 292. And plan ahead to make sure a snack is handy when hunger strikes.

Change One Fast Track

In a hurry to see more weight come off? Choose one or two of the following Fast Track changes to help to speed your progress.

Early to bed

Surprisingly, insomnia or even regularly falling short on sleep by an hour or two may keep you from reaching your goal. Some researchers suspect that overtired people unwittingly compensate for their lack of energy by eating more.

Being short of sleep can also make people more susceptible to stress, and thus more likely to overeat. Whatever the reason, weight-loss experts recommend trying to get seven or eight hours of sleep every night.

If you've been burning the candle at both ends lately, say good night to late nights this week. If you find yourself repeatedly waking up in the night no matter when you go to bed – especially if you're a heavy snorer – talk to your doctor. You could have sleep apnoea, a common problem that can be treated easily. Being overweight is a common risk factor for this condition.

Have some fun

This weekend set aside time to do something fun that also involves moving around. Walking, tennis, gardening, cycling, swimming – anything that takes your fancy, as long as it's active. Make it a family outing, if you like. Invite a friend. Or choose something you want to do just for yourself. Set aside at least an hour for activity.

Open your diary

Keep a food diary, again or for the first time. We've recommended it before, and we're recommending it again for one simple reason: research shows it's the single best way to jump-start your diet.

Now that you're adding supper to the other *ChangeOne* meals, keeping a record of what you eat will help you to see how far you've come in changing your diet. It's also a great way to spot trouble: certain times of the day when you eat more than you'd like, or situations that trigger hunger cues. You'll find a sample food diary form on page 307.

Chew on this

Buy some packs of sugarless gum and place them everywhere: your kitchen, your desk, your car, your handbag, your briefcase. When you're tempted to reach for a snack, take a piece of gum instead. You may find that the act of chewing relieves your snacking impulses. Also, try chewing a stick of gum while you're cooking meals – there's no way you can sample things with gum in your mouth.

Take the fitness challenge

Cutting back on calories is the quickest way to start losing weight. But studies show that the best way to keep the weight off is to increase the number of calories you burn by becoming more active. Exercise will also help you to replace fat with muscle, and that will make you look and feel trimmer.

If you aren't as active as you'd like to be, start the *ChangeOne* eight-week fitness challenge this week – the details begin on page 236. This week-by-week plan offers a simple and easy way to ease yourself into a more active lifestyle.

Knowing when enough is enough

Paying attention to satiety signals is just one more way to make sure that you keep portion sizes under control. And in the end, portion size is really the key to the success of any slimming diet. Some dieters discover that once they learn to stop eating when they're no longer hungry – before they're too full – they automatically eat reasonable portions.

Learning the art of knowing when you're satisfied takes time, though. And it doesn't work for everyone. So practise memorising those portion sizes. The easiest way to get a sense of what several grams or ounces of different foods look like is to prepare meals at home as often as you can this week, and to use our suggestions of everyday objects for comparison and to judge portion sizes.

To follow the recipes in *ChangeOne* you won't need anything more exotic than kitchen scales, a measuring jug and standard measuring spoons. Kitchen scales that can be adjusted to zero after you place a bowl or plate on top make it quick and easy to weigh out the correct portion of pasta, for instance. Alternatively, you can divide up a 500 g (1 lb 2 oz) packet of pasta into six equal servings. A variety of individual portion-sized storage containers will also come in handy. (For more on helpful kitchen tools, take a look at pages 302 to 303.)

> Vegetables are so low in calories, you can consider them 'free' foods.

Behind the *ChangeOne* supper menu

Each of the suggested *ChangeOne* suppers contains between 400 and 460 kcals. By following *ChangeOne* breakfast, lunch, snack and supper recommendations, you'll total roughly between 1300 and 1600 kcals a day – a level, as we promised before, that will guarantee you'll lose weight at a reasonable, healthy pace.

How can *ChangeOne* suppers be so thrifty with calories? A big reason is that each supper includes at least two servings of vegetables. Vegetables are so low in calories – 90 g (3¼ oz)

continued on page 94

Grilled kebabs

What could be more delicious than marinated seafood, meat or tofu threaded onto skewers with colourful vegetables and then grilled to perfection?

Prawn kebab feast

2 skewers prawn and pepper kebabs

Sesame broccoli (cupped handful)

Wild and white rice (cricket ball)

kcals 450, fat 9 g, saturated fat 1.5 g, cholesterol 100 mg, sodium 2002 mg, carbohydrate 55 g, fibre 4 g, protein 37 g, calcium 280 mg.

PRAWN AND PEPPER KEBABS

Serves 4
450 g (1 lb) raw king or tiger prawns, marinated for at least 1 hour
1 green and 1 red pepper, cut into 2.5 cm (1 in) squares
2 teaspoons olive oil
8 skewers

1. Microwave the peppers for 1 minute or until soft.

2. Thread the prawns and peppers onto skewers. Brush with olive oil.

3. Grill for 5 to 7 minutes or until the prawns are cooked (turning pink).

Portion bonus (extra food, few extra calories): Add extra peppers and other vegetables to make 3 or 4 more skewers, and help yourself to an extra one.

WILD AND WHITE RICE

Serves 4
225 g (8 oz) mixed basmati and wild rice
Pinch of salt

1. Bring a large saucepan of water to the boil. Add the rice and salt. Bring back to the boil and stir well, then lower the heat so the water is simmering. Cook for about 20 minutes or until the rice is tender.

2. Drain well, then allow to stand for 2 minutes before serving.

SESAME BROCCOLI

Serves 4

350 g (12½ oz) broccoli florets
4 tablespoons chicken stock
2 teaspoons sesame oil
1½ tablespoons sesame seeds

1. Place a medium-sized non-stick frying pan on medium heat until warm.

2. Add the broccoli and stock, and sauté for 7 to 10 minutes or until the florets are just tender. Remove from the heat.

3. Drizzle with the sesame oil and sprinkle with the sesame seeds.

Portion bonus: Add extra broccoli and stock.

Instead of prawns

- Firm-fleshed fish, such as monkfish or salmon, 115 g (4 oz) (palm of hand)
- Skinned chicken breast, 115 g (4 oz), cut into strips (palm of hand)
- Skinned chicken thigh meat, 85 g (3 oz), cut into chunks (palm of hand)
- Lean steak, 85 g (3 oz) (palm of hand)
- Lean lamb, 85 g (3 oz) (palm of hand)
- Extra-firm tofu, 85 g (3 oz) (palm of hand)

Instead of peppers

- Aubergine, in 2.5 cm (1 in) cubes, sprinkled with salt, rinsed after 15 minutes and sprayed with cooking spray
- Button or open-cap mushrooms
- Cherry tomatoes
- Button onions*
- Red onion, in wedges*
- Garlic cloves
- Courgettes, in 5 mm (¼ in) slices
- Carrots, in 2.5 cm (1 in) pieces*

* Microwave for a couple of minutes to soften before grilling.

TIPS FOR GRILLING KEBABS

Let your imagination run riot with kebabs. The combinations of seafood, meat, poultry and vegetables are virtually endless. If you're grilling for a crowd, make all-vegetable and all-meat kebabs so it will be easier to time the cooking.

- Brush kebabs with fresh marinade during cooking for more intense flavour (but remember not to use the sauce you soaked them in). If you're using a sweetened marinade, move kebabs away from direct heat to prevent the sugar from burning.
- Turn kebabs over so that both sides cook evenly.
- Cover the ends of wooden skewers with foil to prevent burning, or invest in a set of metal skewers.

ABOUT MARINADES

Marinating imparts great flavour without many calories. It also may fend off the formation of cancer-promoting compounds that form on meat and other animal proteins grilled at high temperatures. It's best to make your own marinades from ingredients such as oil, vinegar, lemon juice, yogurt, herbs and spices. If you buy a ready-made mixture, check that the calorie count and fat content are not exorbitant.

- To marinate, place your kebab ingredients in a bowl or resealable plastic bag. Add about 4 tablespoons of your favourite marinade – teriyaki, lemon-pepper, lime-ginger – and mix well. Refrigerate for at least an hour.
- Discard the marinade after removing marinated items.

Speedy stir-fry

There's no cooking method that's faster, healthier or easier than stir-frying. You'll love blending vegetables with poultry or meat (or with fish, nuts or tofu) for a fast sauté, and then creating sauces in the pan as you go.

Italian-style stir-fry

Chicken and broccoli stir-fry with basil
(2 cricket balls)

Orzo, or basmati rice (1 cricket ball)

kcals 441, fat 12 g, saturated fat 2.5 g, cholesterol 50 mg, sodium 504 mg, carbohydrate 53 g, fibre 7 g, protein 33 g, calcium 125 mg.

CHICKEN AND BROCCOLI STIR-FRY

Serves 4
3 teaspoons groundnut oil
3 spring onions, thinly sliced
340 g (12 oz) skinless chicken breasts, cut across the grain into 1 cm (1/2 in) pieces
675 g (1 1/2 lb) broccoli florets

150 g (5 1/2 oz) red pepper, diced
125 ml (4 fl oz) chicken stock
1/2 teaspoon grated lemon zest
1/2 teaspoon salt
1 teaspoon cornflour blended with 1 tablespoon water
1 tablespoon olive oil
25 g (1 oz) chopped fresh basil or 1/2 teaspoon dried basil

1. In a large non-stick wok or frying pan, heat 2 teaspoons of the groundnut oil over medium heat. Add the spring onions and sauté for 1 minute or until wilted. Add the chicken and sauté for 3 minutes or until it is no longer pink.

2. Add the remaining groundnut oil and the broccoli, and sauté for 2 minutes.

3. Add the red pepper, stock, lemon zest, salt and 125 ml (4 fl oz) water, and bring to the boil. Reduce to a simmer and cook uncovered for 2 minutes or until the chicken and broccoli are cooked through.

4. Stir in the cornflour mixture, olive oil and basil, and cook, stirring, for 1 minute or until the sauce is lightly thickened.

Portion bonus: Use more spring onions, broccoli, red pepper.

ORZO

Serves 4
250 g (8½ oz) orzo (rice-shaped pasta)

1. In a large pot bring 3 litres (5 pints) of water plus 1 tablespoon salt to the boil. Add the orzo and cook for 10 to 12 minutes or until al dente.

2. Drain the orzo in a sieve or colander, shaking it to remove all the water.

Instead of chicken

You can use one of the following in the above recipe for about the same number of calories:
- Salmon fillet, 265 g (9 oz)
- Pork fillet, 280 g (10 oz)
- Firm tofu, 265 g (9 oz)
- Beef fillet, 225 g (8 oz)
- Boneless leg of lamb, 225 g (8 oz)
- Cashews, 70 g (2¼ oz)

ABOUT WOKS

If you don't have a wok, is it worth getting one? Yes. A wok is perfectly designed for low-calorie cooking, using little oil, and cooking vegetables and meat so quickly that they stay tasty and keep their flavour and nutrients. A wok is not just for Asian cooking. Use it anytime you need to sauté something quickly. When shopping for a wok, you'll have a number of choices:

- **Non-stick, flat bottom** Our favourite because it fits on any cooker and washing-up is easy. However, it doesn't conduct heat as well as a traditional steel wok.

- **Traditional carbon steel** The traditional wok from Chinatown conducts heat extremely well, and the concave design makes it simple to keep the food cooking evenly. However, it requires regular seasoning with oil. A pre-seasoned carbon steel wok is easier to keep clean. For both types, wash and dry thoroughly after each use, then wipe with a little vegetable oil to avoid rust.

TIPS FOR STIR-FRY

Most of us associate stir-frying with Chinese cooking, but this low-fat cooking method can be used to create healthy meals with flavours from round the world. Use this supper menu's Italian-themed stir-fry recipe to create other international delights:

Cuisine	Instead of broccoli, red pepper	Instead of olive oil, basil
Mexican	Assorted peppers, sweetcorn	Squeeze of lime juice, fresh coriander
Chinese	Green beans, mushrooms	1 tablespoon soy sauce, ½ teaspoon sesame oil
Thai	Unchanged	2 tablespoons each lime juice and peanut butter
Greek	Aubergine, assorted peppers	2 tablespoons each lemon juice and olives

Succulent stew

Every culture in the world has a recipe for slow-cooking chunks of meat with lots of vegetables. A traditional British beef stew can take pride of place.

Beef stew supper

Beef stew (2 cricket balls)

Egg noodles (1 cricket ball)

kcals 420, fat 12 g, saturated fat 3.5 g, cholesterol 90 mg, sodium 360 mg, carbohydrate 52 g, fibre 5 g, protein 26 g, calcium 63 mg.

BEEF STEW

Serves 4
225 g (8 oz) carrots
115 g (4 oz) parsnips
115 g (4 oz) celery
150 g (5½ oz) potatoes
1 tablespoon olive oil
340 g (12 oz) lean stewing beef, cubed
2 medium onions, cut into quarters
½ teaspoon dried thyme
Salt and pepper to taste
500 ml (16 fl oz) beef stock

1. Cut the carrots, parsnips, celery and potatoes into 2.5 cm (1 in) cubes. Heat the oil in a large flameproof casserole.

Add the beef cubes and brown on all sides. Drain off excess fat.

2. Add all the remaining ingredients, cover and simmer for about 45 minutes or until the beef and vegetables are cooked.

3. Check seasoning. Serve over egg noodles.

Portion bonus: Increase stock and all vegetables (except potatoes).

EGG NOODLES

Serves 4
200 g (7 oz) egg noodles
1 tablespoon salt

1. In a large saucepan, bring 3 litres (5 pints) of water to the boil. Add the noodles and salt and cook according to packet instructions, until al dente.

2. Drain the noodles in a colander, shaking so that all water drains out. Refrigerate any extra.

Instead of egg noodles

If you'd prefer to use pasta made without eggs, here are suggestions:

- Plain noodles, fettuccine or tagliatelle
- Farfalle (bow-ties)
- Penne (short, straight quills)
- Fusilli (spirals)
- Rigatoni (short, ridged tubes)
- Rice sticks (flat Chinese noodles)
- Soba (Japanese buckwheat noodles)
- Chinese wheat noodles

ABOUT STEWING BEEF

Beef for stewing – chuck, blade, round, brisket and flank – is from flavourful, less expensive, tougher cuts that become tender when cooked slowly in liquid. All are similar in calories and nutrients. Cooking slowly in moist heat breaks down the tough connective tissue that is abundant in meat for stewing. Generally, the longer the cooking time, the more tender the result. It's best to buy a whole piece of beef and cut it up yourself, discarding excess fat as you go. Browning the cubes of beef in a small amount of oil (and then draining off the excess fat) before adding liquid will caramelise the surface of the meat and add a richer flavour to your stew.

TIPS ON ROOT VEGETABLES

Carrots, parsnips, turnips, onions and potatoes are abundant over the winter months when other fresh, locally grown produce is in short supply. All supply fibre, along with an assortment of vitamins and minerals. Root vegetables such as these are particularly well suited to stewing, as their fibrous flesh stays firm during the cooking process. Try these other ways of preparing root vegetables too:

- **Roast.** Cut into 2.5 cm (1 in) chunks, toss with a bit of olive oil and roast in a shallow tin at 230ºC (450ºF, gas mark 8) for 30 to 45 minutes until soft and caramelised.
- **Mash.** Cut into 2.5 cm (1 in) chunks, then boil or microwave for 3 to 5 minutes or until soft. Mash or purée with milk or stock, a pinch of salt, freshly ground black pepper and a small knob of butter until smooth.
- **Braise.** Cut into 2.5 cm (1 in) chunks, place in a pot with just enough stock to cover and simmer, covered, for about 15 minutes or until the liquid is absorbed and the vegetables are soft.

ABOUT STOCK

Stock is a must-have ingredient for healthy, slimline cooking. It adds lots of flavour and moisture, with very few calories.

- Homemade stock, made by simmering bones (chicken, beef, veal or fish) or seafood shells with vegetables and herbs in water to cover, has a rich flavour. Bought chilled fresh stock is an alternative, although it is quite expensive.
- Best vegetables for stock include carrots, onions, leeks, celery and garlic. Avoid cabbage, broccoli and other members of the cabbage family, as they will make the stock bitter, and strong-tasting vegetables such as parsnips, swede and Brussels sprouts, which tend to dominate.
- If you don't have time to make stock, or have none in the fridge or freezer, you can use stock made from bouillon powder or paste or good-quality stock cubes.

continued from page 87

of cooked spinach contains only 13 kcals, for instance, and 80 g (scant 3 oz) cooked sliced carrots just 20 – that you can think of them as 'free' foods and help yourself to as much as you want.

One exception is vegetables that are creamed or sautéed in butter or oil. Another is fried vegetables. In these cases pay attention to serving sizes. Weight for weight, the fat in butter, cream and oil has more than twice as many calories as either protein or carbohydrates. So even small amounts can drive up the calorie total. A teaspoon of butter (about 5 g) packs 34 kcals; a teaspoon of oil contains 40 kcals.

With those numbers in mind, the *ChangeOne* menus on these pages have been chosen in part because they're relatively low in fat. But we've been careful to include some fats, especially the unsaturated kinds that can improve cholesterol levels. Fat adds flavour and enjoyment to food. Diets with a moderate amount of fat offer much more variety and flexibility than strict low-fat diets. As long as you keep portion sizes under control, you can eat any kind of food you enjoy, even if it contains fat.

Remember, new research findings show that when you're trying to lose weight, diets with moderate amounts of fat work the best. Several recent studies have shown that slimmers are more likely to stay committed to low-calorie diets if those diets get 25 per cent to 35 per cent of their calories from fat. Very low-fat diets, on the other hand, are so difficult to follow that most people give up and go back to their old ways of eating. Of course, it's wise to eliminate fatty foods that you don't really like or want. It's smart, too, to replace saturated fat with unsaturated fat. You can do this easily by using olive oil instead of butter, for instance, and choosing a reduced-fat mayonnaise. But don't become too preoccupied with fat. Managing portion sizes is a much smarter way to keep calories under control.

Help!

'I often don't get home from work until late – which means I eat supper just before going to bed. I've heard eating before bedtime causes food to go right to fat. Is that true?'

Worry not. As long as you have sensible portions at supper, it won't magically appear on your thighs tomorrow. Despite what some fad diets tell you, the timing of meals makes virtually no difference to whether the calories are burned up or stored as fat. It's the number of calories in a meal that matters, not what time you eat.

Of course, many people don't like the feeling of going to bed on a full stomach. If you're one of them, try moving your supper time back an hour. Choose meals that take a little less time to prepare. Do as much advance preparation as you can, either the day before or over the preceding weekend. After you eat, take a walk. Many people find that walking helps them to digest a meal and encourages sounder sleep.

What about high-protein diets?

We've all heard the buzz about high-protein diets. It's easy to see why they've proven so popular. Any diet that invites you to live on steak and eggs is going to attract attention.

But most doctors remain sceptical about high-protein diets. It's not that these regimens don't help people to lose weight. They do. A 2002 study by scientists at Arizona State University in the US showed that young women who ate a meal high in protein burned more calories during the next few hours than women who ate a high-carbohydrate, low-fat meal. The reason, researchers surmise, is that protein needs more energy to digest than carbohydrates do. That extra energy consumption showed up in slightly raised body temperatures for the women consuming high-protein meals.

Another study, from 1999, found that volunteers were more satisfied after eating a meal with 29 per cent of its calories from protein than after a meal with only 9 per cent of its calories from protein. They also burned more calories to digest the higher-protein meal.

Before you get too excited, though, keep this in mind: you'll burn a lot more calories by taking a 15 minute walk after supper than you will consuming extra protein. And while it's true that high-protein foods seem to satisfy hunger well, complex carbohydrates do the same, often with fewer calories.

High-protein diets may also pose long-term risks if you don't choose the foods in them wisely. Many high-protein foods, like meat, are also high in saturated fat, which can be rough on your arteries. Probably more important when you're controlling calories is that overloading your diet with protein raises the risk that you'll come up short on other nutrients, such as the essential vitamins, minerals and fibre in vegetables. Over the long haul, a very high-protein diet could lead to nutritional deficiencies.

What if I'm losing weight too fast?

Yes, it sounds crazy. But there's a danger to dropping weight too fast. Experts recommend losing no more than 1.35 kg (3 lb) a week.

Why? Because losing weight faster than that means you're burning off muscle as well as fat. Losing muscle tissue will leave you weaker than when you began your diet. It can also lower your basal metabolic rate – the rate at which your body burns fuel to sustain itself – because muscle tissue requires more calories for maintenance than does fat. The result: the less muscle, the fewer calories you'll burn, and the harder it is to maintain weight loss.

If you've lost more than 1.35 kg (3 lb) a week on average – more than 4 kg (9 lb) in your first three weeks – it's time to slow down. Add 200 to 300 kcals to your diet by eating an extra snack or two each day, or increasing portion sizes slightly. And to make sure you don't lose muscle tissue, increase your exercise. You'll find an easy eight-week fitness programme starting on page 236.

Change One First Person

Slowly but surely

'I was losing weight, a little every week. In the beginning I didn't think I was losing it fast enough. But the pounds were coming off, and that was great', says Barbara Deem, an accountant.

'Starting to eat breakfast helped. I hadn't been a breakfast eater before. Watching portion sizes at lunch also made a difference. But the biggest thing for me was supper. It's not what I was eating, it's how much I was eating. That was the big revelation for me. As soon as I began to pay attention to portion sizes, I began to realise, "I don't have to eat that much food to feel satisfied".'

During her first month on *ChangeOne*, Barbara did a lot of weighing and measuring in the kitchen. 'You think you know, but you don't', she says. But soon she began to get a feel for what a reasonable portion should look like – and that also helps a lot when she and her husband go out for dinner.

By following her good example, Barbara's husband lost 1.8 kg (4 lb) during the first week of *ChangeOne*. Her own progress has been slower – half to one kilo (1-2 lb) a week – but steady. By the end of the fifth week she was down 5 kg (11 lb). 'I still have a way to go. But now I actually like the slower pace. I'm starting to feel a difference in how my clothes fit. I'm starting to feel a lot more confident that the changes I'm making are changes I can live with.'

The watchword is moderation. Yes, it sounds familiar. But it's still the best advice around. Protein, carbohydrates and fat – you need them all. Tipping your diet too far in the direction of one or another forces you to cut way back on the variety of foods you get to eat, which makes it harder to stick to a diet. And by loading up on one constituent of food, you'll inevitably fall short on another that may be just as important. We've made sure that the *ChangeOne* plan contains all the protein you need to be healthy and feel satisfied after a meal, but not so much that it bumps other vital components of a healthy diet off the menu.

Cutting back on calories is what really matters when you're trying to lose weight, after all. For most of us, that simply means eating less. That's all there is to it. No magic. Just good common sense about portions.

Goal-setting: it's finally time

Chances are you had in mind the weight you wanted to lose when you started *ChangeOne*. That's great. In fact, this week we want you to put your goal in writing – and sign your name to it.

Now it might seem puzzling that we have waited until the fourth week of the programme to get to the topic of goals. But there are two reasons we waited.

The first is that it is impossible to set a reasonable goal when you are just embarking on a new skill. If you never played golf, for example, how can you predict how good a golfer you can be in 12 weeks? You need to learn some of the skills and practise them before assessing that. Only then will you be able to determine a reasonable path to success.

Help!

'I've been putting in lots of time being active, and I haven't seen any results on the scales. What's wrong?'

Nothing. By being as active as you can, you're doing the right thing. The frustrating fact is that it takes a lot of exercise to lose even a small amount of weight. The average weight loss most people can expect from exercise alone is about 150 g (5½ oz) a week.

So why bother? Try these three very good reasons:

1. Physical activity does burn calories – and those extra calories will help you to lose weight over time.

2. You'll be much more likely to keep the weight off. Almost all the successful dieters in the American National Weight Control Registry say that a big part of their success comes from exercise. On average they burn an extra 2500 kcals a week doing physical activities.

3. Being physically active has been shown to improve people's mental outlook and boost their self-confidence, two changes that can make it much easier to stick to a diet.

Don't stop exercising because you're not losing weight. Stay active and take another look at your diet. Make sure you're not consuming a lot of empty calories in the form of sweetened drinks, including sports drinks and sugary tea and coffee. Readjust portion sizes to make sure yours are still within the *ChangeOne* guidelines.

continued on page 104

Pasta perfect

Who doesn't love the taste and texture of spaghetti and noodles? Our advice:
skip the readymade tomato sauce and experiment for fun and flavour.

Pasta primavera supper

Pasta primavera (2 cricket balls)

Italian salad (2 rounder balls)

kcals 410, fat 13 g, saturated fat 3 g, cholesterol 11 mg,
sodium 690 mg, carbohydrate 54 g, fibre 7 g, protein
18 g, calcium 235 mg.

PASTA PRIMAVERA

Serves 4

140 g (5 oz) small cauliflower florets
140 g (5 oz) small broccoli florets
200 g (7 oz) spinach or plain fettuccine
   or tagliatelle
2 teaspoons olive oil
1 small red onion, diced
2 cloves garlic, finely chopped
225 g (8 oz) mushrooms, thinly sliced
½ teaspoon salt
½ teaspoon dried rosemary, crumbled
1 medium tomato, in 1 cm (½ in) cubes
2 teaspoons plain flour

250 ml (8 fl oz) semi-skimmed milk
25 g (1 oz) Parmesan cheese, grated
15 g (½ oz) chopped parsley

1. In a large pan of boiling water, cook the
cauliflower and broccoli for 2 minutes to
blanch. With a slotted spoon, transfer the
vegetables to a plate.

2. Add the pasta to the boiling water and
cook according to packet directions. Drain
and transfer to a large serving bowl.

3. While the fettuccine cooks, heat
1 teaspoon of oil in a large non-stick frying
pan over moderate heat. Add the onion and
garlic and sauté for 5 minutes or until
tender. Add the mushrooms and sauté for
3 minutes or until softened.

4. Add the remaining teaspoon of oil to
the pan. Add the cauliflower and broccoli,
sprinkle with the salt and rosemary, and
sauté for 1 minute or until the vegetables
are heated through. Add the tomato and
cook for 3 minutes or until softened.

5. Sprinkle the flour over the vegetables, stirring to coat. Add the milk and bring to the boil. Reduce to a simmer and cook, stirring, for 3 minutes or until slightly thickened. Stir in the cheese and parsley. Add to the hot pasta and toss to mix.

Portion bonus: Increase all vegetables.

ITALIAN SALAD

Serves 4

1 cos lettuce, torn into bite-sized pieces
70 g (2¼ oz) stoned black olives, chopped
85 g (3 oz) red pepper, diced
85 g (3 oz) green pepper, diced
35 g (1¼ oz) pine nuts
85 g (3 oz) canned or boiled chickpeas

1. Mix all the ingredients together in a large salad bowl.

2. Toss with fat-free dressing and serve.

ABOUT PASTA PRIMAVERA

With so many vegetables, pasta primavera can be wonderfully healthy:

- Our version supplies 25 per cent of your vitamin A, more than 100 per cent of your vitamin C and 15 per cent of your iron requirements for the entire day.
- Broccoli, a popular primavera vegetable, is a nutrition star. It is among the top suppliers of vitamins A, C and folate. It also is packed with disease-fighting plant compounds.
- To add more fibre, make this dish with wholemeal or buckwheat pasta. Spinach, tomato and other vegetables add flavour and colour, but few additional nutrients.
- Enjoy this dish with frozen vegetables when fresh are out of season. Frozen veggies are just as rich in vitamins and minerals.

Instead of primavera

Although primavera means springtime pasta, this dish is delicious year-round. What makes it so versatile is that you can mix and match ingredients almost any way you like.

Instead of	Try	Why
Fresh cauliflower and broccoli	Frozen mixed vegetables	Always in season
Parmesan cheese	Mature pecorino cheese	Sharper flavour
Milk	240 g (8¼ oz) ricotta cheese Tomato sauce	Creamier Kids may prefer it
Fettuccine	Pizzocheri (buckwheat pasta)	More fibre
Dried rosemary	Fresh basil or oregano	Lighter, fresher flavour

Parcel cooking

It's not a widely used method, but parcel cooking (or 'en papillotte') is surprisingly easy and delicious. Combine healthy foods and flavourings in a sealed parcel, pop it into the oven or onto the barbecue, and then just sit back and wait to enjoy it!

Fish parcels with Spanish rice

1 parcel sea bass and sugarsnaps

Spanish rice (1 cricket ball)

kcals 430, fat 5.5 g, saturated fat 1 g, cholesterol 65 mg, sodium 610 mg, carbohydrate 50 g, fibre 3 g, protein 44 g, calcium 120 mg.

SEA BASS AND SUGARSNAPS

Serves 4
450 g (1 lb) sugarsnap peas
2 tablespoons lemon juice
2 teaspoons olive oil
Salt and black pepper to taste
4 sea bass fillets, 170 g (6 oz) each

1. Preheat the oven to 230ºC (450ºF, gas mark 8) or prepare a barbecue fire.

2. In a bowl toss together the sugarsnap peas, lemon juice, olive oil, and salt and pepper to taste.

3. Coat four 37 cm (15 in) lengths of foil with cooking spray. Place a sea bass fillet on one half of each sheet of foil. Top each fillet with a quarter of the pea mixture. Fold the foil over the fish and peas, and seal by folding over all edges.

4. Place the foil parcels on a baking tray in the oven, or directly onto the barbecue grid, and cook for 10 to 12 minutes.

SPANISH RICE

Serves 4

1 medium onion, finely chopped
1 medium green pepper, finely chopped
1 celery stick, finely chopped
2 garlic cloves, finely chopped
115 g (4 oz) button mushrooms, sliced
125 g (4½ oz) long-grain white rice
250 ml (8 fl oz) tomato juice
250 ml (8 fl oz) chicken stock
½ teaspoon salt
¼ teaspoon black pepper
1 bay leaf
4 plum tomatoes, halved, seeded and diced

1. Lightly coat a deep non-stick frying pan with cooking spray. Sauté the onion, green pepper, celery and garlic for about 3 minutes or until the onion is almost soft. Stir in the mushrooms and rice, and sauté for 2 minutes or until the rice turns golden.

2. Stir in the tomato juice, stock, salt, black pepper and bay leaf. Bring to the boil over medium-high heat. Cover, reduce the heat and simmer gently, stirring occasionally, for 15 minutes. Stir in the tomatoes.

3. Cover again and cook for a further 10 minutes or until the rice is tender and all liquid is absorbed. Fluff with a fork to separate the rice grains. Discard the bay leaf before serving hot.

Instead of sea bass

Sole and plaice (200 g/7 oz per fillet): Parcel cooking works particularly well for delicate fish that tends to fall apart with other cooking methods. Season with a squeeze of lemon juice, along with salt and pepper.

Salmon fillet (115 g/4 oz per portion): Try Asian flavourings like hoisin sauce or sesame oil. Salmon steaks take longer to cook than fillets.

Prawns (170 g/6 oz per portion) and scallops (200 g/7 oz per portion): These shellfish stay moist and succulent with parcel cooking. Flavour with finely chopped garlic and a drizzle of olive oil.

Chicken breast (170 g/6 oz per fillet): Combine strips of chicken breast with sliced red pepper and onion, and flavour with a teaspoon of salsa, for a new twist on the popular Mexican wraps called fajitas.

Lean steak (115 g/4 oz per portion): Stays juicy and flavourful when sliced into strips and tossed with thinly sliced onion. Season with a little teriyaki sauce.

Tofu (115 g/4 oz per portion): Cut into 2.5 cm (1 in) cubes and combine with mangetouts and mushrooms. Marinate first for extra flavour.

TIPS ON COOKING IN PARCELS

Cooking in a parcel retains moisture and flavour and minimises washing-up after cooking.

- Use foil, baking parchment or greaseproof paper to hold the food.
- Add little or no liquid, since the parcel retains all the moisture from the food itself.
- Fold over parcel edges well to prevent cooking juices from escaping.
- Cook in the oven or over a charcoal fire. Cooking time will vary with the type of fish or meat and vegetables you are cooking. Root vegetables like carrots take longer than softer vegetables like peas or mushrooms.
- New potatoes are delicious cooked in a parcel. Scrub, then toss with 2 teaspoons olive oil, salt, pepper and rosemary. Wrap in foil or paper parcels and bake or cook on the barbecue until potatoes are soft (cooking time depends on the size of the potatoes).

Asian noodles

Chinese and South-east Asian cuisines are as rich in noodle dishes as is the cooking of Italy. Brimming with interesting flavours and fresh ingredients, Asian noodle dishes make great one-pot suppers at any time of year.

THAI NOODLE SALAD

Serves 4

225 g (8 oz) rice noodles
1 teaspoon groundnut oil
2 cloves garlic, finely chopped
1 medium onion, thinly sliced
4 tablespoons vegetable stock
25 g (1 oz) spring onions, sliced
160 g (5¾ oz) bean sprouts, rinsed and drained
85 g (3 oz) crunchy peanut butter
4 tablespoons reduced-fat coconut milk
450 g (1 lb) mixed salad greens
15 g (½ oz) fresh coriander, chopped
2 limes, juiced
2 tablespoons chopped peanuts

1. Cook the noodles according to packet directions. Reserve 125 ml (4 fl oz) cooking water. Drain the noodles, then place in a bowl with the reserved cooking water.

2. Heat the oil in a large non-stick frying pan. Sauté the garlic for about 30 seconds. Add the onions and stock and cook for 5 minutes or until the onions are tender. Add to the noodles.

3. Add the spring onions and bean sprouts to the noodles and toss gently to mix.

4. Stir together the peanut butter and coconut milk. Add to noodle mixture. Toss to coat. Before serving divide into four equal portions (cricket ball) and refrigerate extra.

5. Place an equal portion of salad greens on each plate. Top each bed of greens with the noodle mixture and garnish with chopped coriander, lime juice and chopped peanuts.

Per serving: kcals 430, fat 16 g, saturated fat 3.5 g, cholesterol 0 mg, sodium 250 mg, carbohydrate 64 g, fibre 3 g, protein 11 g, calcium 150 mg.

Instead of bean sprouts

If you prefer not to use mung bean sprouts, try one or more of these fresh Oriental-style vegetables (cut into shreds, except for watercress, and sauté or microwave briefly, just until the colour brightens). Alternatively, you can use canned water chestnuts or bamboo shoots.

Try	Features
Pak choy	Thick, light green stalks, dark green leaves, mild cabbage flavour
Chinese mustard	Small leaves, zesty flavour (older, larger leaves are more pungent)
Chinese leaves	Light green leaves, lacy veins, delicate cabbage flavour
Watercress	Small leaves, crisp stalks, sharp and refreshing taste
Yard-long beans	Extremely long, resemble and taste like green beans

ABOUT NUTS AND NUT BUTTERS

If you've been avoiding nuts, give them another look. A growing number of experts recommend nuts as part of a healthy diet. The main form of fat in nuts – monounsaturated – has been linked to lower blood cholesterol levels. Like meats, nuts supply protein along with fibre, a substance not found in meats. Here's the catch: weight for weight, nuts have more than three times the calories of meat, so use them wisely. Here's what you get from some favourites:

Type	Kcals per 2 tablespoons (2 thumbs)
Cashews	94
Peanuts	97
Almonds	104
Crunchy peanut butter	187
Cashew butter	188
Smooth peanut butter	190
Almond butter	203

TIPS FOR ASIAN SEASONINGS

Countries that share a continent don't necessarily share a cooking style, as you see in Asia. Each country uses its own unique combination of sauces and seasonings. Our recipe features the classic flavours of Thailand: coconut, peanut, coriander and lime. To travel through the other cuisines of Asia, consider the flavours of:

China – soy sauce, five-spice powder, hoisin sauce, oyster sauce, garlic

Japan – soy sauce, rice wine, sugar, fish stock, ginger

Korea – soy sauce, sesame oil, garlic, chillies, fermented soya paste

Vietnam – fish sauce, lemon grass, coriander, garlic, shrimp paste

Indonesia – ginger, tamarind, thick soy sauce, coconut, lemon grass

The Philippines – coconut milk, garlic, ginger, vinegar, fermented shrimp paste

continued from page 97

The same is true for *ChangeOne*. These first four weeks you have been learning new skills and practising them every day. We assume you have been losing weight and also reaping other personal rewards. Now that you know your weight-loss strengths and weaknesses, isn't it a smarter time to set a realistic goal?

The second reason for the delay is that goal-setting is serious business. Rightly or wrongly, your performance against your goals defines success for you, motivates you and, too often, lets you down. Goal-setting is so important, in fact, you'll discover that we devote a whole week to it a month from now. But until then it's time for some basics.

Take that initial weight-loss goal you set yourself and think about it for a few minutes. Ask yourself three questions:

1. Is my goal a reasonable one, something I can realistically achieve based on the progress I'm making so far?
2. How long is it likely to take to reach my goal?
3. What weight would I be satisfied with if I can't quite hit my ideal goal?

After you've given these weighty questions some thought, set out your goals for the coming months. We recommend your having a goal in mind for the end of the 12-week programme about two months from now. If that's not *your* ultimate goal, set another target on a longer time frame.

Think TRIM

As you think about workable goals for the coming two months and beyond, keep in mind the acronym TRIM. It stands for:

Time-bound. An effective goal should have a deadline – a time when you expect to reach it. Choose a date two months from now, when you will have completed the 12 weeks of the *ChangeOne* programme. Select a specific date and mark it on the calendar.

Realistic. We've said it before, but it's worth repeating: if you set a goal you can't reach, there's no point in setting it. Choose a target that you're pretty sure you can hit. Odds are you won't go from a size 18 to a size 10 in the next few months. But you could get to a size 16, or even 14.

Inspiring. Your goal should be something that really matters to you – attainable, but ambitious enough to excite you. Maybe you don't really care all that much about pounds on the scales, for instance; what you're concerned about is getting into shape so that you can keep up with the kids on rambles and bicycle rides.

Measurable. A worthwhile goal has to be measurable. If it isn't, obviously, you'll never know when you've reached it. The first step is to make it as specific as possible. The next is to describe exactly how you plan to measure your progress. A few examples:

Instead of	Make your goal to:
Lose as much weight as I can before summer begins	Drop 4.5 kg (10 lb) over the next two months
Be better about my diet	Follow *ChangeOne* at least six days out of seven each week
Get back into shape	Jog for 45 minutes at least three times a week in preparation for 10 kilometre charity run
Try to be more active	Walk at least 30 minutes five days a week over the next two months
Eat fewer sweets	Treat myself to just one pudding a week over the coming month
Feel less embarrassed by the way I look	Lose 4.5 kg (10 lb) and join an aerobics class by Easter

In addition to pounds on the scales, give yourself at least two other goals. Dropping several dress sizes, for example. Or fitting into a pair of jeans you wore two summers ago.

It's not all about the scales

Why have another goal in addition to pounds on the scales? Because while weight is the measure that most people use, it's not necessarily the best one. Who really cares what the bathroom scales say? What most people really want is to look better. And the scales can lie.

For example, let's say you're doing a great job on your slimming diet, dropping calories and burning fat. At the same time, you've become so keen on exercise that you've started going to the gym. You're tightening up flabby muscles and even adding some strength. You look great! You feel terrific!

But when you step up on the scales, you find your weight has barely moved. Why? Because you're replacing fat with

What's your healthy weight?

One target worth keeping in mind is your healthy weight. Since height and weight are related, experts don't rely on weight alone. Instead they use a formula called body mass index (BMI). On page 313 you'll find information on how to calculate your current BMI and the weight you'll need to lose to reach a healthy BMI.

Because individual body types differ, the official BMI chart offers a recommended range, not a single magic number. Having your healthy weight in mind can often serve as a great motivator.

But keep your perspective. If you're overweight, losing just a little will make you healthier. Studies show that people who lose 5 per cent of their body weight significantly improve their blood pressure and cholesterol levels, thereby reducing the strain on their hearts and arteries. They also lower their risk of diabetes. The closer you get to your recommended BMI, the healthier you'll be.

muscle, which actually weighs more than fat, volume for volume. You're changing your body composition for the better. The reflection in the mirror shows it. Maybe you've dropped a waist size or two as well. You feel stronger and fitter. But if you have no other gauge than pounds on the scales, you'll be disappointed.

Once you've settled on realistic and measurable goals, fill out the *ChangeOne* contract on page 307. Why a contract? Because while it's one thing to decide on a set of goals, it's another to really commit to them. Make a deal with yourself in writing. The form even includes a place for you to sign. For extra motivation, get a witness to sign it too.

Silly? You may be surprised. There's something powerful about putting your signature on any agreement, even one you make with yourself. Before you sign it, make sure the goals you've set for yourself pass the TRIM test. Check again to be sure they're goals you are willing and able to work towards over the next few months.

Changes ahead: eating out

More and more of our meals are eaten away from home – in restaurants, pubs and fast-food places. The only problem with eating out these days is that the food is often served in large portions that are loaded with fat and calories. This week, while you focus on supper, make a list of a couple of restaurants you'd like to try. Next week we're going to invite you to go out to practise a few simple strategies to cut those portions down to size.

More supper choices

Can't find something you like from among the seven suggested suppers? Starting on page 268 you'll find more quick and delicious *ChangeOne* supper ideas. Here's a sampler:

Chicken and caramelised onion sauté
page 269

Wine-braised beef
page 272

Homestyle meat loaf
page 274

Sweet-and-sour glazed pork with pineapple
page 277

Soy-basted halibut steaks
page 278

Little chicken and sweetcorn pies
page 280

Barley pilaf with herbs
page 282

Summer ratatouille
page 282

Mangetout and apples with ginger
page 283

WEEK **5**

Eating Out

Even though you're watching what you eat, that's no reason to deny yourself the pleasure of eating out. Certainly, the serving sizes may be large, and in many restaurants the notion of a sauce is one loaded with butter and cream. But if you approach eating out with common sense and confidence, you can order what you want, and exactly how much you want, while sticking with your plan.

This week, eat out at least twice. Order exactly what you want, and don't take no for an answer!

Who knows? You might find it great fun getting the waiter and chef to serve you a more personalised meal. If you don't, just forget the experience and move on. There's no need to feel inhibited – you are the customer, paying to get what you want. So enjoy it, take your time and savour the flavours – as you'd like them.

A *ChangeOne* dinner date

Eating out has become one of the great national pastimes. In 2002, one in four meals was eaten outside the home in the UK, and experts suggest that this will rise to one in two. And never before have we had so many mouth-watering choices, from spicy Thai stir-fries and sizzling Indian dishes to exotic Japanese sushi, an amazing variety of Italian food and ever more adventurous food in so-called gastro pubs.

But there is a downside to eating out. Restaurant food typically contains 22 per cent more fat than food consumed at home, say experts. And portion sizes have spiralled out of control, particularly at fast food places. Portion 'creep' has happened so gradually that most people don't realise exactly how big their meals have become. An American organisation called the Center for Science in the Public Interest (CSPI) began conducting clever sting operations a few years ago. The group studied meals from restaurants just like those many of us eat in regularly. In one operation CSPI sampled

Eating out portions

These meal plans use both standard measurements and the *ChangeOne* portion-size guide. In this chapter we've focused on dinner. It's the meal people typically eat out, and it often delivers the biggest portions. When you're going out for breakfast or lunch, you can review the portion sizes in the preceding chapters. For a complete dinner meal (450 kcals) choose one of each type of food, in the portion suggested:

Type of food	Example	Amount	*ChangeOne* portion
Starch or grain	Rice, hot cooked	140 g (5 oz)	Tennis ball
	Bread roll	Medium	Tennis ball
Protein	Prawns, scallops, crab	115 g (4 oz)	Cricket ball
	Chicken, turkey	85–115 g (3–4 oz)	Surface of palm
	Beef, veal	85 g (3 oz)	
	White fish	170 g (6 oz)	Chequebook
	Oily fish: salmon	85 g (3 oz)	
Vegetables	Green beans, with oil or butter	65 g (2¼ oz)	2 golf balls
	Peas, with butter	80 g (2¾ oz)	2 golf balls
	Steamed or raw	Unlimited	

almost two dozen Chinese restaurants. In another, its investigators ordered from the menus of a variety of Italian restaurants.

What they found made headlines in the USA. Portion sizes and fat content at many American restaurants have become so bloated that many meals are health hazards. In some cases, CSPI found, a single main dish exceeded what many of us should eat in a whole day. At some Chinese restaurants, for instance, an order of kung pao chicken had 1400 kcals. Looking at Italian food, researchers discovered that spaghetti with meatballs at some restaurants came in at almost 1000 kcals. Pasta in a cream and cheese sauce soared to almost 1800 kcals in a single serving. Even half of one of these dishes puts you over your *ChangeOne* supper target. And if you were to eat a couple of pieces of bread spread with butter, or dipped into olive oil, you could add 350 or more kcals to the total.

One study found that, in some cases, a single restaurant main course exceeded the kcals you should eat in a whole day.

If you eat out a lot – and many of us have about four meals a week in restaurants, pubs or fast-food places – numbers like those can be discouraging. But even though the chef rules the kitchen, remember that you rule the table. You're the customer, after all. You choose what to eat and how much of it you want. You decide how quickly or how slowly to enjoy a meal. You say when you've had enough. In some restaurants, you can even give the chef specific instructions as to how you want your meal prepared.

Many of the strategies you'll use to take charge in restaurants are those that you've already been practising: planning ahead. Monitoring hunger and fullness signals. Keeping an eye on portion sizes. This week, keep them in mind when you take yourself out to eat. They'll help you sit down to a *ChangeOne* meal you'll enjoy without regrets.

Do your menu homework

If you're considering a restaurant you've never tried before, stop by and look over the menu before you go in to make sure you'll be able to order the meal you want. Most establishments display their menus outside. Some even post them online. You won't be able to learn much about portion sizes, of course, but at least you'll know whether the menu includes some possible options. You could even pick the safest choices before you go in. That way you won't have to look at the menu and be tempted by fillet steak smothered in hollandaise sauce or tarts made with butter puff pastry.

If you eat out frequently, keep your own personal list of diet-friendly places in your area – restaurants where you know you'll be able to get a great-tasting, low-calorie meal.

Clearly, there are some kinds of restaurants you should avoid altogether – unless you have an iron will. Buffet-style restaurants, carveries, 'all you can eat' places, even sprawling salad bars pose a hazard. Salad bars sound healthy enough, but many of them are stocked with calorie-rich dishes such as pasta salads with creamy dressings. Better to order a simple green salad with the dressing served separately. What about fish and chip shops? Most of what's on the menu there is so high in calories and fat that you'll bust your calorie budget before you satisfy your hunger. Fast-food restaurants? Unless you're willing to eat half a burger or chicken sandwich and wash it down with a diet drink, you'll have a tough time finding a fast-food place that doesn't overdo the kcals.

And remember, you're aiming to have at least two servings of vegetables. With your take-away beefburger you'll be lucky to get a piece of lettuce and thin slice of tomato.

But don't worry. There are still plenty of places where you can sit down to a good meal, as you'll discover as you look through this week's suggestions.

Check-in

What meal do you typically eat out? Breakfast? Lunch? Dinner? All of the above? If you eat out a lot, take a fresh look at the portion sizes in the first four weeks of *ChangeOne* so that when that plate of pasta or a burger lands in front of you, you'll know just how much to eat and how much to leave or take home for later.

Many dieters find that keeping a visual equivalent size in mind – a chequebook or a tennis ball, for example – helps prevent portion creep. If you only treat yourself to a restaurant meal once or twice a month, definitely use the tips in this chapter to guide you when you open the menu. But enjoy yourself, too. Have that steak or chop. If dinners out are an occasional treat, you don't have to worry. Still, pay attention to how full you feel. When you're satisfied, put your cutlery down and savour the feeling of being in control of your eating.

Italian

Antipasto, pasta, main dish, dessert is a standard meal in many Italian restaurants. Can you fit it into *ChangeOne*? Yes, as long as you pay attention to courses, portions and include lots of vegetables. Check out our sample meals below.

Menu 1

Melon with Parma ham

Pasta arrabiata (spicy tomato sauce) with 1 tbsp grated Parmesan cheese

Large mixed salad

2 fresh figs

(Meal pictured above)

Approximate serving info (based on *ChangeOne* sizes)
kcals 450, fat 15 g, saturated fat 5 g, cholesterol 15 mg, sodium 1254 mg, carbohydrate 60 g, fibre 4 g, protein 23 g, calcium 15 mg.

Menu 2

Tomato bruschetta

Small portion of spaghetti with seafood

Granita

Approximate serving info (based on *ChangeOne* sizes)
kcals 500, fat 14 g, saturated fat 2 g, cholesterol 55 mg, sodium 1018 mg, carbohydrate 79 g, fibre 4 g, protein 24 g, calcium 180 mg.

Choosing your meal

Soups

Italian soups are hearty, almost filling enough to be a meal in a bowl if paired with a slice of crusty Italian bread and a green salad. Minestrone – a tomato-based soup with vegetables, beans and pasta – is the best known. Pasta e fagioli features a fibre-rich combination of beans (fagioli) and pasta in a savoury broth. Top either with a sprinkle of Parmesan cheese for richer flavour.

Starters

Often listed as 'antipasto' on the menu, starters run the gamut from marinated seafood salad to deep-fried mozzarella. Choose fresh seafood, steamed or boiled, or a virtually calorie-free fresh vegetable salad. If you're wondering how some of your current favourites stack up, here are some typical portions, ranked from best to worst in terms of calories and nutrition:

Olives (5 stuffed olives)	25 kcals/3 g fat
1 bread stick	25 kcals/0.5 g fat
Melon and Parma ham	150 kcals/5 g fat
Garlic bread (small piece)	200 kcals/10 g fat
Fried squid (starter size)	300 kcals/12 g fat

Main dishes

Portions in many Italian restaurants are big enough to feed at least two. Limit your pasta portion to about a tennis ball. Salad nicoise is a good choice but ask for the dressing to be served on the side. If you opt for pasta choose a tomato-based sauce. Other good main courses include chicken cacciatore, seafood or grilled calves' liver. Avoid cream or cheese-based dishes such as spaghetti carbonara. Here's a sample of Italian main courses and desserts with their nutritional values:

Spaghetti alla carbonara	600 kcals/42 g fat
Spaghetti with pesto	455 kcals/13 g fat
Spaghetti with tomato sauce	300 kcals/6 g fat
Large mixed salad	50 kcals/3 g fat (1 tbsp oil)
Tiramisu	500 kcals/30 g fat
Zabaglione	200 kcals/11 g fat
Granita	100 kcals/0 g fat
1 fresh fig	17 kcals/0 g fat

Chinese

Although the traditional Chinese diet is considered to be one of the healthiest in the world many of the dishes that appear on restaurant and takeaway menus are deep fried, which makes them very high in calories and fat. Because it can be hard to resist temptations like spring rolls, take the agony out of ordering by choosing one of the typical Chinese meals below.

Menu 1

Hot and sour soup

Prawns stir-fried with ginger and spring onions

Small serving plain boiled rice

Fresh pineapple

(Meal pictured below)

Approximate serving info (based on *ChangeOne* sizes) kcals 460, fat 15 g, saturated fat 2 g, cholesterol 263 mg, sodium 1200 g, carbohydrates 47 g, fibre 2 g, protein 34 g, calcium 263 mg.

Menu 2

Chicken and sweetcorn soup

Stir-fried beef or chicken with oyster sauce

Small serving plain soft noodles

Canned or fresh lychees

Approximate serving info (based on *ChangeOne* sizes) kcals 455, fat 17 g, saturated fat 3 g, cholesterol 50 mg, sodium 1600 g, carbohydrates 50 g, fibre 8 g, protein 30 g, calcium 135 mg.

Choosing your meal

Starters

There's no need to say no to starters but it pays to choose carefully. Avoid deep fried dishes such as spring rolls, wontons, deep fried dumplings and prawn crackers. Soups such as wonton or egg drop are a terrific choice – they fill you up without an overabundance of calories. Steamed dumplings (dim sum) are another excellent selection.

Chicken noodle soup	42 kcals/1 g fat
Sesame prawn toasts	70 kcals/6 g fat each
Prawn crackers (bowl)	385 kcals/27 g fat
Spring roll	125 kcals/9 g fat

Main and side dishes

Most Chinese restaurants offer a good selection of healthy low fat main courses. Stir fried vegetables are probably the safest option – with chicken, beef, tofu, pork, or seafood. An average serving of sweet and sour chicken can contain the equivalent of 8 teaspoons of sugar – so is best avoided – as is anything that is covered with batter or contains nuts. Opt for a small portion of plain boiled rice rather than special egg fried rice and boiled rather than fried noodles.

Sweet and sour chicken	585 kcals/30 g fat
Sweet and sour pork (battered)	715 kcals/42 g fat
Chicken chow mein	515 kcals/25 g fat
Stir fry beef with green peppers and black bean sauce	375 kcals/20 g fat
Stir fry vegetables	185 kcals/14 g fat
Egg fried rice	550 kcals/15 g fat
Steamed rice	410 kcals/4 g fat
Szechuan prawns with vegetables	310 kcals/16 g fat
Chicken chop suey	390 kcals/21 g fat
Chicken with cashew nuts	530 kcals/35 g fat

Bistro and pub food

Most good modern restaurants and pubs should have a selection of dishes suitable for the *ChangeOne* diet – simply cooked fish or poultry with vegetables is always a good choice. If you're not sure from reading the menu exactly what a dish is or how it is cooked, ask the waiter or waitress and don't forget you can always request that a dish is served without the sauce or dressing.

Menu 1

Vegetable soup

Griddled tuna or chicken with mango salsa

Fresh fruit salad

(Meal pictured above)

Approximate serving info (based on *ChangeOne* sizes) kcals 450, fat 10 g, saturated fat 2 g, cholesterol 42 mg, sodium 1200 mg, carbohydrate 60 g, fibre 10 g, protein 42 g, calcium 42 mg.

Menu 2

Moules marinière

Smoked haddock fish cakes

Large mixed salad

Summer pudding or fresh berries

Approximate serving info (based on *ChangeOne* sizes) kcals 500, fat 15 g, saturated fat 5 g, cholesterol 20 mg, sodium 1200 mg, carbohydrate 60 g, fibre 2 g, protein 36 g, calcium 512 mg.

Choosing your meal

Starters

Seafood starters are a popular offering in modern British restaurants. As long as the seafood isn't fried or swimming in butter or olive oil, it's hard to go wrong with prawns or steamed mussels. Avoid high fat starters like avocado and pâté. Choose melon, soup, salad, shellfish or smoked salmon, and pass on the accompanying bread and butter. A leafy salad is always an option – try topping it with prawns and dressing with a tomato vinaigrette.

Vegetable soup	75 kcals/1.5 g fat
Smoked salmon	85 kcals/3 g fat
Melon	25 kcals/1 g fat
Marinated prawns	100 kcals/2 g fat
Asparagus with Parma ham	30 kcals/3 g fat

Main dishes

Chargrilling is a popular and diet-friendly cooking technique which disposes of some fat as the food cooks, and imparts delicious smoky overtones. But stay alert: the standard fillet or rump steak may be two or more full *ChangeOne* portions, and that's not counting the potatoes with it. Keep in mind that just one tablespoon (15 g/½ oz) of melted butter has more than half the calories of the main dishes below. Avoid creamy sauces, pastry and anything fried. Vegetarian options may not be lower in calories – watch out for dishes that contain cheese or nuts.

Salmon steak	228 kcals/15 g fat
Tuna steak	160 kcals/6 g fat
Grilled chicken breast	200 kcals/10 g fat
Medium jacket potato	160 kcals/6 g fat
Mashed potato	125 kcals/2 g fat (120g serving)
Summer pudding	150 kcals/1.5 g fat
Lemon sorbet	80 kcals/0 g fat (1 scoop)
Fresh strawberries	50 kcals/0 g fat (1 bowl)
Fresh fruit salad	80 kcals/0 g fat
Ice cream	120 kcals/6 g fat (1 scoop)

Love it or skip it?

Love it	Why?
Blackened	Rubbed with black pepper, paprika and other spices and chargrilled
Steamed	Cooked without fat in a steamer
Reduction	Sauce made by boiling down stock, wine or balsamic vinegar
Brochette	Meat, fish, poultry or vegetables on a skewer

Skip it	Why?
Béarnaise	Sauce made with butter and egg yolks
Beurre blanc	Light-coloured butter sauce
Chateaubriand	Large portion of beef fillet, usually for two
Dijonaise	Dijon mustard and cream sauce

HEALTH IMPOSTERS

- Avocado – especially when served with a high-fat dressing.
- Fruit crumbles – usually low on fruit and high on calorie rich topping.

Indian

Traditionally, Indian food is quite healthy and balanced, with plenty of complex carbohydrate and vegetables, but many western restaurants cater for western palates. At around 700 calories and 40 g fat per serving, dishes like chicken korma, lamb dhansak or anything with nuts or a creamy sauce should be given a wide berth by dieters. But if you choose wisely, healthy options are available.

Menu 1

Chicken tikka

Vegetable curry

Raita

Plain boiled rice or 1 chapatti

Fresh mango

(Meal pictured above)

Approximate serving info (based on *ChangeOne* sizes)
kcals 550, fat 26 g, saturated fat 4 g, cholesterol 151 mg, sodium 757 mg, carbohydrate 51 g, fibre 4 g, protein 31 g, calcium 175 mg.

Menu 2

Vegetable samosa with salad
  (one samosa)

Tandoori king prawns

Lentil dhal

Fresh fruit salad

Approximate serving info (based on *ChangeOne* sizes)
kcals 450, fat 19 g, saturated fat 3 g, cholesterol 83 mg, sodium 900 mg, carbohydrate 37 g, fibre 2 g, protein 36 g, calcium 239 mg.

Choosing your meal

Starters

Tandoori chicken or prawns are the best choice – if you can't resist a bahji or samosa, ask for a half portion or split a starter with your dinner guest. Avoid popadoms unless you're assured that they have been baked, not fried. They can add up to a whopping 200 kcals each before you even start your meal.

Tandoori chicken	260 kcals/8 g fat (starter size)
Samosa	474 kcals/45 g fat
Onion bhaji	355 kcals/24 g fat

Main course

Chicken dopiaza, jalfrezi, tikka or sag are all good choices. Vegetable, fish or shellfish-based curries and dishes like mutter paneer (peas with cheese) and sag aloo (spinach and potato curry) are relatively low in calories and saturated fat as well. Balti-style curries are fairly low in fat and provide useful amounts of iron, absorbed from their cooking pots. Peshwari naan and pilau rice are cooked using lots of ghee (clarified butter), so choose chapattis and plain boiled rice instead. Cucumber raita, made with yogurt, is the best choice of accompaniment.

Lamb biryani	900 kcals/20 g fat
Chicken korma	800 kcals/40 g fat
Chicken dhansak	750 kcals/41 g fat
Prawn biryani	600 kcals/15 g fat
Prawn balti	450 kcals/21 g fat
Tandoori chicken	350 kcals/10 g fat
Chapatti	197 kcals/8 g fat
Plain boiled rice	248 kcals/2 g fat
Pilau rice	391 kcals/10 g fat

Dessert

After a hot spicy meal, there's nothing quite like a fresh fruit salad to cool you down. Many Indian restaurants also offer platters of fresh orange or melon slices following a meal.

Family restaurants

Restaurants and fast food outlets which cater for families with children are a godsend for busy parents but it can be difficult to know what to choose when almost everything seems to fall outside the *ChangeOne* guidelines. But with our menu choices you can relax and enjoy yourself.

Menu 1

Garlic mushrooms

Grilled gammon with pineapple

Jacket potato

Peas

Fresh fruit salad

(Meal pictured below)

Approximate serving info (based on *ChangeOne* sizes) kcal 600, fat 19 g, saturated fat 4 g, cholesterol 20 mg, sodium 1000 mg, carbohydrate 78 g, fibre 12 g, protein 44 g, calcium 86 mg.

Menu 2

Tomato soup

Large mixed salad with low fat dressing

Grilled chicken with potato wedges and tomato salsa

1 scoop ice cream with fresh strawberries

Approximate serving info (based on *ChangeOne* sizes) kcal 600, fat 23 g, saturated fat 7 g, cholesterol 117 mg, sodium 1000 mg, carbohydrate 57 g, fibre 4 g, protein 38 g, calcium 162 mg.

Choosing your meal

If you choose a burger go for a small one and hold the cheese – you'll save greatly on kcals and fat. Don't assume that a chicken sandwich is a healthier option – it's not always the case. Burger King's Chicken Royale sandwich contains more fat and calories than McDonalds' Quarter Pounder with cheese. Vegetable burgers don't really contain significantly less fat or fewer calories than beef burgers but they do have a lot more fibre which helps keep the digestive system in good working order.

In family restaurants grilled chicken, fish or lean meat such as pork is always a safe choice. Avoid anything which is fried or coated with breadcrumbs or batter. Potato wedges are a good alternative to chips – a jacket potato is an even better option as long as you don't smother it with butter. Ask for it to be served plain, with a portion of grated cheese on the side so that you can decide how much to add. Look at the chart below and work out your best choices.

BK Chicken Royale	549 kcals/29 g fat
BK Bacon Double Cheeseburger	523 kcals/31g fat
McDonalds Quarter Pounder with cheese	516 kcals/27 g fat
BK Spicy Beanburger	463 kcals/18 g fat
Quarter Pounder	423 kcals/19 g fat
Vegetable burger	423 kcals/18.6 g fat
Fillet of Fish	389 kcals/18 g fat
McChicken Sandwich	375 kcals/17 g fat
BK Chicken Flamer	300 kcals/13 g fat
Regular fries	206 kcals/9 g fat
Potato wedges	368 kcals/18 g fat
Large chocolate milk shake	516 kcals/13 g fat

Take control of the table

1. Ask and you shall receive

The waiters should know how a dish is made, what the ingredients are and how big the portion size is. So ask. Then have it the way you want it. If you'd like the grilled chicken breast without the skin, say so. If the vegetable side dishes are usually prepared with lots of butter, request yours lightly sautéed in olive oil or better still, steamed. Do you fancy a pizza? They should be more than willing to make yours with half the normal cheese, or none, and with an extra topping of vegetables.

2. Order one course at a time

One of the pleasures of eating out is taking your time. Or at least it should be. Unfortunately, at too many restaurants waiters snatch up one course and rush in with the next before you've had time to put your fork down. There's a reason. Most restaurants want to turn tables round as quickly as they can to squeeze in as many seatings in an evening as possible. That's their business. Yours is to sit back, relax and take the time you need to eat only as much as you want – and no more. If you're worried about being rushed, order just one course at a time, not the whole meal. Once you've finished your starter, look back at the menu to consider what you'll have next. A useful rule of thumb: allot at least 20 minutes per course – the time your body needs to send satiety signals. Do you feel full? You're under no obligation to keep ordering.

3. Draw the line

Ask whether the kitchen can prepare half portions. Many restaurants are more than willing to do so. While you are waiting to order, take a quick look at the size of the portions that other diners are eating. If portions seem very large, you could even ask for a child's portion Don't wait until you've started to nibble. Don't depend on your willpower to eat only half of what's in front of you. This is supposed to be dinner you're enjoying, not a test of your determination.

4. Rule the table

When you're eating out, you're in charge – not only of what you eat but of what's on the table. Lots of restaurants start you off with a basket of bread or rolls. If you're very hungry when this arrives, you'll automatically start eating it, probably slathered with butter and loaded with calories, without even giving it a second thought.

Why waste the calories? Tell the waiter, 'No bread, thanks'. If you're famished when you sit down, order something more sensible to take the edge off your hunger – a side salad, a vegetable side dish or a glass of spicy tomato juice, for instance. At the same time, ask for a glass of water. Or, even better, a jug of iced water or a bottle of mineral water. Then you won't have to wait for anybody to fill your glass, and you can keep drinking plenty of water with your meal. Always remember who's boss. If something arrives at the table that you don't want, politely decline it. No one will mind.

Manage the menu

Order wisely, and you can put together a meal that's long on flavour and short on calories. Here are five things to consider when you open the menu:

1. Be colourful

Meat and creamy sauces are usually beige, aren't they? Where do most dishes get their brightest colours? From vegetables and fruit, of course. Choose the most colourful dishes on the menu, and chances are you'll order the healthiest, lowest-calorie selections. Spicy red salsas, deep purple-red beetroot, leafy green salads, golden yellow sweetcorn, purple aubergine and bright red and yellow peppers all turn your plate into a rainbow of colours. As long as vegetables arrive without lots of added fat, they're free on *ChangeOne*. Help yourself. And there's

Help!

'I'm used to having a glass of wine or beer with dinner. Can I enjoy a drink and still lose weight on ChangeOne*?'*

Yes. But before you raise your glass, remember one key word: moderation. Alcoholic beverages contain calories – about 120 kcals in a glass of wine and 145 in 340 ml (12 fl oz) of beer. In fact, surveys show that the average adult who drinks gets 10 per cent of total calories from alcohol.

But whether those calories 'count' in the same way that food calories count is a subject of debate. Even though drinkers consume more calories than nondrinkers, they aren't more likely to be obese or overweight. What's more, volunteers in controlled studies who are given additional calories in the form of alcohol do not gain weight. If they replace some carbohydrates or fat in their diet with the equivalent number of calories in the form of alcohol, they may actually lose weight.

Why? Researchers suspect that alcohol may alter the way the body burns fat, causing it to 'waste' calories.

That's no reason to start drinking, of course. Even the newly recognised health benefits associated with some alcoholic beverages haven't been enough to convince public health experts to advise nondrinkers to start lifting a glass. The reason: excessive drinking poses big health risks.

Still, if you enjoy a glass of wine or beer with dinner, go on enjoying it. But make sure you have just one glass. Drinking more than that can loosen your resolution to stick to your diet.

Help!

'I know going out for fast food isn't the smartest thing to do. But sometimes there's no other choice, especially if the kids have anything to say about it. Is there any way to order off a fast-food menu and still keep calories down?'

Yes, as long as you can resist the messages to add this and supersize that. Be a contrarian. Choose the smallest sizes. Avoid the secret sauce. Double up on lettuce and tomatoes. Order diet soda or water instead of sugary drinks. Here are 10 meal options to choose from:

- Chicken nuggets (four pieces), sauce (one packet), vegetable salad with fat-free dressing
- Grilled chicken flat bread sandwich (without sauce), vegetable salad with fat-free dressing
- Small hamburger, vegetable salad with fat-free dressing
- Plain baked potato, small Caesar salad with low fat French dressing
- Veggie burger, vegetable salad with fat-free dressing
- Grilled vegetable sandwich (without mayonnaise), bean or lentil soup
- Zesty chicken salad bowl (no dressing)
- Taco salad with salsa
- Minestrone soup with French bread
- Toasted sesame bagel with smoked salmon and salad (no dressing)

another reason for filling your plate with colour. Many of the substances that provide fruits and vegetables with their colours are antioxidants – potent disease-fighters that have been shown to lower heart disease and the risk of cancer.

2. Order starters and side dishes

Another favourite dieting strategy: forgo the main dish section of the menu and order only from the starters and side dishes. With large restaurant portions, a starter or side dish often makes the perfect meal by itself.

3. Dip into the sauce

Ordering salad dressing to be served separately and drizzling it on sparingly is one of the oldest tricks in any slimmer's handbook, of course. Remember that you can order other sauces on the side, too, from gravy to guacamole. Give yourself no more than a tablespoon. And put your fork to good use. Instead of pouring on the sauce or salad dressing, dip the tips of your fork into it and then spear a bite-sized portion. You'll make a little bit of a good thing go a long way.

4. Create your own selection

If you're eating out with friends who share your concern about overdoing it, agree to order and share dishes. If there are four of you, order two or three main dishes. You'll get a chance to try a wider variety of items on the menu and keep portions down to size. Be careful, though: some people offered a lot to choose from end up eating a lot more. Decide in advance to sample only two or three forkfuls of each dish. With lots of dishes on the table, it's especially important to be aware of hunger and satiety signals. Sit back from time to time, take a deep breath and think about whether you've had enough – if you have, put your fork down, raise a glass of water and spend the rest of the time enjoying conversation.

5. Be a discerning food critic

Remember the credo of smart dining: if it doesn't taste great, don't eat it. Yes, of course, you paid for it. Of course it's a shame to waste food. But to finish something you don't really like is the true crime. It only means you won't get to eat something else that you'd really savour. When you're eating out this week, be a tough critic. Pay close attention to the first few bites. Decide whether it's good enough to finish or whether you'd just as soon set aside some calories for something else. If you eat out frequently, consider keeping a diner's diary, with mini reviews and notes on what you had. Use a star system to award top restaurants your own *ChangeOne* rating. You'll find yourself paying closer attention to the food you eat – and enjoying it more.

Changes ahead: weekends and celebrations

Restaurant meals are meant to be savoured and enjoyed. So is the weekend. Whether it's a calm day at home or a wild outdoor excursion, so many of us use weekends for relaxation, family and good food. Once you master the art of restaurant ordering, *ChangeOne* style, your next task will be to take on your weekend eating habits.

For some of us this will be difficult. When we get together with friends and family, food seems to magically appear, in copious amounts. It's time to start thinking about the role food plays in your social and family life. Look back to last weekend and think through all you did and the role food played in things. Where were the temptations, the times when food was too available or the centre of attention?

As you will see, we've been taught that food equals love – that mum serving you an extra plate of pudding is her way of showing how much she cares for you. When you are ready to move on, we'll show you how to say no to all those food offerings, without feeling guilty or sacrificing taste and enjoyment. Plus, you'll learn techniques for handling celebrations and special occasions as well.

WEEK **6**

Weekends
& Celebrations

We almost called this chapter 'Family and Friends'. Why? Because at weekends and on holidays and celebrations, that's who you'll be spending your time with, and these people will have an incredible amount of influence over what you eat – and how much. In many cases they'll be instrumental in determining your long-term dieting success, either through their support or lack of it.

Weekends are also when the usual work-week routine is up for grabs. New temptations arise from every side: fancy dinners out, hot dogs at a football match, Sunday lunches, tempting barbecues and birthday cakes.

This week dive into your weekend with gusto. We're proposing just this one change: focus less on food and more on active fun.

We'll show you that you don't have to hide from friends, family or fun to stick to your new eating habits.

Get together with family and friends

By now you know that the real secret of losing weight isn't as complicated as a lot of diet books would have you believe. Like a lot of the volunteers who tested *ChangeOne*, you may have found that making just two or three changes was all you needed in order to start slimming down.

The same principles that have guided you will serve you well when your routine switches gears at weekends and celebrations. Yes, you'll need to be a little creative. But that's not such a bad thing. Learning to be flexible is important. Life, after all, has a way of throwing us a curve now and then. The more confident you feel about adapting your diet to new situations, the better your chances of success. Weekends and celebrations are a great way to discover that you can control what you eat in almost any situation.

Why not take the weekend off?

If you've tried a deprivation-type diet in the past – the kind built around diet drinks or long lists of forbidden foods – you were probably tempted to take a holiday from it when weekends and celebrations rolled round. But by making a distinction between days when you follow a diet and days when you're on 'holiday' from it, you tell yourself that your diet is some kind of unnatural chore – it makes you eat one way to lose weight, but you really want to eat another very different way in your everyday life. That's the recipe for a diet that will fail. Too many dieters lose weight, then go off their diets and return to the way they used to eat. Almost immediately the weight begins to pile on again.

ChangeOne isn't about deprivation, as you know by now. It's about good food and a rational way of eating that you

Check-in

Frustrated that you're not losing weight faster? There's no need to be, if you're dropping half to one kilo (1 to 2 lb) a week. That's a pace that will keep you on track not only to lose weight but keep it off. Wish you were losing that much? Look back at the Fast Track suggestions in the breakfast, lunch, snack and supper chapters. Choose two to put into effect this week. Fast Track turned out to be one of the most popular features of *ChangeOne* among our volunteers. Many followed them all.

can enjoy every day while you lose weight – and will continue to enjoy and benefit from long after you've lost those kilos. It is a diet you can live with every day.

That's the key. The more consistently you make smart eating choices, the more quickly they'll become second nature to you. That's why it's so important, at weekends and at celebrations, to find ways to use *ChangeOne* strategies to guide you even when your normal schedule is disrupted and you find yourself in situations where plates are piled high and drinks are flowing freely.

If you're celebrating something special – your birthday, an anniversary or a big wedding, for example – live it up. And plan ahead. Strike a deal with yourself in advance. In return for getting the chance to indulge a little, agree to skip snacks during the day; set aside 45 minutes for a calorie-burning activity; put together any combination that lets you, in effect, pay as you go. Keep track of what you eat during the day. Fill in a detailed food diary if you have time.

And remember: one indulgence doesn't mean you've failed. It doesn't even have to bring bad news on the scales. To gain 500 g (1 lb), you have to consume about 3500 kcals more than you burn. That's a lot of calories. Even the biggest holiday feast isn't likely to pack that many. The truth is, a big blowout isn't what typically spells trouble for slimmers. The real danger is eating a little too much every day or every weekend. If you do indulge yourself this weekend, just make a pact to follow the *ChangeOne* meal plans more closely during the coming week and you'll be fine.

When food is love

One big reason weekends and celebrations are difficult is that in all the world's cultures, food equals love. Food is a reward. Food is comfort. How do we celebrate Valentine's Day? With chocolate hearts. What do we do for someone's birthday? Bake a cake. How do we mark a wedding? With a feast. The simple act of offering someone food is a way to show love and affection. There's nothing wrong with that. We just need to keep a clear view of why we're eating.

This week and at the weekend, notice the role that food plays for you when you are with your family and friends. If the people who love you encourage you to eat more

Practising the art of saying 'no thanks'

'Eat', your doting mother-in-law says. 'You're going to waste away if that's all you have.'

'What?' your Aunt Ellen says. 'Didn't you like my casserole? You've always loved my casserole. Come now, just one more little helping. Pudding? But it's a special occasion. You can't say no!'

Of course you can say no – but sometimes only at the risk of hurting someone's feelings. Or so it may seem. But you don't have to let well-meaning urgings to eat cause you to overeat. You can always say no thanks. And by being diplomatic you won't hurt any feelings in the process. Here's how:

Be honest. Casually mention to everyone in advance that you're on a diet and watching portion sizes. Make it clear that you don't want to offend anyone, but that it's very important for you to keep an eye on how much you eat.

Compliment early – and often. If you're oohing and aahing after the first bite, it won't seem as if you didn't appreciate the dish when you turn down seconds later.

Pace yourself. If you know Aunt Ellen's feelings will be hurt when you don't sample her apple pie, plan your meal accordingly. Help yourself to smaller portions of the main course so you have a little extra room – and some extra calories to spare – when dessert is served.

Say yes to a little. Sometimes it's easier to say yes to a little than to say no and find yourself staring at an empty plate while everybody enjoys something sweet. But be sure that you control the serving size, not your Aunt Ellen.

Use delaying tactics. Sometimes you can avoid offending people by saying, 'Maybe later'. Or, 'I'm so full right now I wouldn't be able to enjoy it. Let me wait a little while.' Once the plates are cleared away and the festivities move on to the next stage, no one will remember that you didn't have dessert.

> 'I'm so full right now I wouldn't be able to enjoy it.'

Take it home. Another strategy to avoid eating more than you want is simple flattery. When the offer for seconds comes along, rave about how great everything was – and ask if you can take a serving home rather than have seconds now. Remember: taking seconds home doesn't mean you have to eat them. If you don't intend to, make sure you dispose of them right away. We won't tell.

than you want or need, look for alternatives. If your mother says, 'Eat, eat', to show she cares, say: 'No thanks, mum, I'm full right now – but let me help you clear the dishes so we can have a chance to talk'. If your friends' main device for getting together is meals out, suggest alternatives that don't have to centre round food: playing cards or a board game, or even badminton or tennis, for instance, or a walk in a nearby park.

continued on page 134

Eggs on Sunday

A leisurely Sunday breakfast or brunch with family or friends is among life's great pleasures. And since you're combining two meals in one, you have a lot more calories to play with. These two menus feature egg dishes as the centrepiece.

The Sunday omelette

- 1 vegetable cheese omelette
- 1 portion chunky oven chips (see opposite)
- 1 wedge of melon

kcals 470, fat 21 g, saturated fat 7 g, cholesterol 483 mg, sodium 461 mg, carbohydrate 43 g, fibre 5 g, protein 31 g, calcium 400 mg

VEGETABLE CHEESE OMELETTE

Serves 1

2 eggs
2 teaspoons chopped fresh herbs (eg dill, basil, parsley)
salt and freshly ground black pepper
30 g (1 1/4 oz) fresh baby spinach leaves, cut into small strips
1 large tomato, chopped
2 tablespoons grated reduced-fat Cheddar cheese

1. Whisk together the eggs, herbs, 1 teaspoon water, and salt and pepper to taste in a bowl. In another bowl, toss the spinach with the tomato and cheese, and set aside.

2. Lightly coat a non-stick omelette pan or small frying pan with cooking spray and set over medium heat for 1 minute. Pour the egg mixture into the pan and cook until the eggs begin to set on the base. Lift up the edge of the omelette and push the cooked part towards the centre to let the uncooked portion run onto the pan. Cook until the omelette is almost set and the base is lightly browned.

3. Spread the spinach filling over half of the omelette, leaving a 1 cm (1/2 in) border and reserving 1 tablespoon for garnish. Fold the omelette over in half and cook for 2 more minutes. Slide the omelette onto a plate and garnish with the reserved filling.

Quiche with fruit bread

1 slice asparagus and Cheddar quiche

1 slice peach and yogurt loaf (recipe on page 256)

150 ml (5 fl oz) orange juice

kcals 350, fat 11 g, saturated fat 4 g, cholesterol 100 mg, sodium 370 mg, carbohydrate 48 g, fibre 3 g, protein 17 g, calcium 245 mg

ASPARAGUS AND CHEDDAR QUICHE

Serves 6

1 tablespoon dried breadcrumbs
225 g (8 oz) potatoes, peeled and very
**   thinly sliced**
2 teaspoons olive oil
450 g (1 lb) asparagus, trimmed
100 g (3½ oz) reduced-fat mature
**   Cheddar cheese, grated**
3 spring onions, sliced
1 can (about 350 g) reduced-fat
**   evaporated milk**
2 eggs + 2 extra egg whites
2 teaspoons melted butter
1 teaspoon dry mustard
salt and freshly ground black pepper

1. Preheat the oven to 200°C (400°F, gas mark 6). Coat a 23 cm (9 in) flan tin with cooking spray and sprinkle with the breadcrumbs. Beginning in the centre, arrange the potato slices in slightly overlapping circles to cover the bottom. Lightly brush with the olive oil and press down gently. Bake for 10 minutes.

2. Set 8 to 12 asparagus spears aside. Cut the rest into 2.5 cm (1 in) pieces.

3. Sprinkle the potato base with ¼ teaspoon salt and a third of the Cheddar. Cover with the asparagus pieces, then sprinkle with the spring onions and another third of the cheese. Arrange the whole asparagus spears on top.

4. Whisk together the evaporated milk, eggs and whites, butter, mustard, and salt and pepper to taste. Pour into the tin and sprinkle with the remaining Cheddar. Bake for 35 minutes or until a knife inserted in the centre comes out clean.

ABOUT EGGS

Although eggs contain relatively high levels of cholesterol, it's the amount of saturated fat in a food rather than the amount of cholesterol that has the most impact on cholesterol levels in the blood. A medium egg (the standard for recipes) contains about 75 kcals and 30 times more cholesterol than 25 g chocolate, but because the chocolate contains about twice as much saturated fat as the egg it's more likely to raise blood cholesterol levels. And eggs have a lot to offer nutritionally – they're one of the few dietary sources of vitamin D and also provide good amounts of vitamins A, E, B_2 and B_{12} (one medium egg provides almost 100 per cent of the recommended adult daily intake of B_{12}).

Chunky oven chips: For each serving, cut a scrubbed baking potato (with skin) into thick chips or wedges. Put into a polythene bag with 1 teaspoon olive oil and salt and pepper to taste, and shake to coat the potatoes. Spread out in a hot roasting tin and bake in a 240°C (475°F, gas mark 9) oven for 45 to 50 minutes, turning once or twice, until crisp and well browned.

Seafood on Saturday

Saturday brunches are often casual affairs enjoyed with friends. Simple, no-fuss dishes, like fish cakes and smoked salmon with bagels, are perfect.

Fishcake brunch

2 crab cakes

tossed green salad with vegetables and non-fat dressing (unlimited)

1 crusty bread roll

125 g (4½ oz) seasonal berries (eg raspberries, strawberries and blueberries)

kcals 440, fat 13 g, saturated fat 2 g, cholesterol 145 mg, sodium 836 mg, carbohydrate 60 g, fibre 5 g, protein 32 g, calcium 17 mg

CRAB CAKES

Serves 4
25 g (1 oz) fresh breadcrumbs
1 celery stick with leaves, finely chopped
45 g (1½ oz) red pepper, finely chopped
2 tablespoons finely chopped shallot
1 tablespoon chopped parsley
2 tablespoons grain mustard
2 tablespoons reduced-fat mayonnaise
1 egg
1 teaspoon mixed dried herbs
450 g (1 lb) white crab meat
50 g (1¾ oz) plain flour
2 teaspoons vegetable oil

1. Mix together the breadcrumbs, celery, red pepper, shallot, parsley, mustard, mayonnaise, egg and herbs in a large bowl. Gently fold in the crab meat.

2. Preheat the oven to 180ºC (350ºF, gas mark 4). With floured hands, divide the crab mixture into 8 and shape each portion into a small cake. Dredge the cakes in flour.

3. Lightly coat a large non-stick frying pan with cooking spray and set over medium-high heat until hot but not smoking. Add 4 crab cakes and cook for about 2 minutes on each side or until browned. Immediately after turning the cakes over, drizzle 1 teaspoon oil around them and gently shake the pan to spread the oil. Transfer the cakes to a plate lined with kitchen paper. Repeat with the remaining crab cakes and oil.

4. Lightly coat a baking tray with cooking spray. Place the crab cakes on the tray and bake for 8 to 10 minutes or until very hot in the centre. Serve hot.

5. One serving equals 2 crab cakes.

Smoked salmon and bagel brunch

1 bagel, any flavour, split in half and topped with:

1 tablespoon reduced-fat cream cheese
3 slices smoked salmon
2 slices tomato
2 slices red onion (optional)
Capers or caviar (optional)

225 g (8 oz) fresh fruit salad

1 Buck's Fizz (equal parts orange juice and champagne or sparkling water)

Coffee or tea

kcals 610, fat 7 g, saturated fat 3 g, cholesterol 17 mg, sodium 1521 mg, carbohydrate 110 g, fibre 5 g, protein 17 g, calcium 192 mg

HEALTH TIP

When shopping for reduced-fat cream cheese, check the labels to compare the calorie and fat contents of the different brands. They can vary considerably.

BRUNCH MENU TIPS

Try some or all of these ideas for your brunch menus:
- A basket of mini-muffins or crusty rolls

Salad variations:
- Baby spinach with reduced-fat dressing
- Sliced cucumbers tossed with rice vinegar, sesame oil and a sprinkle of caster sugar
- Cubed tomatoes drizzled with balsamic vinegar and extra virgin olive oil
- Baby lettuce and watercress

Cheese choices:
- Low-fat cottage cheese mixed with chopped cucumber, peppers and radishes
- Ricotta flavoured with pure vanilla extract, cinnamon and caster sugar
- Assorted sliced reduced-fat cheeses

Fruit treats:
- Fresh fruit salad
- Tri-colour melon ball salad (Charentais, watermelon and honeydew)
- Sliced peaches drizzled with Amaretto

continued from page 129

When you do find yourself at the table with friends and family, remember that you don't have to overeat to show you care. Food is only part of what makes sitting down with friends and family a pleasure. We get together to talk and laugh, to catch up on the latest news, to reinforce the ties that bind by expressing our feelings for one another. If you're engaged in conversation, no one will notice that you've put your fork down and are sipping from your water glass. Food may nourish our bodies, but it's laughter and expressions of caring, after all, that nourish our souls.

Nurturing yourself

Family and friends aren't the only people who urge food on us as a reward or show of affection. Some of us do it to ourselves. We eat to reward ourselves, or to feel better when we're a bit low. Especially if you grew up being offered food to feel better, you may have internalised the same reflex. Feel bad? Eat. The trouble, of course, is that you'll almost certainly overeat. When you do, you'll feel bad. And what do you do then? Well, eat some more.

> Music, quiet, a phone call, a walk – all serve as small personal rewards.

How to escape? You may already have found part of the answer in becoming aware of genuine hunger cues, and distinguishing them from environmental and emotional triggers. But if you still have trouble resisting the urge for food rewards, make a list of alternatives to edibles. What else will make you feel better? If your day is full of stresses, reward yourself with five minutes of quiet time to relax and de-pressurise. (You'll find more stress-busting strategies in Week 9, Stress Relief, which begins on page 180). If you love music, take a few minutes out to play a favourite piece. If you really, really, really want something to eat, reward yourself with a stick of sugar-free gum, a suggestion we've made before because it *really* works. Make it a habit, in fact. Over time, whenever you get the urge to treat yourself to food, you'll think 'sugar-free gum'.

Have a plan in place

Routines may change at weekends and when you're celebrating, but that doesn't mean everything is thrown up in the air. It's likely that you've already made at least a few plans for this weekend. Before it gets underway, think ahead. Write down a schedule for breakfast, lunch and supper, and fill in as many blanks as possible. Think of it as a reverse food diary. Let's say your weekend plans include a trip to your mother's house to celebrate her 70th birthday with a big family do. Your schedule might look something like this:

Saturday:

Breakfast: *ChangeOne* breakfast at home
Lunch: on the way
Supper: Mum's house

Sunday:

Breakfast: Mum's house
Lunch: family celebration
Supper: on the way home

Smart holiday tricks

When the Christmas season arrives, there's often no way to avoid being stuck in the house with lots of relatives and friends – and food everywhere. Here's how to cope:

Be helpful anywhere but in the kitchen. This is tough, especially if you're at the in-laws' house. It's all too easy to nibble when you're surrounded by food in various stages of preparation. Volunteer for other duties: clearing up, setting the table, fixing drinks, running errands – anything that doesn't involve food.

Be the activity director. Take the lead in suggesting non-eating activities that the family can do together, from playing a game of Scrabble or making decorations.

Grab a water bottle. When there are lots of high-calorie drinks around, it helps

Volunteer for any job that doesn't involve food.

to have an alternative available. Keep a glass or bottle of water handy.

Keep 'free' snacks and drinks on hand. Satisfy your hunger before the meal with low-calorie crudités – carrots, celery, peppers, radishes, cucumber and diet drinks. That way you won't have to rely on your will-power to steer clear of all those diet-busting rich foods.

Stay with the kids. If all the adults are circling the food table, spend time with the children. At most ages, kids are more likely than adults to be doing something active. Their energy and playfulness can help distract you from food.

Go out. If the sight and smell of all that food becomes just too much for you, excuse yourself and get out of the house. Take a walk or go for a drive.

Bowling over the calories

After losing 8 kg (18 lb) in her first five weeks on *ChangeOne*, Meredith Ross wasn't about to let a big weekend throw her off track – even two big weekends in a row, as she showed when she competed in her regional bowling tournaments. 'I'm the sort of person who has breakfast, lunch and supper same time every day,' says Meredith, an information technology expert and topnotch amateur bowler. 'When those tournaments come along, that schedule goes flying right out of the window. Instead of having supper at my usual seven o'clock, I'm sitting down with friends at one in the morning.'

And as much as she loves bowling, Meredith is the first to admit that the food usually available isn't exactly inspiring. 'It's all sausages, beefburgers, chips. Totally bad food.'

So Meredith set off for the big weekends prepared, carrying a big water bottle and a supply of cereal bars. When she and her friends sat down to meals together, she'd pick and choose to find something that measured up to *ChangeOne*. Breakfast at the hotel was easy: porridge, juice and a glass of milk. When supper rolled round she skipped the fried foods and had soup and a salad. At lunch she asked the cook to make her a lettuce and tomato sandwich.

Her smart choices paid off. When she stepped onto the scales on the Monday following the two back-to-back weekends, she'd lost 1 kg (2.2 lb). 'I was thrilled,' says Meredith. 'I realised that, for me, the biggest change was learning what to eat. I've never been someone who ate a lot of food. But before I started *ChangeOne* I didn't know which foods to choose. Now I know. Vegetables. Whole grains. Grilled instead of fried. Even when my routine goes out of the window, I know now that I just have to remember those few rules and I can stay on my diet.'

Once you've written up a schedule, identify meals that are likely to pose the toughest challenge and think up ways to prepare in advance to make them easier. In the example above, Saturday breakfast is a breeze, but lunch on the way could be treacherous, given the sorts of places to eat that you are likely to come across. Family suppers are always a challenge – too much food, too many people urging you to eat. And a celebration lunch on Sunday! The table will be laden with all the family's favourite dishes.

Never fear. There are plenty of ways to plan ahead for a weekend like this. Here's what to consider:

1. Do it yourself

The best way to control what you eat is to make it yourself. If there's not much chance you'll find a healthy meal en route, consider packing your own in advance. You'll save money, frustration and time. If the weather's good and you can find a nice place to stop, you can turn a packed lunch into a picnic. When the weekend includes a shared meal, where everyone brings something, contribute a *ChangeOne* dish. Fix two if you have the time. That way you'll have a choice of dishes you know you can rely on to be low in calories. Don't forget to bring along sugar-free drinks or sparkling mineral water.

2. Celebrate special occasions with special food

At most big family gatherings and celebrations, people lovingly prepare home-made delicacies like Aunt Margaret's raised chicken pie or your grandmother's baked custard tarts. Spend your calories wisely by skipping crisps, nuts and other savoury snacks before the meal, and choosing only the most special foods for the special occasion.
As much as possible, plan your entire meal in advance.

3. Practise your pace

The big meal over the Christmas holidays is one time when everyone relaxes and enjoys a leisurely feast. It's a great chance to practise all your best tortoise skills. For a long meal, you may have to use every delaying tactic in the book. Drink a sip of water between each bite. Put your fork down frequently. Sit back in your chair and enjoy the conversation for a few minutes without eating anything.

4. Watch the alcohol

Wine, punch, beer and other alcoholic drinks have a way of flowing freely at special meals. Don't let too much alcohol dissolve your best intentions to stick to your diet. Limit yourself to one glass with your meal. The rest of the time, have sparkling mineral water with lemon or lime, or sugar-free soft drinks. Want an icy cold lager on a hot summer's day? Obviously, 'lite' or alcohol-free beer or lager are options, and they're getting better and better.

5. Get out and about

The extra leisure time at weekends offers a great opportunity to plan activities that involve burning more calories – gather your relatives for a ramble, a bicycle ride, a walking tour of a nearby town or stately home, cricket, tennis, a fun run in the park, throwing a Frisbee, frolicking with the dog. Burn 500 extra kcals this weekend and you can treat yourself to a big piece of blackberry and apple pie without worrying about upsetting your calorie balance. Activities that the whole family can join in – from croquet to badminton – are also a great way to enjoy time together that doesn't centre around food.

6. Take time for bedtime

Weekends are a wonderful opportunity to catch up on sleep you may have lost during the week. Remember: lack of sleep can erode your will-power and your determination. Obesity experts believe it can even cause you to put on weight. Get to bed a little early one night this weekend. If that doesn't work, allow yourself to sleep a little later than usual one morning.

7. Fine-tune your expectations

If the coming week holds a crowded schedule of holiday parties, be realistic about your goals. Instead of trying to continue losing weight, for instance, relax your goal and aim to maintain your current weight. Then, when the holidays are finished, you can start shedding weight again. Setting standards that are impossible to meet is setting yourself up for failure. Unless you have an upcoming modelling session for the cover of *Vogue* or *GQ*, odds are you don't have to lose a certain amount of weight by any particular date. Remember, this is a plan for your entire life. Don't put yourself under more pressure than you need. It's far better to take a little while longer reaching your goal than to put yourself under unnecessary stress.

Should you enlist family and friends?

A bit of encouragement, a helping hand, even someone joining you on your walk round the village can be a great morale booster. So can a shoulder to lean on when things aren't going your way. Help from family and friends can also take the pressure off and eliminate unnecessary stresses in your life.

How important are the people around you when it comes to slimming success? At first, behavioural scientists assumed the answer would be 'very'. The more support dieters had, the assumption went, the better their odds of losing weight and keeping it off. But the results of studies looking at social support and weight loss have been mixed. Some people do better when they have a strong social network. Others do just fine on their own.

Knowing whether you tend to be a team player or a solo flyer is the first step in finding the kind of support and encouragement you need to succeed. To find out, answer the questions in the quiz on page 145.

Your friends in need

Social support comes in many forms, from the neighbour who joins you on your morning walk to the partner who decides to do the *ChangeOne* programme along with you. The first step in getting the help you need is deciding what kind of help you need. Tick one or more of the following categories.

❏ An activity partner
❏ Someone to talk to when I'm feeling down or discouraged
❏ Someone who can answer specific diet questions
❏ Help in the kitchen
❏ Help around the house
❏ A lunch or supper companion
❏ Other: _____

continued on page 144

139

Cooking outdoors

What better way to entertain than with a barbecue. But prepare yourself: meals you make for friends and family at weekends tend to be larger than everyday meals, so eat less at the other two meals that day.

Barbecued chicken feast

Crudités platter (unlimited)

Spicy chicken (1 breast, or 1 drumstick plus 1 thigh)

Grilled summer vegetables (coffee mug)

Warm potato salad with Dijon vinaigrette (2 golf balls)

2 sesame breadsticks

1 piece Chocolate Snacking Cake (recipe on page 284)

kcals 540, fat 8 g, saturated fat 2 g, cholesterol 85 mg, sodium 1170 mg, carbohydrate 84 g, fibre 9 g, protein 37 g, calcium 150 mg

GRILLED SUMMER VEGETABLES

Serves 4

2 small fennel bulbs, about 225 g (8 oz) each

1 aubergine, about 450 g (1 lb), cut lengthways into 1 cm (½ in) thick slices

4 tomatoes, halved

3 large peppers, preferably 1 each green, red and yellow, cut into 1 cm (½ in) wide strips

1 red onion, cut into 8 wedges

½ teaspoon salt

½ teaspoon freshly ground black pepper

1 tablespoon orange juice

8 fresh basil leaves, very thinly sliced

1 small garlic clove, very finely chopped

1 teaspoon grated orange zest

1. Prepare a charcoal fire (or preheat the grill or a ridged cast-iron grill pan).

2. Cut the leafy tops off the fennel bulbs and set aside. Trim the bulbs and cut vertically into 1 cm (½ in) slices. Coat the fennel, aubergine, tomatoes, peppers and onion with cooking spray, or a very light coating of olive oil, and sprinkle with the salt and pepper.

3. Barbecue (or grill) the vegetables for about 4 minutes on each side or until tender and browned. Transfer to a serving platter and sprinkle with the orange juice.

4. Finely chop the reserved fennel tops and mix in a bowl with the basil, garlic and orange zest. Sprinkle over the vegetables.

5. Serve warm or at room temperature.

SPICY BARBECUED CHICKEN

Serves 4
1 chicken, 1.1–1.35 kg (2 ½–3 lb)
3–4 tablespoons dry spice rub, made with equal parts paprika, onion and chive seasoning and garlic granules, plus salt and pepper to taste
1 can beer or lager

1. Prepare the barbecue, placing the coals around the outside edge. If using a gas barbecue, leave one burner off.

2. Rub the chicken inside and out with the spice mixture. Loosen the skin slightly and sprinkle a bit of the spice rub between the skin and the flesh.

3. Open the can of beer and pour out half. Place the beer can on the barbecue, in the centre if using charcoal or over the unlit burner on a gas grill. 'Sit' the chicken on top of the beer can (the can should fit inside the chicken cavity) with its legs spread to form a 'tripod' on the rack.

4. Close the barbecue lid and cook the chicken for 45 to 60 minutes or until thoroughly cooked. Carefully remove the chicken and can from the barbecue.

5. Cut the chicken into 6 pieces – 2 thighs, 2 drumsticks and 2 breasts. One serving equals one thigh plus one drumstick, or one breast. Remove the skin before eating.

WARM POTATO SALAD WITH DIJON VINAIGRETTE

Serves 4
450 g (1 lb) red-skinned or waxy new potatoes scrubbed and quartered
3 smoked turkey rashers
1 small onion, chopped
3 tablespoons cider vinegar
1 ½ tablespoons caster sugar
1 tablespoon grain mustard
½ teaspoon olive oil
¼ teaspoon salt
½ teaspoon freshly ground black pepper
45 g (1 ½ oz) finely chopped sweet-and-sour gherkins
45 g (1 ½ oz) finely chopped red pepper
4 tablespoons chopped parsley

1. Cook the potatoes in a large saucepan of boiling water for about 10 minutes or until tender. Drain and keep warm.

2. At the same time, cut the turkey rashers in half, then cook in a large non-stick frying pan until crisp. Transfer to kitchen paper, then crumble. Sauté the onion in the same pan (add cooking spray if necessary) for about 7 minutes or until golden.

3. Shake the vinegar, sugar, mustard, oil, salt and pepper in a screwtop jar, then whisk into the onion in the pan. Bring to a simmer and cook for about 2 minutes. Add the potatoes, half the turkey rashers, the gherkin and red pepper, and cook, stirring, for about 2 minutes or until the potatoes are coated and hot. Sprinkle with the parsley and the remaining turkey rashers.

4. Serve warm or at room temperature.

Holiday classics

Holidays and food go hand in hand, and most of us look forward to enjoying the same foods year after year. It's fine if you choose to leave *ChangeOne* behind for a feast day celebration. To continue following *ChangeOne* during the holidays, check out our sample menu and some new variations on old favourites.

Christmas lunch

85 g/3 oz apple-stuffed turkey breast
(pack of cards)

4 tablespoons turkey gravy, bought or home-made (golf ball)

2 tablespoons cranberry sauce
(table tennis ball)

Orange-glazed carrots and sweet potatoes (2 golf balls)

green salad with fat-free dressing
(unlimited)

1 small crusty bread roll

kcals 410, fat 7 g, saturated fat 1 g, cholesterol 25 mg, sodium 959 mg, carbohydrate 75 g, fibre 4 g, protein 25 g, calcium 104 mg (Note: Figures do not include starter, dessert and drinks.)

ABOUT FEEDING A CROWD

- Select at least two starters, one vegetable (like stuffed mushrooms or a crudités platter) and one based on low-fat or reduced-fat cream cheese.

- Offer a green salad as a low-calorie filler. Make the dressing optional, and offer a fat-free alternative.

- Main course choices should include one or two dishes, a starch side dish (pasta, rice, potatoes), rolls or bread and one or two cooked vegetables.

- Prepare each recipe for about half the number of people expected. For example, if you have 16 guests, prepare each dish to serve 8.

APPLE-STUFFED TURKEY BREAST WITH ORANGE MARMALADE GLAZE

Serves 8

1 whole turkey breast joint on the bone (1.35–1.6 kg/3–3½ lb)
1½ teaspoons salt
1 teaspoon freshly ground black pepper
2 celery sticks, cut into 2.5 cm (1 in) pieces
2 large dessert apples, peeled and thinly sliced
1 large onion, thinly sliced
5 sprigs fresh thyme, plus 1 teaspoon chopped fresh thyme
2 teaspoons olive oil
500 ml (16 fl oz) apple juice
150 g (5½ oz) low-sugar orange marmalade
125 ml (4 fl oz) white wine or apple juice

1. Preheat the oven to 180ºC (350ºF, gas mark 4). Rinse the turkey, pat dry with kitchen paper and rub the skin all over with salt and pepper.

2. Combine the celery, half the apples and onion, and 3 thyme sprigs in a roasting tin, piling in a mound in the centre. Toss the chopped thyme with the remaining apples and onion in a bowl. Stuff half of the mixture under the turkey skin; place the remaining mixture in the neck cavity.

3. Set the turkey on top of the vegetable mixture in the tin. Lightly brush the turkey with olive oil and top with the remaining thyme sprigs. Pour the apple juice into the tin. Roast for 1 hour. Discard the thyme sprigs, and baste the turkey with half the marmalade. Continue roasting for about 15 minutes or until the turkey is golden brown and cooked through, basting twice with the remaining marmalade. An instant-read thermometer inserted in the thickest part of the breast, not touching bone, should reach 75ºC (170ºF). Transfer the turkey to a platter and allow to rest for 10 minutes, then carve. Discard the skin.

4. Stir the wine or juice into the apples and vegetables in the tin and boil, scraping up the browned bits from the tin, until liquid is reduced by half. Serve with the turkey.

ORANGE-GLAZED CARROTS OR SWEET POTATOES

Serves 8

900 g (2 lb) carrots or sweet potatoes, peeled
1 can (about 170 g) frozen orange juice concentrate, thawed
2½ teaspoons ground coriander
1 teaspoon salt
175 ml (6 fl oz) water
1 tablespoon olive oil
20 g (¾ oz) fresh mint, chopped

1. If using carrots, halve lengthways and cut into 5 cm (2 in) lengths. If using sweet potatoes, cut into eighths lengthways and then cut into 5 cm (2 in) lengths.

2. Combine the carrots or sweet potatoes, orange juice concentrate, ground coriander and salt in large frying pan. Add the water and bring to the boil over medium heat. Reduce to a simmer, cover and cook for 15 minutes.

3. Uncover the pan, increase the heat to high and cook for a further 7 minutes or until the vegetables are tender.

4. Add the oil and cook for 1 minute, tilting the pan to swirl in the oil, until the vegetables are glossy and the sauce is creamy. Stir in the mint and serve. One serving is 2 golf balls.

continued from page 139

Now, make a list of possible candidates to fill the positions you've ticked. Keep in mind: sometimes support comes from unexpected places. A work colleague may be more useful to you than a close family member. A neighbour you meet on one of your walks – someone who's also trying to slim down – may offer more help than a close friend.

If you're looking for emotional support, identify someone you're willing to confide in, even if that means admitting weakness or failure. If you're looking for practical help around the house, you probably already know who to ask. So ask. Be specific about what you need, and why you need it. If you're asking someone to do a real favour, think about – and ask – what you can do in return.

Beware of saboteurs

In a perfect world, family and friends would support you 100 per cent. But we live in an imperfect world. Sometimes the people closest to you may be threatened by your efforts to change.

Often it's especially the people closest to you, in fact, who have trouble with your decision to lose weight. A husband or wife, for example. A brother or sister. Why? If your husband or wife tends to be jealous, your decision to lose weight could be interpreted as a desire to be found attractive to other people. If your spouse could stand to lose a little weight, too – but isn't willing to try right now – he or she may resent your determination and success.

There are plenty of reasons that don't take a psychiatrist to figure out, of course. Following a diet requires changes in the kitchen and at the table. Some family members may not want to be bothered by those changes. They may not like the extra time you spend planning lunches or suppers. They may feel uncomfortable finishing everything on their plate when you eat only half of what's on yours.

Take a moment to think about the people closest to you. Among them, is there anyone who:

- Urges food on you even when you say that you're not hungry?
- Belittles your efforts to lose weight?
- Throws obstacles in the way of your being more active?
- Seems resentful or threatened by the fact that you've begun to lose weight?

Change One Quiz

Team player or solo flyer?

Some people need the support and advice of people around them. Others do best on their own. To determine whether you're best suited be a soloist or a team player, answer the following true or false questions. Your score will help you choose the best strategies to overcome obstacles and to keep your motivation high.

1. I'm comfortable talking to other people about my weight.
- △ True
- ☐ False

2. If things aren't going well for me, I typically turn to family or friends for advice.
- △ True
- ☐ False

3. I'm embarrassed talking about my feelings with other people, even people close to me.
- ☐ True
- △ False

4. Getting a little pat on the back now and then would help motivate me right now.
- △ True
- ☐ False

5. When I set my mind to do something, I don't really need other people to push me.
- ☐ True
- △ False

6. I have at least one person in my life with whom I can talk about almost anything.
- △ True
- ☐ False

7. I tend to keep my personal feelings to myself.
- ☐ True
- △ False

8. The people around me are part of the reason I've had trouble losing weight in the past.
- ☐ True
- △ False

9. I've always tended to tackle problems on my own.
- △ True
- ☐ False

10. I'm not really sure that the people around me have my best interests in mind.
- ☐ True
- △ False

11. Just being able to talk things over with someone when I've got a problem can make things seem better.
- △ True
- ☐ False

12. I'm very uneasy about letting people see my weaknesses.
- ☐ True
- △ False

13. I've joined groups in the past, and they've really helped me.
- △ True
- ☐ False

14. Frankly, I don't really trust people to be honest with me or tell me what they're really thinking.
- ☐ True
- △ False

Turn to next page to add up your score.

145

Quiz score

Add up the number of coloured shapes you ticked according to colour.

△ Blue _____

☐ Green _____

△ Blue triangles show team players, people who benefit from the support of others. The more you've ticked, the more likely you are to benefit from a strong support network of friends and family. If you wish you had a little more help from those around you now and then, read on for tips on how to get the support you need.

☐ Green boxes indicate solo flyers – people who typically go it alone. The more you've ticked, the more likely you are to depend on yourself.

Most of us are a little of both, of course – we turn to friends or family sometimes and depend on ourselves at other times. So don't be surprised if your score falls somewhere in the middle. Read on for advice on how to strengthen your social network, along with tips on how to make a better job of helping yourself.

■ Gets angry or frustrated when you leave food on your plate?

■ Undermines your efforts with negative messages, saying things like 'I don't know what makes you think you'll be able to lose weight this time', or 'Once the holidays start you're going to gain it all back again anyway'?

■ Constantly reminds you that you're on a diet and clucks over every bite you eat? That's not help, it's a constant irritation that could wear you down over time.

If so, you may be struggling against someone who's trying to sabotage the change that you want to make. Often the hardest part in dealing with a saboteur is acknowledging that your personal relationships aren't perfect, and that someone close to you may be standing between you and the improvements that you want to make. It's easier to blame yourself or your lack of will-power. But it's crucially important to recognise when someone is making life harder for you rather than easier. Otherwise, they can undermine your chances of success.

Talk it over

This week, if you spot a problem like that and you think it comes mainly from a lack of communication, ask your problem person for a heart-to-heart talk. Explain why losing weight is so important to you – and why the sincere support and enthusiasm of people around you matters so much. Point out things that make it hard for you or hurt your feelings. And be specific about the kind of help you need. For instance:

- 'I'd rather you didn't offer me more. When I say no, I feel as if I'm hurting your feelings. But it's very important to me right now to cut back on the amount I eat.'

How to be your own best friend

Can't find a support team? Doing just fine on your own? Whether you're a soloist or a team player, a few strategies can help you get through the inevitable rough patches. The key is to be your own best friend. Here are four ways to do that:

Banish negative thoughts. Most of us have heard that little voice that whispers: 'You're never going to be able to do it' or 'You just don't have what it takes'. Learn to recognise such negative thoughts and replace them with the kinds of positive messages a good friend would offer. 'Yes, you can do it.' 'One slip-up is no big deal.' 'Keep up the good work.'

Keep a journal. If that negative voice in your head just won't let up, try carrying a small notebook with you this week and jot down every negative thought that occurs to you. You may be surprised to find that the simple act of writing these thoughts down makes you see how irrational they are. If you can't dismiss them, take a moment to come up with a positive counter-message.

'I'm trying to improve myself.' 'I've stayed with a diet for five weeks, which isn't bad.' 'No one's perfect. I'm doing my best.' By keeping a diary, you'll also become aware of the situations and circumstances that trigger negative thoughts. Avoid them if you can. If you can't, have your positive counter-messages ready.

> 'No one's perfect. I'm doing my best.'

Reward yourself for a good job. When you reach one of your goals – even if it's something as simple as sticking to *ChangeOne* through a long holiday weekend – give yourself a reward. For a little extra motivation, decide in advance what the reward will be: a new pair of walking shoes, a new item of clothing, a spa or massage treatment, or tickets to a big match or concert.

Learn to laugh at your foibles. Having a sense of humour can go a long way when you're trying to make a big change in your life. Take yourself too seriously and you'll slip into the kind of all-or-nothing thinking that makes people give up before they've even given themselves a chance.

- 'I'd really like you to join me for a walk after supper instead of watching television. Maybe we can make a list of the programmes we really want to see and work out a schedule around them.'
- 'It would help me a lot if we put snack food in the cupboard rather than on the worktop where I see it all the time. I have a tendency to eat when there's food out.'
- 'It really hurts my feelings when you say that I never stick with things. I'm really trying this time. Your encouragement means a lot to me.'
- 'I appreciate that you want to help me lose weight, but continually reminding me I'm on a diet is driving me to distraction. For the most part, I want to handle this on my own. Let me ask for help when I need it.'

Ask your spouse or partner to talk about their own feelings. Explore what you can do to make the situation easier. If a loved one feels threatened, make it clear that your love hasn't changed.

Be sure to have fun at weekends. It makes healthier eating so much easier.

In some cases, you may know that all the talk in the world isn't going to solve the problem. Then the best strategy is learning to recognise acts of sabotage and to find ways to defuse them. This week, try to avoid tense situations that involve food. Spend less time in the kitchen, for instance, and more in other parts of the house. If leaving food on your plate is a flash point, serve yourself only as much as you want to eat.

No advice will fit every situation. Use your best judgment. And remember: if you can't get the support from one source, you can often find it from another. And you can always learn to lean on yourself for motivation and encouragement, too.

Enjoy yourself

It should be easy to enjoy yourself at weekends, during the holidays and at times of celebration. But if you're constantly worried about being tempted by too much food, it's easy to forget that the whole point of weekends and celebrations is to relax and have a good time. The meal suggestions on these pages offer plenty of great flavour and portions guaranteed to satisfy even a weekend appetite.

So this weekend, make sure you relax and have fun. Being physically active at weekends and on other days off also adds enjoyment and gives you an opportunity to relax.

Why make a point of having a good time when you're on a diet? Because the more you're able to find pleasure in food, the easier you'll find it to stay on the programme, turning healthy eating into a lifelong habit.

Changes ahead: fixing your kitchen

Some of us love to cook, the rest of us don't. But cook we must, almost every day. Next week, we will be focusing on having a kitchen that is as friendly and simple as can be, so that making *ChangeOne*-style meals is child's play.

So even as you work through your strategies for weekends and celebrations, ponder your kitchen set-up. Are you over-stocked with snacks and unhealthy prepared foods? Or is your storecupboard so bare that making a healthy, fresh meal guarantees a trip to the shops? Do you own a can of cooking spray? If yes, is it easier to get to than the butter in the refrigerator?

We think you'll be surprised at how much easier cooking healthy can be, once you make a handful of small tweaks to the way you buy and store your food and supplies.

WEEK **7**

Fixing Your Kitchen

'On days when warmth is the most important need of the human heart', the author E.B. White once wrote, 'the kitchen is the place you can find it…'. These words still hold true. Even in today's world of take-away pizzas and microwave meals, the kitchen is still the warm heart of most households.

This week you'll transform the kitchen by tossing out the devilish foods on hand, replacing them with *ChangeOne* choices, and rearranging for easier, healthier cooking.

Why the changes? Because we don't ever want you to think of a kitchen as a place to be avoided. In *ChangeOne*, we want the kitchen to remain a place of warmth, a place that encourages happiness and healthy eating at the same time.

150

Stocking up

Making sure you have plenty of food in your storecupboard may sound like strange slimming advice. Who wants more temptations around when you're trying to eat less?

In fact, as many dieters discover, a bare cupboard can actually spell trouble. No matter how scant your provisions are, chances are there's a bag of crisps from last week's party or a box of chocolates left over from a dinner party lurking somewhere. And if that's all there is to eat, guess what you're going to grab if you get hungry enough. Exactly.

By keeping plenty of healthy foods around, you'll have plenty of choices, not just for snacks but for every meal of the day. And with some clever kitchen organisation, you can make sure the best choices are in front of you when you open a cupboard or the refrigerator door. What's more, a well-stocked, well-organised kitchen can save you time and spare you frustration. With the right selection of essentials on hand, you can put together a simple and delicious meal without having to rush out to the corner shop for provisions. Many home cooks are inspired to make interesting dishes simply by opening the refrigerator, checking what's there and conjuring up tasty combinations. (You'll find three from-the-storecupboard recipes on pages 156, 159 and 162.)

> Ask yourself, 'Would I eat this?' Then, 'Should I eat this?'

How can your kitchen help you? To find out, answer the questions in 'Inspecting Your Kitchen'.

The first step in designing a diet-friendly kitchen isn't shopping; it's clearing your shelves. So get the rubbish bags ready, along with a box for items you can give away to a charity shop. It's time to get rid of food you don't want and don't need around to tempt you.

Start with the storecupboard. Ask yourself for each item, 'Would I eat this?' If yes, then ask, 'Should I eat this?' Keep in mind your family's tastes, of course. But don't be too generous. If you shouldn't eat it, chances are your loved ones shouldn't, either. Focus in particular on items that have sat around for more than six months.

Move to the refrigerator and freezer next. Clear out those old jars of condiments, those squishy old peppers, those eight-day-old leftovers.

If it feels good to clear the shelves, it should. And it'll feel even better when you fill up the space with foods that are healthier, fresher and more interesting.

Go shopping

Your next step is a trip to the supermarket to buy essentials. Exactly what those essentials are will depend on your taste, how often you prepare meals at home and the kinds of foods your family likes. You'll find a master shopping list of storecupboard essentials on page 157 to use as your guide. You won't want them all, of course. The more choices you have on hand, though, the easier it will be for you to put together a *ChangeOne* meal or snack on the spur of the moment.

Before you go to the supermarket this week, keep in mind the seven essential strategies for smart shopping.

1. Have a snack before you leave. You'll get some exercise pushing your trolley down the aisles and hauling bags, so go ahead and take the hunger edge off before you get there. An empty stomach can make you empty-headed. Nothing weakens will power faster than being hungry. You've probably seen shoppers so hungry that they dip into the bag of crisps or packet of biscuits even before they've reached the check-out. Avoid trouble by shopping after you've eaten a meal. If you absolutely have to shop for supper on an empty stomach, help yourself to a *ChangeOne* snack before you set off for the supermarket.

2. Start with a list – and stay with it. Your local supermarket is full of temptations that can be hard to resist. Supermarkets are in the business of selling food, especially items with a big profit margin. The biggest money-makers are often the items that are prominently displayed at eye level or at the ends of aisles around the store. The chances are you'll see row after row

Check-in

Is someone making it harder rather than easier to eat as you should? If you realised last week that you have a saboteur in your midst, consider taking an extra week to resolve the situation as best you can. Keep a diary and write in it every time someone says or does something that seems designed to sabotage your efforts. At the end of each day, look over your entries and devise ways to free yourself. Strategies include avoiding situations that involve food, countering negative messages with positive ones, or simply learning to ignore criticisms or unwanted enticements. The best approach sometimes is to talk about it. At other times, separating yourself from the source of trouble is a better solution. Use your judgment. Just remember: you're in charge of what you eat – no one else. Be considerate of other people's feelings, but stick to your resolution.

Inspecting your kitchen

How diet-friendly is your kitchen? There's only one way to find out. Put on your kitchen inspector's cap and fill out the following checklist.

1. What are the first three things you see when you open the refrigerator door?

1. _____
2. _____
3. _____

2. What are the first three things you see when you open the freezer?

1. _____
2. _____
3. _____

3. List the three handiest snacks in your kitchen:

1. _____
2. _____
3. _____

4. How many different kinds of fresh vegetables does your refrigerator or vegetable rack contain?

❑ None
❑ One or two
❑ Three or more

5. Is there a bowl of fresh fruit on the work surface?

❑ Yes
❑ No
❑ Usually, but not today

6. Do you have the makings of a *ChangeOne* supper in your storecupboard and refrigerator?

❑ Yes
❑ No
❑ Usually, but not today

7. Where do you keep your shopping list?

❑ Posted on the refrigerator door or in another prominent place
❑ Tucked away somewhere in the kitchen
❑ What list?

8. Rate your collection of storage containers

❑ Plentiful, in a variety of different sizes
❑ Enough for a few leftovers
❑ What storage containers?

9. How many 'too-tempting-to-resist' foods are stored in your kitchen right now?

❑ None
❑ One or two
❑ Three or more

10. Which of the following are absent from your kitchen?

❑ Measuring spoons
❑ Kitchen scales
❑ A non-stick frying pan or wok
❑ A set of sharp knives
❑ A vegetable steamer
❑ Microwave oven
❑ Rice cooker
❑ Set of small bowls and plates

Turn to next page to add up your score.

Quiz score

Assessing your answers:

1, 2, 3. If the first items you see fit on the *ChangeOne* menu, your kitchen is in great shape. If not, your kitchen is working against you. Either get rid of the stuff you'd rather not be tempted by, or tuck it away where you have to work to get it.

4. Vegetables are free, so keep a tempting variety that will make it easy to throw together a low-calorie meal without having to the shop.

5. Put a bowl of fruit out where everyone in the family can see it. That way, it will be the first place everyone goes when a snack attack strikes.

6. If you don't have the ingredients for a *ChangeOne* meal in your storecupboard, you should. If you do, you'll be ready for anything, from a stormy night to a surprise visitor.

7. Invest in a wipe-clean shopping list you can mount on the refrigerator. It's a great way to keep track, so you won't be caught short when you want to cook a quick and simple meal.

8. Keep plenty of storage containers handy. They're great for keeping leftovers. But you can also use them to divide up giant-sized packets into reasonably sized portions as soon as you get home.

9. Why drive yourself mad keeping foods you can't resist? Throw them out. Or put them so far out of reach that you'll have to make a really big effort to get them. One of our *ChangeOne* volunteers tucked his treat foods behind a couple of rows of wine glasses.

10. For a list of terrific time-saving, slimmer-friendly kitchen tools, take a look at page 304.

of snack foods, crisps, biscuits, soft drinks and highly sweetened cereals. Steer your trolley down almost any aisle and you'll be surrounded by brightly-coloured packages specifically designed to entice you to grab them and pop them into your trolley. All natural! Two for one! Giant family-size economy pack! Choose me!

To avoid the hard sell, put together a shopping list in the quiet and comfort of your own kitchen. Build your list around recipes and meal plans. Use the guide to kitchen essentials on page 157, along with our lists of shopping strategies on pages 302 to 303.

Once you get to the supermarket, stick to your list. If fresh peaches or perfectly ripe tomatoes are in season, help yourself. Don't be afraid to tweak your meal plan if you find something irresistible in the produce section or a good bargain at the fish counter. But don't reach for that jumbo-size bag of cheesy wotsits just because it's on special offer this week. If it's not on your list – or your diet – it doesn't belong in your trolley. If you don't find what you're looking for, talk to the manager. Most supermarkets are happy to stock what customers want.

3. Steer your trolley around the perimeter.

In most supermarkets, the healthiest choices are arranged around the perimeter of the store. That's where you'll find dairy products, the produce section, and the meat and fish counters. Processed foods, including those rows upon rows of brightly coloured snack food packets, are usually in the centre of the store. The more shopping you do around the perimeter, the less processed food you're likely to eat – and the more food that fits your *ChangeOne* diet.

4. Think small.

Giant food cash-and-carries have grown up around the notion of saving money by buying in bulk. There's nothing wrong with saving a few pounds. But if you have a hard time stopping yourself once a big bag of crisps is open, take heed. If you're buying food to eat right away, buy a small packet – preferably a single-serving size. If you buy jumbo sizes to save money, divide them into single-serving-size resealable plastic bags or containers as soon as you get home.

5. Read the small print.

With few exceptions, all processed and packaged foods are required to carry detailed food labels that list ingredients and nutrition information. Learning to read a label will help you shop wisely. When your goal is to lose weight, the most important number on the label is calories per serving (but do look at fat and fibre too). Be sure to check how the label defines a serving size. The amount can vary widely even within the same category.

continued on page 158

Managing your food

1. Use opaque storage containers for 'treat' foods so you won't be tempted by the sight of the contents.
2. Put notes on food containers to remind yourself of what a sensible portion should be.
3. Decide in advance how much you plan to eat—before you open the container.
4. Attach a list of your favourite *ChangeOne* snacks to the refrigerator door as a reminder.
5. Put a date on leftovers – and a reminder on your calendar of when you plan to eat them.
6. Once a week tour your kitchen, ensuring the healthiest foods occupy the most prominent positions.
7. Keep a list of essential items that are running low so that you won't be caught unprepared.

Storecupboard stew

Here's an easy vegetarian dish made from the storecupboard and freezer.

Easy midweek supper

Chickpea and pasta stew (2 cricket balls)

1 slice garlic bread (palm-size)

kcals 400, fat 7 g, saturated fat 2 g, cholesterol 5 mg, sodium 700 mg, carbohydrate 67 g, fibre 8 g, protein 20 g, calcium 200 mg

CHICKPEA AND PASTA STEW

Serves 4

2 cans (about 400 g each) chopped tomatoes, plain or flavoured
1 can (about 400 g) chickpeas or other beans or pulses, drained and rinsed
300 g (10½ oz) frozen mixed vegetables
155 g (5½ oz) small pasta shapes such as elbow macaroni, conchigliette or ditalini
½ teaspoon dried oregano
½ teaspoon dried basil
500 ml (16 fl oz) water, plus additional water as needed

1. Combine all the ingredients in a medium-size saucepan. Place over medium heat and bring to the boil.

2. Reduce the heat to low and simmer for 20 to 30 minutes, stirring occasionally, until the pasta is al dente. Add more water during cooking if the stew looks dry.

GARLIC BREAD

Serves 4

4 slices ciabatta or French bread (palm-size)
2 cloves garlic, finely chopped
2 teaspoons olive oil
4 teaspoons grated Parmesan cheese

1. Preheat the grill. Mix together the garlic and olive oil. Spread one-quarter of the mixture on each slice of bread. Top each slice with 1 teaspoon grated Parmesan.

2. Grill for about 1 minute or until the topping is golden brown.

Kitchen essentials

U se this guide to make sure your kitchen has all the items you'll need for healthy snacking and quick, easy-to-cook meals. Here we list some everyday staples, the basic provisions you should have on hand to be sure you can always put together a meal from a well-stocked storecupboard and refrigerator. For a guide to perishables – the fruits, vegetables, dairy products and meats that you use in *ChangeOne* meals – look at the shopping strategies on pages 302 to 303.

In the storecupboard
- Oils – olive, groundnut, sesame and sunflower
- Herbs, dried
- Any spices, dried
- Stock cubes or powder – chicken or vegetable*
- Flours – wholewheat, plain and self-raising
- Sugars – white and brown
- Tomatoes, canned*
- Tomato sauce*
- Tuna, canned*
- Baking powder
- Bicarbonate of soda
- Soups – mushroom, minestrone or vegetable, canned*
- Vinegars – balsamic, red wine
- Cocoa powder, unsweetened
- Cornflour
- Vanilla extract
- Cooking spray
- Peanut butter*
- Mushrooms, dried

Condiments
- Salt and pepper
- Ketchup*
- Mayonnaise, reduced fat*
- Mustards* – Dijon, English
- Soy sauce
- Tabasco sauce
- Pickles and relishes*
- Capers*
- Olives*

Cereals, grains and beans
- Cereal – ready-to-eat, wholegrain
- Porridge oats
- Couscous
- Legumes (kidney beans, chickpeas, black beans, etc), canned or dried
- Pasta
- Rice – brown and white
- Polenta

Snacks
- Digestive biscuits
- Water biscuits
- Nuts, mixed
- Popcorn kernels
- Wholegrain snacks like oatcakes

Fruits and vegetables
- Fruit canned in juice*
- Fruit, assorted fresh
- Raisins
- Garlic, fresh
- Onions
- Potatoes – new, baking or roasting
- Celery
- Peppers, green or red

In the refrigerator
- Butter
- Cheeses for grating, such as Parmesan
- Eggs
- Milk – low-fat or nonfat
- Yogurt, plain – low-fat or nonfat

In the freezer
- Bagels – normal or mini
- Breads – wholewheat and pitta
- Berries and other fruit, frozen
- Fruit sorbet or fruit/juice lollies
- Beef or chicken bones for homemade stock
- Chicken breasts, individually portioned
- Minced turkey or lean ground beef
- Veggie burgers
- Pizza bases, frozen
- Prepared dinners – reduced-calorie, frozen
- Vegetables, frozen

Miscellaneous
- Carbonated water
- Vegetable juices
- Sugar-free drinks
- Herbs, fresh
- Tomato salsa
- Green chillies
- Tortillas – corn and flour, small

These items may need to be refrigerated after you've opened them.

157

continued from page 155

Some cereal boxes list 30 g as a serving, for example, others 40 g. Some foods may look as if they're low in calories – until you discover that their suggested serving size would fit into a thimble.

6. Keep treats as a treat.

Don't buy high-calorie items you have trouble resisting once they're under your roof. Do you really want them tempting you all the time? To ensure that treats remain treats, make them part of a special occasion. When the family wants ice cream, say, go out to get it. Don't make it too easy by keeping tubs in the freezer. Kids clamouring for biscuits? Take them to the bakery section of the supermarket and buy a couple of good ones. Decide in advance how much you'll have. One small bite of everybody else's ice cream will let you sample a range of flavours and still keep you within the recommended serving size for dessert. A nibble or two on the kids' biscuits will satisfy your sweet tooth.

> SPECIAL OFFER
> ICE CREAM!
> Uh-oh.

Breaking the chain

The single most important change for many of our *ChangeOne* volunteers was learning to shop smartly. If you prepare a lot of your meals at home, the decisions you make at the supermarket go a long way towards determining what you eat and don't eat.

To understand how important smart shopping is, visualise a chain. Scientists who study behaviour talk about chains of behaviour – individual decisions that connect like links on a chain. Let's say you give in to temptation one night and eat that whole 500 ml container of toffee pecan ice cream in the freezer. At first, that may seem like a single impulsive act. But in reality, it's the end of a long chain of choices.

Think back to the beginning. That toffee pecan ice cream didn't find its way into the freezer on its own, after all. The links in the chain might look something like this:

- You go shopping when you're hungry.
- Rushing out of the door, you forget to take your shopping list.
- At the store, you see a sign that says SPECIAL OFFER ICE CREAM! Uh-oh.

continued on page 160

Quick beans and rice

A dish of beans and rice goes with just about anything – here we've served it alongside grilled chicken. You can make the dish mild or spicy.

Chicken, beans and rice

Quick beans and rice (2 golf balls of rice and tennis ball of beans)

1 grilled chicken fillet

Mixed green salad (unlimited) **with 2 tablespoons fat-free dressing**

kcals 450, fat 11 g, saturated fat 2 g, cholesterol 86 mg, sodium 566 mg, carbohydrate 52 g, fibre 7 g, protein 40 g, calcium 90 mg

QUICK BEANS AND RICE

Serves 4
2 teaspoons olive oil
1 red pepper, diced
½ medium onion, diced
1 stick celery, diced
1 clove garlic, finely chopped
1 can (about 400 g) black or red kidney beans, drained
1 tablespoon chopped green chilli or 1 teaspoon Tabasco sauce (optional)
400 g (14 oz) hot cooked brown rice

1. In a large non-stick frying pan, heat the olive oil and sauté the pepper, onion, celery and garlic for about 5 minutes or until soft. Add the beans and chilli or Tabasco sauce, and heat until warmed.

2. Combine with the brown rice. Serve hot.

GRILLED CHICKEN FILLET

Serves 4
4 skinless chicken fillets, about 150 g (5½ oz) each
2 teaspoons olive oil
lemon juice
freshly ground black pepper

1. Place the chicken fillets in a shallow dish in one layer. Sprinkle with the olive oil, and lemon juice and freshly ground black pepper to taste (or use your favourite marinade). Set aside for 10 minutes.

2. Cook under the grill or on a ridged cast-iron grill pan for 7 to 10 minutes or until cooked through. Turn once.

continued from page 158
- You pop a container in your trolley.
- You pop that same container into the freezer, telling yourself you'll only have a little, and only on special occasions.

Change One First Person

Lots of little packets

'I know I could probably find something a little grander, or maybe a little healthier for me,' says Paul Rodriquez, 'but for me, convenience matters a lot. If something takes too long to put together, I'm not going to do it.'

So after trying a variety of *ChangeOne* breakfasts during the first few weeks, Paul finally settled on the ultimate in convenience: individual-sized breakfast cereal packets that he can buy 30 to a box at the local cash and carry. 'I can have one at home or take it to work if I'm running late. I don't have to worry about pouring a certain amount into a bowl.'

The same solution helped steer him away from the high-fat, high-calorie snacks he used to eat. Paul now buys oat-based cereal bars – 100 kcals each – in bulk at the same shop. He takes one or two with him every day.

'Maybe later I'll want to branch out and be a little more creative. But right now it helps not to have to decide what I'm going to have for a snack. If I get hungry, I just reach for a cereal bar. It's been great.'

After years of putting on weight, Paul was thrilled to see it beginning to slip away – 7 kg (15 lb) over the first five weeks.

- You're feeling low one night. You know you should get up and out for a walk to feel better, but...
- You're hungry. You open the refrigerator door, but because you haven't gone shopping recently there's not much there that you want.
- You open the freezer door and what's this? A container of toffee pecan ice cream! It leaps into your hands.
- You know you should serve up just one small scoop and put the container back, but you're feeling lazy, so you open the lid and grab a spoon.
- You know you should sit down at the table and eat the ice cream, savouring every bite. But the TV is on and you wander into the sitting room. Instead of paying attention to the ice cream, you eat while you're watching TV. The next thing you know, the whole 500 ml is gone.

How can you make sure that doesn't happen? Of course you can break the chain at any one of its links. You can get the ice cream home, realise your mistake and give it away. Or you can pause with your spoon in hand and decide not to dig in. Yes, you can *but* if you're like most people, the best time to stop the chain is at the supermarket. You won't have to resist eating something you didn't buy. That's something to remember the next time you're tempted by something you know could overwhelm your willpower and set your diet back.

Put food in its place

Once you're back from your shopping trip, it's time to take a serious look at your kitchen. The strategy is simple. Put the healthiest choices in the most prominent places on your kitchen shelves

Help!

'I have three teenage kids, and the kitchen is filled with foods they love – crisps, soft drinks, ice cream and all the rest. How can I slimmer-proof my kitchen against that kind of temptation?'

You can't, not entirely, but you can certainly make your kitchen more comfortable for yourself. If your teenagers are tall enough, ask them to keep their snack foods on the upper shelves. Assign them a shelf out of reach for soft drinks and other sweetened beverages in the fridge. Insist on reserving the most accessible shelf in the refrigerator for foods that are on your menu. Ask the kids not to leave bowls and packets of junk food lying around. When they've finished eating, tell them to put the food away.

Don't stop there. Try to encourage the rest of the family to follow your example and eat food with fewer empty calories. Yes, it can sometimes be an uphill struggle. But many kids these days are surprisingly health conscious. And since weight problems typically begin early in life, you'll be doing them a favour.

Sit down with your kids and explain why losing weight really matters to you. If your children are still young, you can nudge their tastes in the right direction. Only keep healthful choices around, and in no time, they'll be eating them without a battle. One *ChangeOne* participant regularly offered his four and six-year-olds wholemeal bread rolls, broccoli, asparagus, grilled fish and, well, macaroni cheese. Okay, so it was lots of macaroni cheese. But getting the kids to eat broccoli and asparagus was a big victory.

Tuna noodle bake

Just add vegetables to these storecupboard staples for an easy supper.

Tuna bake supper

Tuna noodle bake (2 tennis balls)

Rocket salad (4 cricket balls)

kcals 400, fat 12 g, saturated fat 1 g, cholesterol 50 mg,
sodium 1217 mg, carbohydrate 44 g, fibre 3 g, protein
32 g, calcium 92 mg

TUNA NOODLE BAKE

Serves 4
2 cans (about 200 g each) tuna in water
1 can (about 400 g) 98%-fat-free cream of
   mushroom soup
125 ml (4 fl oz) evaporated skimmed milk
75 g (2½ oz) stoned black olives, sliced
85 g (3 oz) drained canned pimientoes,
   chopped
200 g (7 oz) cooked noodles

1. Preheat the oven to 190°C (375°F, gas
mark 5). Spray a medium-size baking dish
with cooking spray.

2. Combine all the ingredients. Place in the
dish and bake for about 30 minutes.

ROCKET SALAD

Serves 4
400 g or more rocket tossed with
   4 teaspoons olive oil and balsamic
   vinegar to taste

Instead of	Try
Tuna	Canned salmon
	Cooked peeled prawns (450 g/1 lb)
	Tofu
Mushroom soup	98%-fat-free cream of asparagus or tomato soup
Egg noodles	Pasta shapes

and in your refrigerator. Put 'treat' foods – the items you only want to reach for now and then – out of sight, even out of reach.

Let's say you like to treat yourself to an oat and raisin biscuit from time to time. Now imagine that those biscuits are stored in a clear glass jar on the kitchen counter. Every time you come into the kitchen for a snack, they're the first thing you see. Which means every time you enter the room you've got to rely on your willpower to resist turning a special treat into an everyday occurrence.

Why put yourself through that? Imagine, instead, that you keep a bowl of fruit on the counter and a few plastic containers with carrot and celery sticks at the front and centre of the refrigerator. The biscuits are safely stored away on the very top shelf of the cupboard in a container with a lid that snaps shut – high enough that you need to get the step ladder when you want them. Suddenly it's easy to grab something low in calories and rich in nutrients – an apple or a handful of carrot sticks.

By the end of this week your kitchen will be a place where you can relax, not a place where you have to constantly feel you have to resist temptations.

Changes ahead: how am I doing?

In a typical conversation about weight loss, you talk about kilograms or pounds. It's the easiest, clearest measurement of how you are progressing. But is it the best measurement? Certainly not.

Once you have your kitchen under control – and it might be wise to take extra time on that task, given how important it is, and how many habits might need tweaking – we'll turn to the subject of measuring progress.

Sounds too simple to be important? Not at all. Self assessment is a tricky business. We tend to be very hard on ourselves. We forget the important criteria – energy, attitude, overall appearance – and focus on unrealistic statistical measurements. So to prepare for this examination, think again about why you really want to lose weight. Think about how you judge your success or failure. And be prepared to look at yourself in a whole new way.

WEEK **8**

How Am I Doing?

'How long does getting thin take?' Pooh asks anxiously in A.A. Milne's classic children's book. You may be asking the same question just about now. You probably have other questions too. Why do you seem to lose weight some weeks and not others? Are you making reasonable progress towards your goal? What can you do to kickstart your diet when weight loss stalls?

This week, you'll assess how you're doing and find ways to get over or around trouble spots.

To get you started, take the Seven weeks of progress quiz on the opposite page. You will use its questions in this chapter to focus on the best ways for you to overcome your unique weight-loss challenges.

Change One Quiz

Seven weeks of progress

Circle the appropriate number in the right-hand column to track your score.

1. How do you feel about your weight-loss progress so far?

Very satisfied	3
Satisfied	2
Disappointed	1

2. How would you rate your energy level since you began *ChangeOne*?

Improved	3
About the same	2
Slumped	1

3. How would you rate your self-confidence while on *ChangeOne*?

Better	3
About the same	2
Worse	1

4. How many days last week did you closely follow the *ChangeOne* menu for breakfast, lunch, supper and snacks?

All or most	3
About half	2
Fewer than half	1

5. How often are you able to stick to sensible portions when you eat out?

All or most of the time	3
About half the time	2
Less than half the time	1

6. Planning is crucial to dieting success; how well are you doing when it comes to planning where and what you'll eat?

Very well	3
Good	2
Only so-so	1

7. Feeling hungry can whittle away at anyone's will power. How would you describe your experience on *ChangeOne* so far?

Hunger isn't a problem for me	3
Now and then I get so hungry that I eat more than I should	2
Hunger is a problem for me a lot of the time	1

8. How often do you experience strong cravings for specific foods (chocolate, ice cream, salty snacks or sweets, for instance)?

Never	3
Now and then	2
Frequently	1

9. What phrase best describes your family and close friends?

Behind me 100 per cent	3
Somewhat supportive	2
Not very helpful	1

10. How would you rate your overall motivation right now?

Excellent	3
Good	2
Shaky	1

11. Stress can often get in the way when people are trying to change. How are you dealing with it?

Very well	3
Well enough	2
Not very well	1

continued on page 166

continued from page 165

12. **Sometimes it seems there's food everywhere. How would you rate your ability to deal with temptations?**

I'm getting better at eating only if I'm hungry	3
I give in to temptation now and then, but not as much as before	2
I still have a very tough time saying no	1

13. **Where did you eat in your house during the past week?**

Kitchen and dining room only	3
In front of TV or in the bedroom	2
Both in front of TV and in the bedroom	1

14. **How many days during the past week did you fit in at least 30 minutes worth of physical activity (walking, jogging, bicycling, gym workouts, etc)?**

All or most	3
About half	2
Fewer than half	1

Quiz score

Scoring:
Add up the sum of the numbers you've circled and use the guide below to start evaluating your progress:

A score of 32–42: A big gold star for you. Put a tick beside any questions that you scored as 1 and read the corresponding tip below for advice on how to move ahead.

21–31: A little extra help could improve your chances of success. Mark the questions you scored as 1 and read the numbered tips that follow for advice.

14–20: Okay, you're having a tough time. Many people do when they first try to lose weight. Put a tick beside responses you scored as 1 and read the numbered tips in the section that follows for advice on dealing with these trouble spots.

Succeeding your way

No single diet works for everyone. Even diet experts have been surprised to find how many ways there are to succeed, or fail, at slimming. Some people like to be told exactly what to eat, then follow a strict plan. Others can take a few basic principles and handle the rest. Some people need a lot of support from family and friends. Others go it alone.

We've seen the same thing among the volunteers who tested the *ChangeOne* programme. Some began to lose weight right away with breakfast; others didn't hit their stride until they changed their approach to supper. There were people who began to lose weight as soon as they changed the way they snacked. Others had the greatest success by paying attention to hunger cues. For some, *ChangeOne* was a breeze. For others it wasn't always easy.

The quiz you completed should help to clarify the challenges you've encountered on *ChangeOne*. To help you to overcome these challenges, we'll review the questions in detail, offering tips and advice as we go, to make sure you are getting all you can out of your efforts.

1 Disappointed in your results?

Reassess your goals. Renew your commitment.

If you've lost 3.6 kg (8 lb) or more since starting *ChangeOne,* there's no reason to be disappointed. Most experts say a healthy weight-loss plan should average 450 g–1.3 kg (1–3 lb) a week. Eight weeks into *ChangeOne*, in other words, you can expect to have lost 3.6–11 kg (8–24 lb). Losing weight more quickly than that means losing muscle tissue along with fat – and that, in turn, could slow your metabolism and make it harder to maintain your weight loss.

If you haven't started seeing the progress you'd like, there may be several reasons. If you've significantly increased the amount of exercise you're doing, you may be losing fat but adding muscle. That's fine. In fact, it's the sure-fire way to look firmer and shapelier. But because you're trading fat for muscle, you may not see much difference on the scales. One sign that you're making progress is your waist size. If it's going down, you're changing for the better.

The most important thing now is not to get discouraged. Make a pact with yourself to take a little extra time and expend a little extra effort this coming month to reach your goal – and make sure it's realistic. (We'll be assessing goal-setting in more detail later in this chapter.)

2 Energy at a low ebb?

Have a snack – and get moving.

While people usually feel much better when slimming, some people do experience periods of fatigue when they begin to lose weight. As you take in fewer calories than you burn, you force your body to turn to the energy it has stored as fat. Falling short on calories can make you feel tired and even grumpy. There's another kind of fatigue: some people begin to get tired of dieting. You don't have to allow either kind of fatigue derail your weight-loss programme.

If you're feeling deep fatigue every day, talk to your doctor. But if you simply have occasional slumps and less energy than you used to have, try eating smaller meals more frequently during the day. Save the piece of fruit from breakfast to eat midmorning. Keep aside the sliced vegetables you brought for lunch and have them as soon as you feel hungry in the afternoon. Eating more frequently can steady your blood sugar levels so you won't feel a slump when your energy supplies run low.

Eating more frequently can stabilise your energy levels, and being active can actually *increase* them.

Another way to combat fatigue is to fit extra physical activity into your daily schedule. It seems paradoxical to be more active when you feel you have less energy, but research shows that physical activity can actually make people feel more energetic rather than less. Activity provides a psychological boost that can banish the blues. Getting up and moving also increases your self-confidence. And regular exercise increases stamina, so you'll build reserves of energy for more activity.

3 Need a boost of self-confidence?
Celebrate small victories.

It's easy to lose confidence if you're not reaching the goals that you have set and you're not quite sure why. There's always the temptation to blame yourself. You know how it goes. You tell yourself that you just don't have the staying power, or the will power, to lose weight. Banish those negative thoughts. You haven't failed just because the weight is proving more stubborn than you'd expected. For the moment, focus on your successes.

Here's a trick that worked for some of our volunteers. Let's say you've managed to lose 2.3 kg (5 lb) so far, which may not sound like a lot. The next time you're at the supermarket, grab a 2.5 kg bag of potatoes. Carry it round the store under your arm as you shop. Getting heavy? That's the amount of excess weight you used to carry around all the time. On the scales 2.3 kg (5 lb) may not seem like a lot; but when you carry that much in your arms, and think of it as the fat you've lost, you'll realise what a big accomplishment you've achieved already. Remember, too, that kilograms and pounds aren't the only measure of success. Make a list of other benefits you've gained by following *ChangeOne*. Maybe your clothes feel a little more comfortable. Maybe you're moving around more easily. Maybe you're simply eating a healthier diet. Whatever your successes are, celebrate them. And remember: if you can make one change, you can make two. If you can make two changes, you can make three.

> If you are not satisfied, take another week to master the meal that's giving you trouble.

4 Struggling with a particular meal? Go back for seconds.

If you're pleased with your weight-loss progress so far but you aren't following the *ChangeOne* menu for all of your meals, don't worry. Some people find they need to make only one or two small changes – giving up chips or switching to sugar-free drinks, for example – to start losing weight. If you're not satisfied with your progress, go back to the meal that's giving you trouble and take another week to master it. Set aside enough time so that you can follow that chapter's meal plans to the letter, at least for one week. Try a few suggestions you didn't try the first time round. Too rushed to have breakfast? Get everything ready the night before. Eating too many snacks during the day? Distract yourself for a few minutes with something other than food – a short walk, an errand or a household chore.

5 Is eating out your downfall? Zero in on portion control.

If your parents praised you for cleaning your plate, you may still have trouble leaving food behind – especially when you've paid good money for it at a restaurant. With today's portion sizes, eating out can be a major challenge. Don't let the size of the serving put down in front of you determine how much you eat. Keep in mind the *ChangeOne* portion size guidelines we've been visualising – a tennis ball or a pack of cards, for example – to remind yourself what a reasonable amount of food should look like. Ask the waiter to take away what you don't want to eat (and perhaps pack it so you can take it home). Pay attention to hunger and fullness cues. And eat slowly. For more tips on navigating restaurants, turn to Week 5 (page 108).

6 Trouble planning ahead?
Make a list. Check it twice.

Knowing where your next meal is coming from is critical to successful dieting. If you're having trouble planning ahead, try this: set aside 15 minutes the night before or first thing in the morning to make a list of what you'll need to do that day to stick with *ChangeOne*. Your list might include a quick shopping trip to buy what you'll need for supper, a reminder of when and where you plan to get some exercise during the day, or a note to book a table for lunch at a restaurant where you know you'll be able to order a sensible meal. Or look for a frozen meal that meets the *ChangeOne* guidelines. Keep several in the freezer. If you're having trouble finding time to pack a lunch, choose a meal that's quicker and easier to prepare: for instance, a macaroni salad you can make in advance and even divide up into single-serving containers.

7 Famished?
Eat more often.

It's fine to be hungry just before your next meal. But if you're getting so famished that you're tempted to give up the whole idea of losing weight, it's time for a reassessment.

For starters, this week fill out a Hunger Profile for a few days (you'll find it on page 308). Keeping tabs on your appetite will highlight when you typically feel the hungriest during the day, and what you do about it. Next, begin helping yourself to a snack during those moments when you're feeling especially ravenous. Choose low-calorie, fibre-rich snacks as these will fill you up without putting you over your calorie target. If you're still hungry after lunch or supper, help yourself to an additional serving of vegetables. Keep an eye on your weight. If you continue to lose weight, even if it's a little more slowly than before, that's fine. You're more likely to stick to a diet that doesn't

> You're more likely to stick to a diet that doesn't force you to go hungry.

force you to go hungry. If your weight remains steady, that's fine, too. Consider attacking the other side of the calorie equation by increasing your activity level by adding 15 minutes of walking a day to what you already do. Keep this in mind, as well: many of our volunteers reported feeling hungry at first. But very quickly, their appetites adjusted to *ChangeOne* portion sizes, and they began to feel perfectly satisfied. So don't give up.

8 Caving in to cravings?
Forge a new association.

Food cravings aren't hunger pangs. When you're genuinely hungry, you want food and any food will do. Food cravings are usually for something special – chocolate, ice cream or a salty snack, for example. Sometimes food cravings are part of emotional eating. You want chocolate because it makes you feel better when you're a bit low. Food cravings can also be reactions to environmental triggers. You want ice cream after supper or popcorn when you get to the cinema simply because all the cues remind you of a certain food.

The solution is teach an old dog a new trick by creating a different, healthier association. Instead of having dessert after supper this week, get up from the table and go for a 15 minute stroll. Instead of popcorn at the cinema, bring along a *ChangeOne* snack. It won't take long before you associate cinema-going with a cereal bar or a piece of fruit instead of popcorn. For more on food triggers, emotional eating and environmental cues, look back at Week 6, which begins on page 126.

9 Need a helping hand or a friendly word?
Ask for it.

When the going gets tough, the tough often call on friends and family. If you're not getting the support you need, take this week to explore ways to enlist help and encouragement. The best way to get what you need is by asking for it. Be specific about the kind of help you need. Ask if there's anything you can do in return. Need to cast a wider net? Be creative. If you're looking for an exercise partner, for

> Food cravings aren't hunger pangs. They are caused by emotional and environmental triggers.

instance, put up a notice at work or at the newsagents. Wishing you had an eating partner? How about starting a *ChangeOne* supper club?

And keep in mind that even though the support of people around you can smooth the way, making a lasting change is ultimately up to you. Even without the active support of family and friends, you can make it on your own. Look back to 'Talk it over' on page 147 if you need more encouragement.

10 Motivation in need of a service?
Think back to the beginning.

Once the first flush of excitement is over, it can be tough to stay motivated on any diet. Now's the time to remind yourself why you wanted to lose weight in the first place.

> Remind yourself why you wanted to lose weight in the first place.

Write down your three top reasons for starting *ChangeOne*. Below that, make a list of the benefits you've noticed so far. These may include the way you feel, the weight you've managed to lose, the way your clothes fit, or the fact that you're getting more exercise than before. Assign each one a rating of one to three stars, depending on how important it is to you.

Put up your list somewhere where you'll see it every day (on the refrigerator door, for instance). By reminding yourself of the reasons you started *ChangeOne*, and the benefits you've already gained, you may strengthen your motivation.

11 Feeling frazzled?
Find a way to let off steam this week.

Being on a diet can be stressful. Add to that the other strains and stresses in your life and the combination can seem overwhelming. If stress is threatening to derail your efforts to eat a healthier diet, it's time to take action. Next week, we'll zero in on ways to deal with stress.

For this week, think of one change you can make in your life that will relieve some of the pressure. Ask someone to take on one of your responsibilities at home or the office. Rearrange your schedule to find time to relax. During this week, experiment with different ways to let off steam.

Listen to your favourite music. Sit quietly and concentrate on your breathing. Take up yoga. Go for a walk or a workout. Exercise eases stress and burns extra calories in the bargain.

12 Surrounded by temptations?

Take control of your surroundings.

If your will power is being tested every time you turn round, it's time to take charge of your environment. At home, put occasional treats out of sight and make sure the calorie-efficient choices, like fruit and vegetables, are the centrepiece of your kitchen. At work, don't keep food around your desk or work area. If you find yourself in a situation where you can't remove the temptations, remove yourself – go for a walk, do an errand or choose a *ChangeOne* snack. Remember, the less you have to rely on sheer will power to avoid temptation, the more likely you are to reach your goals.

Give your will power some help – don't make cheating easy.

13 Eating all over the house?

Practise the 'one room, one chair' rule.

If you eat in practically every room of the house, you're creating associations with food everywhere you go. You'll have no escape from the urge to binge. Set aside one room and one chair for eating at home. This week, make a pact with yourself to go there for every meal and every snack you eat at home.

14 Sitting on the sidelines?

Get in on the action

You don't have to start running marathons. All you have to do is find opportunities to walk. This week, work out how to add at least 15 minutes of walking during the main part of the day – before breakfast, in the lunch hour, running errands, or an evening stroll.

Goal-setting, part II

Back in Week 4 of the *ChangeOne* programme, you signed a goal-setting contract with yourself. It's time to pull it out and give it a read. Were you fair on yourself? It's all too easy to have unrealistic expectations when you decide to lose weight – especially when it's the first time you've tried it in earnest. Even people who have dieted in the past tend to set goals that are tough to reach. And when they don't reach them, they give up.

By now you're an expert on what it takes to lose weight. You also know what you're willing and able to do. This is the perfect time to take a clear, no-nonsense look at what you want to accomplish from now on. In addition, by revisiting your goals and committing yourself to them afresh, you'll take a big step towards staying motivated. To start off, fill in the questionnaire, 'How do you spell success?' opposite.

Don't mistake success for failure

Almost anyone who sets out to do it can lose weight on a diet. The crazy thing about many slimmers is that when they succeed, they often don't realise it. Many people who succeed end up thinking they've failed. The reason: they get their minds wrapped round an unattainable goal and never see what they've achieved.

You probably guessed where we're going with the questions in 'How do you spell success?' Most people have several goals in mind when they decide to lose weight. A super-ambitious goal is great if it fires you up at the start. But if it's just too ambitious, and you begin to think you'll never reach it, you can begin to feel frustrated, then disillusioned. You may actually succeed in losing a lot of weight and getting all the good that goes with it – looking and feeling better, for instance – but if you didn't reach that goal, you may consider the diet a failure. Then you might give up, go back to your old patterns of eating and gain back all the weight you'd lost.

To test the reality of the typical slimmer's expectations, researchers at the weight loss clinic of the University of Pennsylvania in the US carried out a clever experiment. They asked a group of women at the start of a diet programme to describe four different goals. The categories will sound familiar. We borrowed them for the quiz you just completed.

How do you spell success?

Part I

1. How much did you weigh when you began the *ChangeOne* plan? _____

2. What is your dream weight? _____

3. Let's say you can't reach your dream weight. What's the most you can end up weighing and still be happy with the results? _____

4. If you can't reach your 'happy' weight, what weight would you describe as acceptable? _____

5. Let's say that you lose weight, but still don't reach an 'acceptable' weight. What ending weight would leave you feeling disappointed? _____

Part II

1. Look again at your 'dream' weight. What is the number based on?

❏ The lowest my weight has been as an adult

❏ My ideal weight given my height

❏ What I weighed when I was at school or college

❏ The lowest weight I've been able to reach on a slimming diet

❏ A healthy weight for me according to my doctor

❏ Other

_____

2. Numbers on the scales aren't the only way to measure the success of a diet. Besides weight, what other measures are important to you? On a scale of 1 to 5 – not important to very important – rate the following items:

Smaller dress or trouser size	1 2 3 4 5
How my clothes feel	1 2 3 4 5
How I feel (slimmer, more energetic, more attractive)	1 2 3 4 5
Specific health measures (blood pressure, for example)	1 2 3 4 5
Overall sense of health	1 2 3 4 5

3. If dress or trouser size is an important measure of success for you, what goal do you have in mind?

Dress size: _____

Waist size: _____

4. What else do you hope to achieve by slimming? On a scale of 1 to 5 – not important to very important – rate the following:

Feeling more self-confident	1 2 3 4 5
Feeling sexier or more attractive	1 2 3 4 5
Being happier about myself and what I look like	1 2 3 4 5
Feeling more in control	1 2 3 4 5
Not being embarrassed by my weight	1 2 3 4 5
Feeling fitter	1 2 3 4 5

Answers

Congratulations! You got every question correct. There are no wrong answers to the questions we just asked; they are too personal for that. But your answers do say a lot about your expectations. For insights on your comments and some thoughts about whether you are being fair to yourself, read on.

The researchers asked the women to specify:

- **Their dream weight** – the amount they would like to weigh if they could choose the ideal number.
- **Their happy weight** – a number on the scale that, even if it wasn't perfect, would make them happy.
- **Their acceptable weight** – the number that they'd be willing to accept if they couldn't reach either their happy or dream weight.

Weight loss goals: myth vs reality

Myth 1: Your ideal weight is what you weighed when you were first married (or at college, or before you had children...)

If you're hoping to get back to what you weighed a year or two ago, fine. There's a chance you really might get close to that weight again. But if this was 15 or 20 years ago, you might want to reconsider. Many people put on weight as they get older. And no matter how hard they try, they have a hard time being as active as they might have been in their early twenties. Don't live in the past. Set a weight-loss goal that's appropriate now.

Myth 2: Your ideal weight is the number listed on a standard height and weight chart.

True, height and weight are often related. Taller people weigh more than shorter ones, all things being equal. But all things are never equal. Many other factors play a role in determining what you weigh. For example, your body type: big-boned and solid, small-boned and light, or in between. Your metabolism: whether you naturally burn brightly and move a lot, or take things more slowly. The number of fat cells you have. How much your parents and other relatives weigh. The number listed for someone your height on a standard weight and height chart is just an approximation of what your healthy weight should be. Don't let them determine if you've succeeded or failed.

Myth 3: Your ideal weight is the lowest weight you've been able to get down to in the past.

Okay, so you've lost that much weight. But the fact that you're slimming again says you gained at least some or even all of it back again. If you set a weight-loss goal that's too low for you to maintain, you'll get caught in the trap of yo-yo dieting – losing weight, gaining it back, and then trying to lose it again. The best weight goal is one you can live with.

Myth 4: The less you weigh, the healthier you'll be.

Not true. In fact, many studies show that if you're overweight, even seriously overweight, losing just 5 to 10 per cent of your current weight is all you have to do to get the bulk of the health benefits associated with weight lose: lower risks of heart disease, stroke, diabetes and even some forms of cancer.

Myth 5: If you don't reach your dream weight, you'll never be happy.

You don't believe that, do you? A number is just a number. And if it's a number that leaves you frustrated and stuck in an endless cycle of losing and gaining weight, it's time to replace it with a more reasonable one.

> Don't live in the past. Set a goal for the present.

■ Their disappointed weight – a number that, even though it was less than what they currently weighed, would leave them feeling disappointed.

The women in the experiment had high hopes. They began the programme weighing an average of 99 kg (218 lb). Most of them hoped to get down to 68 kg (149 lb) – a 31 kg (69 lb) loss. If they couldn't have their dream weight, most said, they'd still be happy if they got down to 70 kg (155 lb). If all else failed, they'd accept a final weight of 74 kg (163 lb). They'd be disappointed if they ended the diet at a weight of 82 kg (181 lb), an average loss of 17 kg (37 lb).

How did they do? The women in the six-month programme lost an average of 16 per cent of their starting weight. Most experts would call that a success. The average weight loss at that point in a successful diet programme is around 10 to 15 per cent.

Though the researchers were thrilled, the women were not. Their 'disappointed' weight would have required losing 17 per cent of their starting weight. Even the number they described as merely acceptable represented a 25 per cent drop. Their dream weight would have required a 32 per cent weight loss.

Think about it. These women did fantastically well. They lost a significant amount of weight. But without a realistic goal to measure their progress by, most of them were likely to consider the diet a failure. That's crazy.

Divide big goals into milestones

'Oh no', you're probably thinking just about now. 'This is where they tell me I can't lose as much weight as I'd like.'

Not for a second. All we want to do is urge you to make sure your first goals are achievable. Especially if you have a lot of weight you'd like to lose, it's helpful to think in terms of milestones rather than the ultimate weight you want to be. Once you reach your first milestone, you can celebrate your success, take a deep breath and head on to the next one. This approach helps you to gain confidence. It also makes it easy to measure your progress step by step, rather than in a single leap. And that's what *ChangeOne* is about.

What's a reasonable first milestone? Many experts say you should first set your sights on losing about 10 per cent of your starting weight. To calculate that number, take your weight when you started *ChangeOne* and knock the last

177

A comfy pair of leggings

**'I didn't really have a specific goal in mind when I started
ChangeOne,' Peg Ho remembers. 'I certainly didn't have any fantasies
of becoming a magazine model. I'd reached 50 and was chubbier
than I wanted to be. For health reasons, mostly, I
thought it was time to get into shape.'**

An information technology manager, Peg couldn't
have been happier when she saw the numbers on
the scales go down. By the eighth week on
ChangeOne she'd lost 7.2 kg (16 lb). But about half
way through the programme, something else began
to matter to her a lot more than those numbers.

'One of the first changes I wanted to make was to
become more active. I made up my mind to walk as
often as possible when I got home from work. I
bought myself a pair of stretch leggings to walk
in. But I was so embarrassed by the way I looked in
them, I wore a long sweatshirt so no one would see.
It must have been a week or two later that I began
to notice that they were fitting better. They just felt
more comfortable. Even my husband said he could
really see the difference.'

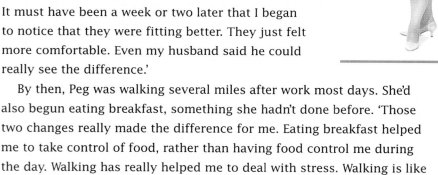

By then, Peg was walking several miles after work most days. She'd
also begun eating breakfast, something she hadn't done before. 'Those
two changes really made the difference for me. Eating breakfast helped
me to take control of food, rather than having food control me during
the day. Walking has really helped me to deal with stress. Walking is like
meditation for me. I love it.'

Something else she loves is how comfortable her new leggings have
become. 'For me now, it's not so much a weight thing. Maybe I'll get
down to my ideal weight, maybe I won't. But I know just by the way my
clothes feel that I look better. And when I'm out there walking I know
that I feel better. For me, that's enough reason to stay motivated.'

number off. If you weighed 100 kg (222 lb), for instance, 10 per cent is about 10 kg (22 lb).

Once you reach your first milestone, allow yourself a few weeks to savour the new, slimmer you and to consolidate the changes you've made. Take the time to enjoy all of the other benefits you're likely to experience, from the way you look in the mirror to the way your clothes fit. Then, when you're ready, set the next milestone for weight loss. For many people weight loss slows as they shed pounds. That's perfectly natural. To avoid becoming discouraged, set subsequent milestones at about 5 per cent of your starting weight – 11 pounds if you started out at 222, for instance.

A contract with yourself

At the end of Week Four, we asked you to sign a *ChangeOne* Contract. Now that you've more experience under your belt – which you've moved up a notch or two, we hope – take a look back at your contract. How are you doing? Do the goals you set back then still seem reasonable? Are they the goals that matter most to you?

Write up a revised contract if your earlier goals aren't working for you. This is a contract with yourself, after all. You're doing what you're doing – eating better, being more active and losing weight – for your own sake, nobody else's. You decide the goals that mean the most and work the best for you. By putting them in writing, you'll be able to keep them in mind – and gauge your progress along the way.

Changes ahead: stress relief

Our lives are filled with stress, and that's not always a bad thing. Stress comes in many forms and intensity levels, and much of it is normal and healthy. The trouble comes when we are unable to balance our daily stresses with time to recuperate and relax. Next week, we will be looking at how stress can affect the way you eat and sabotage your weight-loss efforts. To prepare for the coming week, think about the ways you deal with stress. Do you turn to food when the going gets tough? Does your day allow for time to relax and enjoy life? Are excessive responsibilities and the interests of family getting in the way of caring for yourself?

WEEK 9

Stress Relief

All we're asking you to do this week is relax. That's right, relax. Take a moment or two to shake off the stresses and strains of daily life.

Sound easy? If only it were so. Life can feel so hectic these days that even taking a minute or two off from the pressures of work and family seems impossible. While achieving a stress-free life is unlikely, you can definitely loosen the hold tension and anxiety have on you.

That's important, especially when you're trying to lose weight. A difficult period at work or tension at home has knocked many dieters off their programme. Stress can rob you of the energy you need to stay focused and motivated. If the pressure gets fierce enough, you may be tempted to say, 'I just can't do this,' and give up your best intentions to stick to a healthier diet.

This week you'll identify sources of stress in your life and try out techniques to manage or even eliminate them.

Take the pressure off

Like a lot of people, you may find yourself reaching for something to eat when the demands get to be too much. That's hardly surprising. Just the act of eating can make you feel better when your nerves are frayed or you're feeling down. Recent studies have shown that eating – especially eating something high in carbohydrates – can lower your level of stress hormones and make you feel less frazzled.

In fact, you may feel better after eating because that's exactly what your body signals you to do: eat something. Scientists are learning that stress itself can actually trigger hunger. Here's how it works. Say you're on your way to a vital meeting. You're already running a little late when traffic comes to a sudden halt ahead of you. Instinctively, your body readies itself to do something to deal with the problem. Your brain signals your adrenal glands to churn out a variety of hormones, including the stress hormone cortisol. One of cortisol's jobs is to trigger the release of glucose and fatty acids, in case your muscles need energy.

Back in our hunter-gatherer days, this system made sense. Stress didn't take the form of traffic jams; instead, it was usually a real physical threat, such as a charging animal. A 'fight or flight' stress response evolved to prepare us, within seconds, to do battle or run away. These days, the challenges we face aren't as straightforward. Yes, you might be tempted to stop the car, get out and run the rest of the way to your meeting. If you did, you'd burn off the energy your body has made available. But chances are you sit there and smoulder until traffic finally begins to move again.

Check-in

At about this point in *ChangeOne*, you're probably having an easier time with some of the changes you've undertaken than with others. That's no surprise. Our volunteers reported the same experience. Your natural reaction may be to target the part that's giving you the toughest time. That's great. But if you get so frustrated that you begin to wonder if it's worth the trouble, ease off. Focus on changes that feel a little bit more do-able right now. If fitting in activity every day just isn't on the cards, don't worry. Concentrate instead on reining in portions. If paying attention to hunger and fullness cues has made a big difference, focus your energy there and don't worry that you're missing breakfast now and then. Go with your strengths. Zero in on the changes that offer the biggest pay-off and concentrate on turning them into easy habits. Go easy on yourself.

Afterwards, the result of your surge in cortisol is an increase in appetite – your body's way of guaranteeing that you'll replace the energy it released in the form of glucose and fatty acids.

A flood of these hormones wouldn't pose much of a problem if it happened only now and then. But a steady tide of tense situations can keep cortisol levels high all day, making you feel hungry almost all the time. As if that's not bad enough, cortisol also triggers enzymes that activate fat cells, priming them to store energy as fat. The most susceptible fat cells are those around your middle, which are particularly sensitive to the effects of cortisol.

You see the problem. Stress makes you hungry. Eating makes you feel better. Stress promotes fat. The result: you put on weight instead of taking it off. Watching your efforts to lose weight come to nothing can then create even more pressure and tension.

Now is the time to make sure you don't get caught in the upward spiral of stress and eating.

If stress is getting the better of you, remember that everyone's life has its hassles, small and large. One major difference between people who succeed and those who don't, psychologists say, is how we deal with everyday tribulations.

To see how well you handle stress, complete the test opposite. Your answers will help you to analyse how you cope with the challenges of daily life.

Help!

'I feel jittery and short-tempered a good part of the day. I thought it might be too much caffeine – but I have only a couple of cups of coffee in the morning, that's all. What's going on?'

Watch the caffeine you're getting from sources other than coffee. The caffeine in coffee is a stimulant, and in some people it can aggravate stress. But there's also caffeine in tea, colas, chocolate and some pain relievers – you may be getting a lot more than you realise. The best way to know if too much caffeine is a problem is to cut back on the amount you consume, but don't cut it out entirely. Caffeine withdrawal can cause headaches and may make you feel even more jittery and short-fused. A better bet is to begin mixing regular coffee with decaffeinated coffee. Over two or three weeks, gradually add more decaf and less of the high-octane brew. Then, if you decide to give up coffee altogether, you'll have an easier time.

Step one: solve problems that *can* be solved

The most direct way to deal with stress is to eliminate the situations that wear you down. Easier said than done? Yes, but the more irritations and annoyances you can unload, the easier it is to tackle the big issues. You may find there are

Stress test

Read each statement below and tick those that apply to you now.

○ A lot of things in my life seem to be out of control right now.

△ I have several good friends I can call if I need to talk something through.

○ When I'm feeling frazzled, I often have the urge to eat.

△ I'm feeling pretty good about my life right now.

○ I often feel overwhelmed with the thought of everything that has to be done during the day.

△ I feel better once I've made a list of what I have to do.

○ Trying to lose weight has definitely added to the pressures I feel.

○ It's really been frustrating for me to try to find time to be more active.

△ Taking control of my diet has made me feel better about myself.

○ Sometimes I resent all the responsibilities I have.

△ I'm pretty good at taking problems in my stride.

○ Lately I notice myself losing my temper when even little things go wrong.

△ Even when things get a little crazy, I still feel as if I'm in control of what's going on in my life.

○ If someone puts me on hold while we're talking, and then doesn't come back on the line fairly soon, it really makes me mad – angry enough to hang up sometimes.

○ I don't have much patience with people who make mistakes.

△ Even though my life is pretty crowded, I'm good at keeping my priorities straight.

△ I don't worry much about things I can't control.

○ When I'm under a lot of pressure, I sometimes find myself running in three different directions at once.

○ I frequently wake up in the night feeling anxious about my life.

△ No matter how hectic the day has been, it's easy for me to relax and unwind once I get home.

○ I wish I had more control over what happens in my life.

△ Exercise is a good way for me to let off steam.

○ Social situations often make me nervous.

△ Frankly, I don't tend to worry about the little things – I reckon they'll take care of themselves.

Quiz score

What your score means:
How many of each colour did you tick? If you tallied more blue triangles than red circles, your responses indicate that you've got the pressures of everyday life well in hand. But if the red outnumber the blue it could spell trouble – stress is hurting your life. If the numbers are about equal – and even if the blue slightly outnumber the red – be aware that a bad day could send you into the red zone. Whatever your score, there are plenty of effective ways to keep cool, calm and collected. Just read on.

plenty of petty aggravations you can quickly fix once you start paying them attention. Every time you find yourself getting agitated, stop and see if you can find a solution. If you can never seem to find the car keys or your specs, for instance, establish a place where you put the keys, spectacles, mobile phone or whatever, every time you put them down. Post a reminder on the door, if you have to, until you get into the habit.

If preparing supper makes your blood pressure rise because half the time you don't have on hand what you need, take time at the weekend to stock up for the week. Make double batches of dishes that can be stored, to cut your cooking time.

Not all problems are that easy to eliminate, of course. Let's say your boss gives you more work than you can manage. On top of that, you haven't been given the authority you need to do the job. That's a classic high-stress dilemma. What to do about it? The direct solution is to talk to the boss and explain the problem. Frame the talk not as a complaint ('You're asking too much of me') but as a search for solutions ('It would help me a lot if we could decide on priorities, and if I had your support for making a few key decisions').

Or say your problems are at home – tension in your marriage, for instance, or trouble with one of the children. Talking it through with the person closest to you might help you get to the source of the pressure and relieve it.

Yes, it can be hard to ask for help – but it gets easier when you first ask yourself, 'What am I getting out of letting things go on the way they are?' You might explain to your spouse or kids why reducing tension in the household is so important to you now. If the problems are more complicated than the family can handle alone, consider enlisting the help of a counsellor.

Only you can know which problems you can confront directly and which you may have to learn to live with. Almost certainly there are going to be irritations and worse that you can't eliminate – at least at the moment. But you can learn to live with them without being overwhelmed by them, and without letting them derail your diet.

If you can't stand the heat...

For people who compulsively reach for food when tensions reach boiling point, the simplest solution is to get away from food. If there are problems at home, don't deal with them in the kitchen. Go to another room of the house to sort them out, and don't take food with you. Under pressure at work? Keep snacks out of easy reach. This week, remember a simple rule: don't eat to relax. Try one of these techniques first. Then wait 5 or 10 minutes to see if you're still hungry. If so, then go ahead and eat.

Step two: accept the things you can't change

There are people who can shrug off almost any setback. Others get frazzled when even the smallest things don't go right. In either case, the demands may be the same. The difference is in how you respond to it. Psychologists don't understand all the reasons why people react so differently to stress. Having a sense of humour seems to help many people. Being able to distract yourself is an added bonus. Just having something you really enjoy doing offers a time out from the pressures of life. Playing a musical instrument, solving a crossword, reading a good book, volunteering at a charity shop – all can take your mind off problems and give you a much-needed holiday from fretting.

Naturally, you can't completely change your personality. But experts say you can change the way you react to hassles and frustrations. On the following pages we offer seven ways to cool down when your temper flares or the problems in your life feel overwhelming. This week, try out several of them. If one doesn't seem to work for you, move on to another. Your goal: to have at least two stress-busting techniques you can turn to when the pressure builds and your nerves begin to feel frazzled. Knowing how to relax and let off steam will help you stay focused and motivated.

1. Run away

One of the most effective ways to defuse stress is to run away from it – or at least walk briskly. In a 1998 study that asked 38 men and 35 women to keep diaries of activity, mood and stress, volunteers felt less anxious on days when they were physically active than on days when they didn't exercise. Even when stressful events occurred, people in the study said they felt less troubled on their physically active days.

Why? Exercise acts as an antidote to life's pressures in several ways. First, it is a simple distraction from problems. Second, it may change the chemistry of stress, blunting the effect of hormones like cortisol. Exercise has also been shown to ease the symptoms of moderate depression. That, in turn, may help people deal better with daily hassles. And then there's the fact that exercise burns calories, an added bonus for slimmers. Physical activity makes it easier not only to lose weight but to keep calories in balance once you go off your diet, and that's enough to make anyone feel good.

Virtually any kind of physical activity seems to relieve the effects of stress, although some researchers think that activities that involve repetitive movements – walking, running, bicycling or swimming, for instance – may offer the best defence. Many people consider swimming to be one of the most relaxing of all forms of exercise, a soothing way to literally go with the flow. Repeating a physical movement over and over again somehow seems to ease mind and body.

Think about some ways to make your workout even more relaxing. If you're a walker, be aware of the way your arms swing from front to back and the rhythm of your gait. Repeat a soothing word or phrase each time you exhale.

An ancient cure for frayed nerves

Looking for a simple way to relax, refresh your energy, become more limber and tighten up muscles at the same time? Yoga may be the answer. Exercise scientists have long known that yoga offers a great way to stretch, increase strength and improve balance. Now psychologists are discovering that it can also ease a troubled mind.

When researchers at the University of Wurzburg in Germany tested 12 women before, during and after a 60 minute yoga class, they found that the women's heart rates dropped dramatically during yoga practice. The women also reported feeling less irritable than they did before the class.

Another recent study showed that yoga may be one of the best stress-easers around. At Oxford

Yoga is among the best stress-busters around.

University, a psychologist divided 71 men and women into three groups. One group practised simple relaxation techniques like deep breathing. The second visualised themselves feeling less tense. The third did a half-hour yoga routine. The relaxers and the visualisers felt sluggish afterwards. The people in the yoga group reported feeling more energetic and more emotionally content.

How to get started? On pages 243 to 246 you'll find a simple stretching routine that includes several modified yoga poses. Give it a try this week. If you enjoy the routine, you may want to sign up for a yoga class. Many fitness centres or yoga studios offer them. You'll also find helpful instruction in yoga videos or instruction books.

If you work out on an exercise cycle or stair machine at a health club, you probably find yourself parked in front of a bank of television sets. Watching TV can prevent you from getting into the soothing rhythm of your workout. Studies show that watching television makes people more jittery, not less. So ignore the screen. Concentrate on your breathing and the repetitive movement of your arms and legs. If the gym plays music that gets on your nerves, bring a personal stereo with headphones and your own favourite music or use noise-blocking earplugs and enjoy a quiet interlude.

> You'll find plenty of aggravations you can fix if you take the time to recognise them.

2. Do one thing at a time

Chances are you've heard of Type A behaviour—the hard-driven, competitive, take-no-prisoners personality type once thought to be linked not only to high levels of stress but to a greater risk of heart disease. The original term for Type A behaviour was hurry syndrome, because Type As tend to do everything faster than more relaxed personality types. Type As feel so rushed, in fact, that they often try to do three things at once. They're the ones you see eating lunch, talking on their mobile phones and driving – all at the same time.

If you find yourself falling into this behaviour, make an effort this week to focus on the task in hand. Instead of balancing your accounts while you're talking on the phone, give the phone call your full attention, then turn to the figures afterwards. If you're constantly being interrupted by phone calls while you're trying to work on something, let the answering machine take messages, instead of picking up the phone. Ring people back when the time is right for you. Do one thing at a time and you may feel your stress meter reading begin to fall.

3. Put out the fire

Anger can be stressful, especially the 'hot-headed' kind that lashes out and doesn't solve the problem that ignited it. However, never expressing your anger can be harmful to you as well. If you feel your temper about to flare, stop, take a deep breath and ask yourself three quick questions suggested by Dr Redford Williams, a researcher at Duke University in the USA, who pioneered work in anger control:

187

ChangeOne First Person

Taking control, one week at a time

Dianne Barnum was no stranger to dieting or diet books. 'I've read lots of them, and tried lots of programmes,' says Dianne. Three and a half stone heavier than she wanted to be, she'd never found a plan that worked for her. When *ChangeOne* came along, she was among the first to sign up.

'Frankly, I wanted a lot from a diet. I wanted a programme that was based on solid advice and the kind of foods I like. But I also wanted it to be doable. No counting calories all the time. No adding up food points. I didn't want to have to spend all my time writing things down. I wanted to be able to go on living my life – going out to restaurants with my husband, socialising – and make sensible eating part of it. But I also really wanted to start shedding pounds.'

She did. She dropped 17 pounds by the end of Week 9, and by the end of the first 12 weeks she was down 22 pounds. But she didn't stop there; after five months on *ChangeOne* she'd lost 40 pounds. 'The most important thing I learned was how to take control. It's easy to blame other people or the things around you when you're overweight. But the simple truth is, you're the one who decides what you're going to put in your mouth, no one else. Once I realised that, all I needed was knowledge about smart choices and sensible serving sizes.'

On course to lose the 50 pounds she set as her goal, Dianne continues to look for one change a week to keep her on track. 'It may be something as simple as finding a new recipe I haven't tried. Or experimenting with a new food. I'll vary my exercise programme just to keep it interesting. Whatever it is, every week I try to make one more change. And what a difference that's made in the way I look and feel. I look at myself in the mirror now and see a different person. And I love it.'

■ **Is this really important to me?** If the answer is no, leave what sparked your anger behind. If the answer's yes, then ask yourself:

■ **Am I justified in being angry in this situation?** Argue the pros and cons, as if you had to make your case in court. If your answer is, 'No, I don't really have much to moan about', you're likely to feel your anger and stress dissolve. Of course the answer may be, 'Yes, damn right, that bloke nearly ran me off the road, and he's so busy talking on his mobile phone he didn't even notice it!' Then ask yourself just one more question:

■ **Is there anything I can really do about it?** Honking the horn like crazy isn't going to change anything. It's only likely to make you feel even angrier. Here's a case where the best response is to let it go, take a deep breath and keep out of the bloke's way.

If your answer to the last question is 'yes', then you're in luck. You have the chance to make a real change for the better. Let's say you're angry because one of the kids keeps leaving junk food out on the worktop in the kitchen when you've specifically asked them to put it away. Lay down the law. Explain why you don't want junk food lying around. Get angry if you have to. Then let your anger go. If you have trouble doing that, ask yourself the first question again, but with a little twist: 'What do I get out of staying angry?' Chances are the answer is not much, except a load of unpleasant aggravation.

If all else fails, try this: imagine this is your last day alive and write down how you'd be dealing with the situation if you knew, assuming that you still have to go to work and do normal things. You're likely to find out you have better things to do than stay angry and tense.

4. Phone a friend

Of course, it sounds a little soppy. But talking to someone else – even just phoning someone to say a quick hello – does more than take your mind off your troubles. It can be powerful medicine. Swedish researchers recently reported that people with a strong sense of social connection to other people were almost one-third less likely to die after they'd had a heart attack than those who were socially isolated.

Don't watch TV when exercising. It distracts you and hurts your rhythm.

Part of the reason, researchers believe, may be the stress-easing effect of close relationships. If you don't have a circle of friends to turn to, consider beginning to build one by volunteering for a local community charity, joining a club or a church group, or signing up for an exercise class.

5. Talk to yourself

Sometimes we're our own worst enemies. Instead of easing our pressures, we add to them by thinking in terms of absolutes, using words like 'never' or 'should' or 'always'. 'I should never have done that.' 'Things always go wrong for me.' 'I'll never be able to lose weight at this rate.' If that sounds like you, be alert to moments when you're being unreasonably hard on yourself and try to lighten up. Counter the negative messages with positive ones.

Don't be embarrassed to say them out loud if you're alone. 'Stop now. Easy there. Give it a rest.' Replace the harsh absolute with a more reasonable and forgiving thought: 'So it's going to take a while to lose the weight. So what? No one's pushing me but myself. I'm doing fine.' Take the broad view. Things don't always go wrong for you, after all.

The truth is, things occasionally go wrong for everyone. And when they do, everyone has the same challenge: to sort things out and get on with life.

'What do I get out of staying angry?' Chances are, not much.

6. Laugh it off

Laughter can be strong medicine, say researchers. The act of laughing eases muscle tension and relieves stress and has even been shown to lower the risk of stress-related illnesses such as heart disease.

In a study published in 2001, researchers at the Center for Preventive Cardiology at the University of Maryland Medical Center in the US tested 300 volunteers' propensity to laugh at everyday events. The scientists found that those with a ready laugh were less likely to have heart problems than those who rarely smiled. Even among people with elevated blood pressure or cholesterol levels, the ability to laugh offered protection against heart attacks.

Now it's not always easy to laugh when things go wrong. But if you need a good chortle, try renting the video of a favourite comedy film, watching your favourite sitcom or keeping a humorous book handy. A collection of cartoons –

say, *The Far Side* – offers plenty of laughs. If you frequently fume in rush-hour traffic, try listening to an audio book – preferably a funny one.

7. Practise relaxation

Another proven way to ease stress is what cardiologist Dr Herbert Benson of Harvard University calls the relaxation response. According to Benson's studies, the method taps an innate mechanism that can be used to counteract the human 'fight-or-flight' response that underlies stress. His research shows that it can lower blood pressure and ease muscle tension. Benson suggests setting aside 20 minutes and following these six simple steps:

Find a quiet place where you won't be disturbed. Sit in a comfortable position, one that allows you to relax your body. Close your eyes.

Starting with your feet and progressing upwards through the body, relax your muscles. End with the muscles of your face. Take a moment to experience the feeling of being completely relaxed.

With your eyes still closed, breathe in and out through your nose, concentrating on each breath.

As you exhale, begin to silently repeat a short phrase or single word, such as 'peace' or 'calmness' or 'easy does it'. Choose a word that helps you focus your mind and banish distracting thoughts.

Continue repeating your soothing word or phrase and concentrating on breathing. The experts usually recommend doing this exercise for 10 to 15 minutes. Don't set an alarm, though, or you'll constantly be thinking about when it will go off. Have a watch or clock handy and open your eyes now and then to check the time. And don't be discouraged from doing the relaxation routine if you don't have a full 15 minutes. Even a few minutes will help.

Sit quietly for a few more minutes, first with your eyes closed and then with them open. Enjoy the way your body and mind feel.

Sound easy? In fact, most of us have a hard time letting our minds go quiet and our bodies relax. You may need to practise relaxing a few times before you master the art. But with some practice, you'll find that you can slip quickly into relaxation and away from stress.

Most of us have a hard time letting our minds go quiet and our bodies relax.

191

Making the change

Choose at least three of the strategies in this chapter to try this week. You probably already have an intuitive sense of which ones are best suited to your temperament. But don't be afraid to try at least one that sounds a little far out. You may be surprised at how effective it can be.

Whatever you choose, don't put added pressure on yourself by thinking you have to squeeze yet one more change into an already crowded schedule. Most of these stress-busting techniques take no time at all. Even those that do, like practising the relaxation response or exercising, are well worth the extra time. By taking a few minutes to relax, you may find you're more focused and productive when you get back to work. Certainly, you'll feel calmer. And that's a change that will help you stay in charge of your diet and your life.

Changes ahead: staying active

When someone says they don't have the time to do something, what they often mean is they choose to spend their time doing something else. It's all a matter of priorities.

So when you say you don't have the time to exercise more, what priority of yours is higher than exercise? It's a question worth pondering this week as you work on de-stressing your life.

We realise that we've already asked you this week to invest time in relaxation, and that meant setting aside some other task. Next week we're going to ask you for even more time. But as you'll learn, you can grab exercise time in small pieces throughout the day, and with surprisingly little sacrifice. So as you proceed through this week, think of how you spend your time, and whether the TV soap or that fourth phone call of the night is as high priority as good health and maintaining weight loss.

Comfort foods for relieving stress

'Comfort food', we've come to call it: simple, satisfying, home-cooked meals that conjure up relaxed family dinners in a cosy kitchen. Each of us has certain dishes we think of as comforting; usually they're recipes we associate with childhood. Sitting down to one of them can be a great way to relax and recover from a difficult day. Here's a sampler of six *ChangeOne* comfort-food meals guaranteed to transport you to easier times:

Beef stew page 92

Apple-stuffed turkey breast page 143

Tuna noodle bake page 162

Wine-braised beef page 272

Homestyle meat loaf page 274

Little chicken and sweetcorn pies page 280

WEEK 10

Staying Active for Success

Let's face it: most of us have it easy these days. By some estimates, we burn about half as many calories as people did a century ago just going about their everyday lives. Many experts think that shortfall is a major reason so many of us struggle with our weight.

From the first week of this programme we've been pushing exercise on you in subtle and not-so-subtle ways. This week we're getting serious about it.

Over the coming days, find times to squeeze in a little activity, a short walk, a relaxing stretch. Start developing a new habit – moving around, whatever you can.

Becoming more active isn't essential to shedding weight. But it does help. And it becomes even more important when you're trying to keep the weight off. Research shows that an active lifestyle is the single most important key to long-term dieting success.

Rebel against inactivity

Over the past 20 years, health experts have confirmed a simple but profound fact: we were built to be active. Physical activity helps keep arteries clear, hearts strong and immune systems revved up. Evidence shows that the more active we are, the lower our risk of having high blood pressure, high cholesterol levels, diabetes, osteoporosis, depression and even some forms of cancer.

For slimmers, getting up and moving is especially important. Consider this: it takes a 500-kcals-a-day deficit to lose half a kilo (1 lb) of body fat in a week. One way to do that is to eat 500 fewer kcals than you need. Another is to burn an extra 500 kcals a day doing serious exercise. For a 91 kg (200 lb) man, for example, that's about 40 minutes a day of steady jogging at five miles per hour, seven days a week.

Some people favour exercise. Others eat less. But most successful dieters find it's a whole lot easier to split the difference: to eat roughly 250 kcals less a day and to burn an extra 250, for a grand total of 500. That way, your diet doesn't have to be quite so spartan. And you don't have to spend every free moment working up a serious sweat on a stair machine or treadmill at the gym. In fact, as you'll see, you don't even have to become a formal exerciser.

But burning calories is only one reason to include physical activity in your *ChangeOne* programme.

We were built to be active. Exercise makes us less susceptible to almost every major disease

Improving your long-term odds of success

By adding physical activity to a weight-loss programme, especially 10 weeks into it, you definitely enhance your chances of continuing success. Dieting may be the best way to lose weight initially, but exercise turns out to be the best way to keep it off. In a landmark 1996 study in the US, researchers compared three weight-loss approaches: diet only, exercise only, and a combination of exercise and diet. At the end of the first year, the combination group had lost the most weight, followed by the diet-only group, with the exercise-only group trailing in third place.

But during the second year, a dramatic turnaround occurred. The diet-only group regained all the weight they'd lost, and more. The combination group regained some of the weight they'd lost, but still remained slimmer than when they'd started the programme. The exercise-only group fared best of all, regaining only a little bit of the weight they'd lost. Why? People get weary of pure slimming and eventually give it up, the experts surmised. Being physically active, on the other hand, becomes a pleasure – something people are willing to make a part of their lives.

Tame hunger

In a study published in 2002, researchers at Stanford University in the US compared volunteers in a diet-only programme with a programme that combined exercise with diet. After a year, people in the combination group reported feeling less hungry than those in the diet-only programme. They also found it easier to make sensible food choices and avoid temptations. One reason is simple. When you expend more energy through exercise, you can eat more without gaining weight. Also, research shows that exercise itself can suppress appetite.

Maintain the burn

One of the drawbacks to eating less is that your body compensates by burning fewer calories. That's why people often find it difficult to continue to shed weight while dieting. The best way to make your body burn enough calories even as you lose weight is through physical activity.

Preserve muscle

Another drawback to dieting is that your body may obtain energy by burning not only fat but also muscle cells. That's a problem for three reasons. First, muscle gives you a

Don't slow down

You may have heard that certain kinds of aerobic exercise are better than others at burning off fat. Don't believe it.

It's true that leisurely exercise of roughly 40 minutes or longer will prompt your body to start tapping into fat cells for energy. But fitness experts say that increasing workout intensity will better serve your weight-loss goals over the long haul.

There are several problems with taking it too slowly: most people don't exercise long enough to begin burning into their fat stores; by going at a slower pace, they burn fewer calories; and since everyone's squeezed for time these days, longer, slower workouts just don't make a lot of sense.

The best reason to exercise vigorously is that you'll burn more calories while you're working out, and the high intensity means that you'll continue to burn some calories after you stop. Remember, you want to create a calorie deficit, and the more energy you expend during (and after) exercise, the bigger that deficit. Work out as hard as you comfortably can.

shapelier physique. If one of your goals is to look better in the mirror, you definitely want to keep muscle – maybe even add some. Second, well-toned muscles help you to keep your balance and stay strong enough to work and play with ease – in short, they keep you agile. Third, when you lose muscle tissue, your metabolism slows down, because muscle tissue requires a lot of energy to maintain. The more you have, the more calories you burn, even when you're doing nothing.

Lose fat faster

Add exercise to your weight-loss programme and you'll speed your fat-burning rate. Scientists at Queen's University in Canada recently compared the effects of diet versus exercise in 30 men. Over three months, volunteers in both groups lost more than 7 kg (16 lb). But the exercisers lost almost 1 kg (2.2 lb) more body fat than the others did.

Look and feel better

A recent study from the University of Maryland in the US offers further evidence of the many benefits you get by combining a weight-loss programme with even moderate exercise. Researchers asked 24 overweight, inactive women to begin walking three times a week. At the same time the women also cut back on calories. The diet advice was simple: the women were asked to cut 250-350 kcals a day from what they were eating before while following nutrition guidelines very much like those of *ChangeOne*.

Check-in

It's been six weeks since you first drew up a *ChangeOne* Contract and two weeks since you took time out to assess your progress. Now, look back at the commitment you signed. Make sure the goals you set still make sense and are workable. If not, adjust them in any way that makes sense. This is a long-term contract you're making with yourself. Push yourself hard enough to stay motivated, but not so hard that you get frustrated and give up.

After six months, the volunteers had lost 8 per cent of their body weight. For an 82 kg (180 lb) woman, that's a loss of 6 kg (14 lb). That's great. But in addition their total body fat had fallen by 15 per cent. That means they'd shaved off 12 kg (27 lb) of fat, replacing about half of it with muscle. (And muscle doesn't show up on your hips or tummy.) They'd also become much fitter. Their aerobic capacity – a measure of their lungs' ability to take in oxygen – jumped 8 per cent. In short, thanks to the diet and exercise combination they were slimmer, stronger and had more stamina.

Making the change

Most people who disavow exercise discover that they actually enjoy it, once they get into the swing of things. So keep an open mind. Here's how to get started.

Convince yourself it's worth a try. Beyond weight loss, experts say, there are some 50 proven benefits to exercise, from a healthier heart to a rosier outlook on life. Think about the benefits you're looking for and make a list of five that matter most to you.

Help!

'I'm just not an exercise person. Never have been, never will be. Isn't it possible to lose weight and keep it off without having to work up a sweat?'

Yes, it's possible. But maybe you're reacting to the myth that exercise has to involve gyms, pumping iron, skintight gear and girly aerobics. As you'll see in this chapter, you can get plenty of activity without weights or spandex. Your day provides lots of opportunities for walking, stair climbing and other activities – if you know where to look.

And those short bursts can be particularly long-lived. In a study at the Cooper Institute in Dallas, Texas, scientists recruited 235 men and women. Half agreed to do a standard gym workout several times a week. The others incorporated physical activity into their everyday lives. Both groups burned about the same number of extra calories and lost the same amount of body fat, on average. But the everyday-activity group turned out to have one big advantage over the gym-goers. They were more likely to continue exercising long after the official study ended.

Picture yourself on the move. Top athletes often visualise themselves performing their moves in order to fine-tune their performance. The same technique can help jog you into action. Picture yourself happily riding a bicycle, doing water aerobics or walking on a local footpath. Imagine all the pleasant things you'll experience, from beautiful scenery to a surging sense of self-confidence.

Tell all. Announce your activity plans to friends and family. Knowing they know will encourage (or shame) you into following it through.

Leap the hurdles. Look for clever ways to get over the inevitable obstacles. Pressed for time? Lay out your exercise clothes the night before. Travel on business a lot? Choose hotels with exercise facilities or running tracks nearby. Preoccupied with family matters? Find activities you can do together, like walking, tennis or cycling.

Turn quiet time into a moving experience

Of course, you never have any free time. Don't be so sure. No matter how busy you are, chances are you have plenty of opportunities to be more active. This week, start by completing the Personal Time Analyser form on page 311. Make a couple of copies. On at least two days this week, preferably a weekday and a weekend day, fill out a time analysis. Write down what you do and how much time you spend doing it, hour by hour. Mark whether you're sitting still or up and moving. Active pastimes include walking, hoovering, digging the garden, climbing stairs, riding a bicycle – any activity that requires enough effort to make you feel a little winded. Inactive pastimes involve standing around, sitting or stretching out on the sofa.

Once you've filled in the form, identify at least two opportunities during the day when you can get up and get going. The goal: to turn at least 30 minutes of inactive time into activity by the end of the week every day. Why 30? Because studies show that you'll get the weight-loss benefits you want by doing at least 30 minutes worth of moderately strenuous activities – such as brisk walking – most days of the week. Start with 10 to 15 minutes a day for the first half of the week, then add another 10 to 15 minutes. You don't have to do 30 continuous minutes. Eventually you can divide it up any way you want to: three 10-minute walks, for instance, or 10 minutes spent climbing stairs coming and going from work and a 20-minute walk in the morning.

Some opportunities may be obvious. If you commute by bus, train or underground, get off one or two stops early and walk the rest of the way. If you take the lift or escalator on the way to the office, use the stairs instead. If you often park yourself in front of the television after supper, choose a half-hour programme you can miss and go for a walk. At the very least, do a few exercises during the adverts.

With a little ingenuity, you'll find other ways to turn quiet time into active time. Do you love to read? Consider getting that latest thriller on tape and listen while you take a walk around the block. Are you a devoted sports fan? That doesn't mean you have to become a couch potato when your favourite matches are on; get a Walkman-style radio

continued on page 201

You choose...

Here are some everyday activities and the amount of calories burned every 30 minutes. The figures are based on an 82 kg (180 pound) woman's expenditure:

Activity	Kcals burned
Watch a cricket match	66
Play cricket	240
Shop online	66
Walk around the shops	141
Drive to the car wash	66
Wash your own car	129
Watch ballroom dancing	66
Go ballroom dancing	129
Ride a lawnmower	66
Push a lawnmower	258
Play a video game	66
Play Frisbee	129
Use a leaf-blower	75
Use a rake	171
Sunbathe	66
Go swimming	300

Having a lot more fun

Two weeks before she started *ChangeOne*, Lynn Schmelder joined a gym, hoping to get back into shape for the summer. And for a couple of weeks she was really into it, grabbing time over her lunch hour to work out on one of the heart-boosting cardio machines. It didn't last long.

'I just got bored with doing the same thing over and over. I began to have to force myself to go. And then pretty soon I wasn't going. That's happened to me before – I've joined a gym, all excited, and then stopped going after the initial excitement wore off.'

With a nudge from us at *ChangeOne*, Lynn decided to give exercise one more try. But this time she was determined to ward off boredom by going for variety – lots of it.

'I started doing aerobics, and I found that I really loved it. I like being with other people in a class. I like learning new moves. The instructors are great. So right now I'm going three to four times a week. I do regular aerobics, step aerobics and kick-boxing.

'What a difference! Before, I had to drag myself to the gym. Now I can't wait to get there.'

Staying active has also made a difference on the scales. When she started *ChangeOne*, Lynn weighed 71.5 kg (159 lb); she's now down to 66.6 kg (148 lb). 'My clothes fit better. I have so much more energy. And I'm having a lot more fun.'

And she's also come to realise that, for her at least, the only way to stay active is to find things she really enjoys doing. 'If you have to force yourself to do it, you won't keep it up. Willpower only goes so far. The key is to find things that are fun and interesting, things you really enjoy for their own sake. Then nothing can stop you.'

continued from page 199
and walk while you listen to a live commentary on the game. Is your work day filled with meetings? Suggest to your colleagues or clients a walk and talk session. Do you travel a lot? Ask for a room on the third or fourth floor of the hotel and take the stairs instead of the lift. And when you're waiting at the airport for a flight, don't sit still: take a brisk stroll round the terminal.

Here are other suggestions for fitting in an activity every day this week:

Plan ahead. Decide where and when you'll fit in extra activity, and mark it on your calendar. Treat activity as you would an appointment. Find an open time slot and write in a workout. If you use a computer, programme it to remind you during the day. At the end of each day, total up how much extra activity you fit in. If you fell short of your goal, devise ways to get a little more exercise the following day.

Have a fallback. Let's say Plan No. 1 is to walk for 15 minutes after lunch. That's great – unless someone at the office is celebrating a birthday and you end up being part of the festivities. Then it's time for Plan No. 2: walking for 30 minutes after supper, when you would usually do your second 15-minute walk. Make sure your plans include both weekdays and weekends this coming week.

Make it useful. If you have trouble doing exercise just for the sake of exercise, look for ways to make it useful. Are you planning to do more walking? Find bona fide reasons to go for a walk. Instead of having the newspaper put through your door, for instance, cancel the delivery and walk to the newsagent's. If you typically drive to a supermarket that's not far away, lace up those walking shoes and save on petrol. If there are jobs that need doing around the house or garden, make a list and get cracking. The bottom line is to find a way to stay active, wherever and whenever you can.

continued on page 203

Help!

'The last time I tried exercising, I ended up being so sore the next morning that I could barely get out of bed. Is there anything I can do to prevent that?'

A little bit of soreness is normal. But if you're uncomfortably sore, it means you overdid it. This time around, don't try to go from zero to 60 in 10 seconds. Ease into an exercise programme a little at a time. Starting on page 236 you'll find an eight-week fitness programme designed to get you into shape slowly but surely. Another tip that may help: try doing a few stretching exercises before and after you walk or do other physical activities. You'll find a quick and simple stretching routine on pages 243 to 246.

Walking: your best bet

Walking is the exercise of choice for most dieters. No wonder. You don't need to be a member of a gym. You can walk almost every-where – around the block or around the shops, for example. It's gentle on joints, and you can burn a surprising number of calories. On level ground, a half-hour walk can burn 100 to 150 calories, depending on your weight. Hike up some hills and you can spend 200 to 250 calories. Here's how to prepare:

Find shoes that fit

The only equipment you really need is a decent pair of walking shoes. Finding them is easy. What matters most is comfort. If they feel good on your feet when you try them on, odds are they also provide enough support. When shopping for shoes:

- Wear the socks you plan to exercise in. That way you'll be sure to get the best fit.
- Try on both shoes. Most people's feet aren't exactly the same size. Choose a pair of shoes that fit your larger foot.
- Allow a little extra room. Feet swell when you walk, so buy shoes with about a thumb's width between your longest toe and the end of the shoe. Make sure the heel doesn't slip, though, or you could get blisters.

Hold your head up

Walking comes naturally, and it makes sense to use the technique you've always known. But these tips will help you to stay comfortable and get the most out of your walk:

- Stand up straight. Imagine a string pulling you up from the top of your head. Let that string pull you up as straight as possible. Relax your shoulders.
- Look ahead. Keep your neck straight and your head held high to avoid unnecessary strain to the neck and shoulders. If you have to look down to see where you're going, lower your eyes, not your head.
- Move your arms. Bend your elbows and let your arms swing naturally at your sides. You'll prevent swelling, tingling or numbness – and you'll burn up to 15 per cent more calories by keeping your arms moving.
- Don't carry extra weight. Some people try to get in additional exercise by clutching a couple of light dumbbells, but fitness-walking experts say that's risky: the weights can pull you off balance and strain back or leg muscles.

> All you need is a decent pair of shoes and a safe route.

Stay safe

Walking is one of the safest of activities, but it's wise to take a few precautions:

- If you're walking at night, wear a piece of reflective clothing.
- If the path is dimly lit, take a good torch with a strong beam.
- When the weather is warm, be sure to drink a large glass of water before you set out and another when you return.
- If you have to walk at the side of the road, keep to the right, so you face oncoming traffic.

If your path is rugged or bumpy, protect your ankles, particularly if you have a history of twists or sprains. Consider wearing a comfortable elastic bandage for support, and keep your eyes focused on the path.

continued from page 201
To help you to reach this goal, we've included a Daily Activity Log on page 310, which will enable you to chart your time, effort and progress.

If you still need motivation – and who doesn't? – consider these compelling benefits of regular activity:

To burn more calories. Exert yourself. The minute you get up from the sofa or out of your office chair and start walking, you more than double the number of calories you're burning. An 82 kg (180 lb) woman burns about 2.2 kcals a minute sitting in a meeting or slumped in front of the TV. The same woman strolling around the neighbour-hood at a leisurely pace of 2 miles an hour burns 3.6 kcals a minute. If she increases her pace to 3 miles an hour, she'll hit 4.7 kcals a minute. At a brisk pace of 4 miles an hour – a mile every 15 minutes – she'll burn 7.2 kcals a minute. Fifteen minutes at that pace will burn about 100 extra kcals.

To boost your metabolism. Aerobic exercise – activity that leaves you feeling slightly winded – increases your calorie-burning rate while you're doing it. But if you want to boost your metabolism permanently, add strengthening exercises to your routine. As you know, muscle tissue is metabolically more active than fat tissue, which means it uses more calories just to maintain itself. Dieters who add muscle by doing strengthening exercises help to keep their metabolisms running high.

To look great in the mirror. A combination of aerobic and strengthening exercises is your best bet. Most slimmers focus on the kilograms or pounds on the scales, which is fine as far as it goes. But what the majority of us really want is to look better. And once you begin to shed fat, the reflection in the mirror will look a whole lot better if you begin to tighten up slack muscles and burn body fat.

To become more fit. You'll need to crank the intensity level up a bit. Our 30 minutes a day of moderate exercise is good for overall health, but it is not enough for high-level fitness. One method scientists use to measure exercise intensity is counting heart beats. The harder you're working, the faster your heart beats. To increase your fitness level, most experts say, it's a good idea to exercise for at least 20 minutes at 60 to 80 per cent of your maximum heart rate (to find out your targets, look at the chart on page 204). To track your heart rate during exercise, stop for a minute and find your pulse, either on the inside of your wrist near the base of your thumb or on your neck just to the side of your throat. Count how many times your heart beats in 15 seconds, and then multiply that by four. Or consider buying a heart-rate monitor; they're easy to use, and you can find them at most sporting-goods stores.

Have some fun

If you're already active, devote this week to being a little *more* active. Try an activity you haven't done before. Take a walk in a place you haven't visited. Set up the badminton net that's been collecting dust in the garage. Pull out the bicycle and put some oil on the chain and air in the tyres.

If physical activity hasn't been a big part of your life, give it a serious try this week. Don't push yourself too hard at the beginning. Start by fitting in 15 minutes of walking. Then move on to 30 minutes. Try to make it a pleasure by finding pleasant places to walk in, putting on headphones with your favourite music or inviting a friend to join you. Just getting up from that comfy chair and moving around will get your heart beating a little faster, your muscles working and your calorie-burning engine stoked up.

Targeting your heart rate

As you age, your maximum heart rate decreases. That in turn reduces the intensity at which you should exercise. To learn your target rates, check your age group below:

Age	Maximum heart rate	60% max	70% max	80% max
20	200/minute	120/minute	140/minute	160/minute
25	195	117	137	156
30	190	114	133	152
35	185	111	130	148
40	180	108	126	144
45	175	105	123	140
50	170	102	119	136
55	165	99	116	132
60	160	96	112	128
65	155	93	108	124
70	150	90	105	120

Changes ahead: keeping track to stay on track

We're near the end of the 12-week programme, and by now you should have the key *ChangeOne* skills pretty well in hand. Time to start looking towards the future and at how to maintain your weight-loss successes for the months and years ahead. Next week, we'll help you build a self-monitoring system. In preparation, think through all the ways you monitor your health and weight. Is it through the fit of your clothing? The mirror? The scales? Your moods? Armed with these personal tools, you'll create a warning system to remind you when you might be straying from your desired weight.

WEEK 11

Keeping
on Track

By now you're hitting your stride. You're dropping the weight. The success feels great.

Still, as almost any successful slimmer will tell you, it's crucially important to keep track. The pressures that surround us to eat, eat, eat don't go away. Portion sizes have a way of creeping up. Plans to go for a walk or to the gym can fall by the wayside. And the weight has a way of sneaking back on.

This week you'll devise your own 'first alert' programme to sound an alarm if you begin to get off track.

We're not suggesting that you measure every bowl of cereal or serving of pasta for the rest of your life. But staying alert to how you're feeling, what you're doing and how much you're eating will have a huge payoff in terms of weight, health and self-confidence.

Schedule a regular check-up

With the end of the 12-week programme just around the corner, it's time to take a moment to celebrate how far you've come. If you're like some of our *ChangeOne* volunteers, you may have already reached your target weight. Now it's time to make the transition from a diet that contains fewer calories than you need to one that balances calories you take in with those you expend.

If you began *ChangeOne* hoping to lose a significant amount of weight, you may still have some pounds to go. There's nothing wrong with that. Slow and steady is the best kind of progress to make.

Wherever you are on the path towards your desired weight, start planning ahead. Almost any diet programme will help you to lose weight during the first few months. That's the easy part. If you've slimmed before, you know that the real trick is maintaining weight loss – which requires turning the healthy changes you've made into lifelong habits.

Sadly, that's where most diet plans falter. We've already mentioned one pitfall. Call it the on/off trap. People go on a diet to lose weight and go off it once they've shed the pounds. And unfortunately, that means going right back to the way they were eating before. You know how the story ends. Before long, the numbers on the scales are right back where they started.

There's another pitfall, and one that's probably more common. As people near their desired weight, they begin to ease up a little. They stop paying as much attention to portion sizes. They splurge a little more often on rich desserts. They eat an extra snack. Nothing dramatic. But if they're not watching, all those little nibbles can add up to a pound here, a pound there. Before they know it, they've regained a chunk of the weight they lost.

Regaining a couple of kilos or pounds shouldn't be a big deal. You already know what it takes to lose them. But losing ground can spell real trouble, for several reasons. If you

> Almost any diet will help you to lose weight; the trick is maintaining the weight loss.

begin to gain weight again, it's natural to assume that the diet isn't working and to abandon it completely. Worse, it's easy to begin to blame yourself, to begin replaying all kinds of negative messages in your head. 'I'm a failure.' 'I'll never be able to lose the weight and keep it off.' 'I'm destined to be fat.' Losing weight only to gain it back can also make you reluctant to try again. And if you do try again, you might feel discouraged from the start.

> If your weight is holding steady, get on with your life. Forget about dieting for a while.

Thanks to the careful work you've already put in, this is far less likely to happen to you than it is for people on faddish diets. You've learned that eating can be a pleasure, not something you have to fear. You've seen that you can lose weight and keep it off eating regular food that you actually like to eat. You've discovered on *ChangeOne* that you can eat sensible portions without feeling hungry. Along the way, you've seen which changes have made the biggest difference for you.

Now all it takes to ensure that weight creep doesn't happen is keeping a watchful eye not only on your weight but also how your clothes are fitting, how you feel, how much exercise you're getting and what's on the menu.

The *ChangeOne* first alert programme

Starting this week, you'll take a few minutes once a week to do a quick self check-up. Record your weight. Estimate how much physical activity you were able to fit in. Rate your overall mood. And jot down any issues or problems you may be dealing with. That's all. To make your weekly check-ups even easier, we've included a *ChangeOne* progress log on page 312, which will allow you to track four weeks of check-ups. At the end of these four weeks chart how your weight has changed on the simple graph at the bottom of the form.

We're not suggesting you fill in weight-monitoring forms for the rest of your life. We do recommend logging your progress report for the next two months. If your weight is holding steady and you're comfortable with how things are going, tuck the form away in a drawer and get on with your life. Celebrate your success. Forget about dieting for a while.

But don't forget to pay attention. Weigh yourself at least once a week. Keep track of how your clothes feel or where you notch your belt. Be alert to your moods. If you notice a change for the worse – if your favourite trousers feel a bit snug, or you've added more than a kilo or a few pounds, or you're going through a rocky period at home – take a copy of the progress report and start filling it in weekly.

Remember, most people's weight goes up or down a little, week by week. You probably already know how much yours normally varies. If your weight creeps up by more than 2 kg (5 lb) from your desired weight, it's time to take some action. Don't panic. You haven't failed. And don't give up.

ChangeOne First Person

A new mindset

'Before I started *ChangeOne*, I thought I'd have to see big improvements on the scales – about 2 kg (4–5 lb) a week – to stay motivated. My mindset has definitely changed', says Mary Saltsman, an administrative assistant.

'The first few weeks were the toughest, maybe because I had such unrealistic expectations. But now I'm seeing the weight come off, about half a kilo (1 lb) a week, and that's just fine with me.'

Mary lost 8 kg (18 lb) during the 12 weeks, and she has maintained the weight loss since. Along the way, Mary has made a few important changes. With teenage kids at home, she can't entirely steer clear of fast food. 'But even the kids are beginning to change some eating habits. Chicken nuggets have definitely taken a back seat to salads with my daughter, for instance. At restaurants, I now typically have a hearty soup and a salad. More than anything else, I realise when I'm full now. I know enough to stop.'

You already know exactly what it takes to lose weight. You've done it before and you can do it again.

Add up your activity

Keeping track of exercise isn't as easy as watching kilos and pounds on the scales. True, if you go to a gym, it's easy to write on the calendar each time you go and how long you spend. But if your exercise consists of doing everyday physical activities – taking the stairs, walking from the far end of the car park, doing a circuit round the block during the adverts on TV – keeping track can be trickier.

One approach is to fill out an activity log, adding up the time you spend every day. (Remember, we've included one for you on page 310.) Your goal should be to add up at least 30 minutes of moderately intense activity daily.

Another strategy, which many people come to love, is using a step counter, also called a pedometer. Step counters are devices about the size of a pager that can be attached to your belt or waistband. By way of a mechanical pendulum that moves back and forth with each step you take, the device automatically records your every step.

> If your weight is holding steady, get on with your life. Forget about dieting for a while.

The simplest devices, the ones that just count steps, are the best buy. Pedometers that compute the distance you've covered aren't very accurate; models that claim to tell you how many calories you've burned are even more unreliable, since they can't distinguish between a leisurely stroll and a heart-thumping run. A basic step counter will be reasonably cheap (around £15) and can be found at most sports shops.

Using a step counter

For the first few days, wear the counter but go about your usual day. At the end of each day, jot down how many steps you took. This number will serve as your baseline. Then set your first goal for increasing the amount of walking you do. Without doing anything but going about your daily business, you're likely to take about 3000 steps. Doing roughly 15 minutes' worth of walking, stair climbing and other everyday activities will add about 2000 steps. The optimum goal for weight maintenance is around 12,000 to 15,000 steps a day.

Not quite there yet? Don't worry. Scale up your weekly goals gradually. Start by aiming for 7000 steps one week, for example, and the next week, increase your goal to 9000 steps. Like many people, you may find that using a step counter will give you a little push when you need it. From time to time, check to see how many steps you've taken. If you're barely up to 2000 steps when lunch time rolls round, it's time to consider a brisk walk after you eat. If you've finished supper and are still falling short on steps, turn off the TV and take a walk.

If you decide to use a step counter, include the average number of steps you take on your progress log. That way you'll see your increasing activity at a glance.

Monitor your moods

While you're keeping tabs on your weight, how your clothes feel and how much exercise you get, also be alert to how you feel – happy, sad, enthusiastic, discouraged, busy, bored, really keen, whatever. You'll find a place on the progress log to record what your overall moods were like during the previous week.

Staying in touch with the way you feel is important for several reasons you probably already recognise. For a lot of people, stress, boredom, loneliness or feeling a bit down are triggers for eating. If you're among those emotional eaters, keeping tabs on your mental state will help you begin to see patterns. You may see that the times your weight tends to creep back up again are times when you're bored.

The solution could be as simple as making a list of three or four things to do when you're feeling that way that don't involve eating. Let's say that stress at work is your downfall; every time you start ticking the 'stressed out' box on your progress report, you can almost be sure your weight will start to climb. Simply recognising that familiar pattern can help you change it – by finding healthier ways than eating to deal with stress, for instance, or by increasing the time you spend exercising.

Like many people, you may discover that by paying attention to your moods, you begin to notice early warning signs of trouble. You realise that you're beginning to feel worn down by stress before you become completely frazzled. You notice the first signs of feeling blue. That awareness can help you to remedy the situation before you find yourself in a deep slump. Get together with friends. Schedule time to do something you really love. Set aside extra time for exercise, which is a proven mood-booster. Treat yourself to something special. Turn your attention back to healthy eating as a way to avoid overeating when you're feeling discouraged or down.

The truth is, everyone feels down now and then. Sometimes there's a perfectly good reason for it. Money problems. Relationship difficulties. A bad day at work. But some people find their moods dragged down again and again when there's no good reason except a feeling of low self-esteem. Given the emphasis our society places on being thin, it's not surprising that many people who struggle with their weight end up having a negative image of their bodies.

> Forget the 'perfect' body myth; focus on a healthy, smart weight that fits you.

The problem is compounded by a tendency on the part of many people to think that being overweight is the result of a lack of will-power. It's not that at all. It's the result of a complicated mix of factors, from genes and family eating patterns to body type and psychology.

So here's another reason for monitoring your moods: if your mental state tends to turn sour because you have feelings of low self-esteem, take time to remind yourself of how far you've come in making healthful changes. Remember that not all of us are magazine cover models. Healthy bodies vary tremendously in terms of size and shape. Don't get into the trap of wanting the 'perfect' body. Concentrate, instead, on achieving a healthy, reasonable weight for who you are.

Easier said than done? Of course it is. Sometimes feelings of low self-esteem reach all the way back into childhood, making them very hard to change on your own. Feeling sad or hopeless can be no more than a passing emotion for some people, but for others it can be a symptom of clinical depression. If you find yourself struggling without success against feelings of sadness, hopelessness or low self-esteem, talk to your doctor. There is a proven link between depression and weight gain. And treating depression, studies show, can help people get down to a normal weight.

Back to wearing clothes she loves

'I've never had much luck slimming. But this time around, something just clicked for me', says Tina Settembrino. At the end of the 12-week programme, Tina, a production assistant, is down two dress sizes. 'People stop me all the time and say, "Wow, you really look good". I feel good too, healthier and more confident. I've tried to make a point of being aware of that, so it helps keep me motivated.'

Another big incentive to stick with the programme: being able to wear the clothes she wants to wear. 'Before, I did most of my shopping at a shop that specialises in business clothes for larger women – basically baggy outfits', says Tina with a laugh. 'But now that I'm slimming down, I'm back to shopping in high street shops, buying clingier clothes. It's great.'

Keeping an eye on how her new wardrobe fits helps keep her on track. 'If I feel as if I'm slipping a little, if my clothes feel a little tighter or I think my portion sizes are beginning to creep up, I start right at the beginning, with breakfast. I go through each meal of the day, taking another look at what I'm eating and how much I'm eating. It's a great way for me to take control again without feeling overwhelmed.'

Taking action

If you notice your weight beginning to climb – or your clothes or belts beginning to feel tight – search for the reason. You may know exactly why you're gaining weight. Stress at work, perhaps, or weeks of holiday party-going. Maybe you've just stopped being as strict as you were before about keeping portions under control. The notes you've jotted down should tell you a lot. To do more in-depth troubleshooting, fill in the diagnostic checklist below.

Once you've focused on the specific problem, take action. Don't try to change everything all at once. That's what *ChangeOne* is all about: focusing on one thing at a time.

Having trouble with a specific meal? Check back to the first four weeks of *ChangeOne* for advice on how to take control of breakfast, lunch, supper or snacks. Eating when you're not really hungry? Make a conscious effort to stop and ask yourself whether you're actually hungry, or just responding to an emotional or environmental cue. If you're

Diagnostic checklist

When the first alert warning bell rings, use this checklist to identify the sources of trouble. ☺ A smile means you're doing just fine. ☺ A neutral expression means you're holding your own. ☹ A frown – well, you know what that means. After you're done, look over the categories that scored a frown. These are the areas on which to focus your trouble-shooting efforts.

	☺	☺	☹	FOR HELP:
Breakfast				Page 22
Lunch				Page 38
Snacks				Page 58
Supper				Page 82
Eating out				Page 108
Stress				Page 180
Resisting pressures to eat				Page 129
Emotional eating				Page 66
Environmental cues				Page 62
Self-esteem				Page 212
Stopping when I'm satisfied				Page 84
Motivation				Page 172

not genuinely hungry, distract yourself by doing something else – take a walk, do a chore, phone a friend, brush your teeth or help yourself to a stick of sugar-free gum. Feeling just plain overwhelmed? Your best bet may be that tried-and-true jumpstart for any weight loss plan: the food diary. Keep one for a week. Even if you make no other change, chances are you'll see progress on the scales.

Keeping track is so important that we urge you to set aside a particular time each week to conduct your *ChangeOne* check-up. Many people prefer to do theirs on Sunday evenings. Use whatever day and time works best for you. Just try to stick to it. Put a reminder on your calendar. Post your weekly check-up form on the refrigerator or beside your desk – wherever it's easy to find. If you have a tendency to misplace pieces of paper, record your weight and activity level in a couple of places – in a notebook or on your computer, for instance. That way you'll have a back-up. And if all is going well, then you'll have several reminders to tell yourself, 'Congratulations! Be proud!' By learning the *ChangeOne* way to lose weight, you have changed yourself in untold wonderful ways.

> If you notice the pounds coming back, diagnose the cause and find a remedy.

Changes ahead: *ChangeOne*...for life!

With your own early-warning programme in place, you can begin to relax a little and enjoy yourself without worrying that your waistline will suffer. Next week, in fact, is devoted to making sure that eating remains the pleasure it's meant to be. We're going to invite you to shake things up a little – to try something new in the kitchen or at your favourite restaurant. Treat yourself to something special. Have a blast; you deserve it. Over these past 11 weeks you've made some important changes. You've worked hard. Next week is your chance to celebrate those changes and to look ahead at how to make them last a lifetime.

ChangeOne ...for Life!

It's celebration time. Put down the book for a moment, take a deep breath and let out a victory yell.

You've reached week 12, the end of the formal *ChangeOne* programme. Over the past three months you've done something remarkable. You've redirected your life. You've changed the way you eat. More importantly, you've proved to yourself that you are in control. You've learned that small steps in the right direction can add up to a giant leap forward.

So in this final week, have fun. We want you to be playful with food. At least twice, try a new combination or flavour you've never had before.

Why? Because the enemy of weight loss is boredom. Eat the same way all the time, under tight restrictions, and you'll soon rebel. And if *ChangeOne* is about anything, it's about a love and respect for good food.

Satisfying starters

Little dishes let you enjoy a diversity of flavours and textures as well as cuisines. Plus it's a fun and social way to eat. Here is an Italian approach, with other ideas.

ANTIPASTO SUPPER

100 g (3½ oz) cooked peeled king or tiger prawns (4 to 6) on shredded lettuce topped with 2 tablespoons tomato and chilli relish or salsa

25 g (1 oz) mozzarella cheese (coaster), sliced, interleaved with sliced tomatoes (unlimited) and sprinkled with fresh basil and balsamic vinegar

10 herbed olives

1 slice crusty bread

kcals 370, fat 11 g, saturated fat 4 g, cholesterol 100 mg, sodium 2800 mg, carbohydrate 43 g, fibre 4 g, protein 34 g, calcium 97 mg

VARIATIONS

For balance and calorie control, pick one item from some or all of the following:
- **Protein foods.** Instead of prawns, try 2 skewers satay (Thai grilled chicken or beef strips); 55 g (2 oz) smoked salmon or gravad lax; 3 thin slices Parma ham; or 18 steamed mussels.
- **Vegetables.** Unlimited, as long as they are not prepared with added fat. Roasted or grilled peppers are one idea, delicious with these flavours.
- **Nibbles.** Instead of olives, add gherkins, pickles, chutney, capers or a handful of nuts.
- **Grain.** Instead of bread, try 3 crispbreads.

Reward yourself

Give yourself a big pat on the back, but don't stop there. Reward yourself with something special. Make it a complete extravagance, if you want – a weekend away or a night on the town. Or choose something that reinforces your changes, your results and the new you: running shoes, a new bicycle, a series of yoga classes or an enticing cookery book.

Why make so much of rewarding yourself? Because too often we tend to be aware of when we've fallen short and take our progress for granted. Even people who have lost weight and made healthy changes in the way they live may think they've failed – unless they celebrate their successes.

Acknowledging a job well done also serves as a way to mark those milestones we talked about before – the small steps you take that add up to a giant leap forward. Unless you celebrate them, you may not even be aware of how far you've come. And when we say celebrate your victories, we mean all of them. Some of your successes are easy to recognise. Eating a healthier breakfast, for instance. Or taming runaway snacks. But other positive changes may be more subtle, though more important: discovering that you can decide on a plan of action and stick to it; gaining self-confidence; banishing a negative voice that used to sound in your head; learning that you can slip for a day or two and get yourself back on track.

Small steps? Yes. But each one makes an important difference. This week take a little time to think about the obvious and not-so-obvious ways you've changed over the past 12 weeks. Give yourself kudos for every positive step you've taken.

Isn't it the people around us who are supposed to give us a pat on the back when we've done something wonderful? Of course they are. And maybe you're lucky enough to have someone who does give you accolades for what you've accomplished. Still, it's important to give yourself kudos too. As helpful as other people can be, changing for the better is up to you and you alone. You have to be your own best friend. By giving yourself rewards, you also reinforce positive self-messages – a powerful antidote against those discouraging words that can sometimes repeat in your ears.

> Why pat yourself on the back? Too often we emphasise our failures over our successes.

Trust your instincts

Yes, you'll celebrate your success this week. But – and no surprise here – we've included a lesson for the long haul. Relax. It's a lesson you'll love.

First, a question: what's the toughest challenge slimmers face when it comes to keeping the weight off? When we asked our *ChangeOne* volunteers at the beginning of the programme, many of them listed things like 'snacks', 'hunger', and 'a sweet tooth'. Most people starting a diet think the hardest part will be resisting temptation. In fact, as we mentioned at the start, the biggest pitfall slimmers face over the long haul is something more basic: boredom.

People often give up on a diet because it gets tiresome. They grow weary of counting calories or consulting long lists of foods they should or shouldn't eat. They rebel against the rules that most diets include.

We've made sure *ChangeOne* doesn't include a lot of strict rules, banned foods, complex theories and other guidelines that tie you up. A healthy diet, after all, is about eating sensible servings of tasty and (mostly) nutritious food. You can eat just about anything, but if your choice is rich in calories, you'll have to watch portions. It's that simple.

But even with the varied *ChangeOne* menus, you could be feeling restless. So this week shake things up a little. Prepare something you haven't eaten before. Get creative in the kitchen and concoct a dish of your own. Treat yourself to a meal at a restaurant you've been anxious to try. Forget the *ChangeOne* meal plans for a whole day. In fact, take the whole week off, if you want. Imagine that you're taking the stabilisers off and going for a solo spin after 12 weeks of learning how to keep your balance. This week let the principles of *ChangeOne* guide you as you venture out on your own.

To get started, turn the page for a party of festive ideas; then go to page 222 for more eating adventures.

Check-in

Think back to where you were when you started *ChangeOne*. Write a list of the positive changes you've made since then. Put a star beside the changes that have had the biggest impact on how you look and feel. And then, as we suggested back in Week 11, put the list away, out of sight and out of mind. But remember where you put it. If, in the coming months, you find yourself getting off track, look back at it. You'll find listed there the changes that work best for you. Zero in on them and chances are you'll be able to take control of your weight again.

Taco party

Tacos migrated from Mexico to become one of the most popular dishes in the USA and now in the UK too. A taco party is a lot of fun. So set out a buffet of oven-warmed tortillas, vegetables, low-fat cheese and piping hot grilled or sautéed meats or beans, and let everyone create their own taco. A serving is two tacos, filled as suggested below.

How to build a taco:

1. Line your plate with a corn or small flour tortilla (wrap).

2. Top with a golf ball-sized portion of cooked lean minced beef, minced turkey or shredded turkey, or refried beans (see below) or canned kidney beans.

3. Add 2 tablespoons (2 thumbs) grated reduced-fat cheese, guacamole and/or sliced olives.

4. Cover with vegetables – chopped tomatoes, shredded lettuce, diced red and green peppers, sliced red onion, chopped green chillies (all unlimited) – and salsa.

5. Fold over and eat.

For corn tortilla and minced beef taco: kcals 430, fat 22 g, saturated fat 10 g, cholesterol 80 mg, sodium 670 mg, carbohydrate 33 g, fibre 5 g, protein 27 g, calcium 300 mg.

TIPS ON CHEESE

Mexican 'queso fresco' is a soft white cheese with a mild flavour. Mild Cheddar is a good substitute. Wensleydale, Caerphilly and Edam are also good in tacos. To save calories, look for reduced-fat varieties of cheese, and when grating use the fine holes. Chilling the cheese well before grating helps to prevent it from falling apart. To save time, you can grate a large quantity of cheese and then freeze it; it doesn't need to be thawed if you are going to heat it in a savoury crumble or sauce.

ABOUT REFRIED BEANS

Traditional Mexican refried beans, 'frijoles refritos', are made by sautéeing onion and sometimes garlic in lard, then adding cooked pinto beans and mashing. Make your own lower-fat, lower-calorie version by cooking a chopped onion, and an optional crushed clove of garlic, in a non-stick frying pan with 1 teaspoon of olive oil and a splash of chicken or vegetable stock until the onion is soft. Add a 400 g can of pinto or other beans, drained and rinsed, and 1 teaspoon ground cumin, and mash the beans as they heat. Season with salt and pepper to taste.

TIPS ON TORTILLAS

■ Tortillas are very thin, pancake-like breads made either from a wheat flour dough or a special maize meal called masa harina. They are a staple in the Central American diet.

■ Corn tortillas have fewer calories than flour tortillas because they aren't made with added fat. And corn tortillas can deliver another bonus: when they're made with lime, a calcium compound, they can provide some of this important mineral.

■ Crisp taco shells, which can be bought in most supermarkets, are corn tortillas that are folded over in half and usually fried. This gives them about double the calorie count of a soft tortilla.

HEALTH TIP

Keep your total portion of cheese, olives and guacamole to no more than 4 tablespoons. While they add great flavour and texture to tacos, all are high in fat and calories.

221

Try something new

How you'll shake things up this week is up to you. If you've been sitting down to cereal every morning, see how a yogurt parfait appeals. If you've been packing a sandwich, take yourself out for lunch this week. If you've been following the *ChangeOne* supper meal plans scrupulously, pull a couple of cookery books down from your kitchen shelf and try out a few new recipes. Do a *ChangeOne* makeover of an old family standard. Give a big dinner party. Take the family out for a lavish meal. Splurge on a dessert you haven't had for a while. Visit the local farmer's market or greengrocer and take home something you've never tasted before.

Giving yourself a little freedom doesn't mean putting your progress at risk. Last week you set up a first-alert system that will warn you if you get off track. Trust it. And trust your instincts to guide you. Gaining the confidence to make healthy choices is one of the measures of lasting success.

Colourful fruits and vegetables add pleasure to your plate. Look out for the unusual ones in specialist shops or markets. Clockwise from top left: kale; spaghetti squash; pak choy; sprouting broccoli; Chinese long beans – wrapped round (from top to bottom) chayote, yellow passion fruit and kohlrabi – mango; star fruit, plantain; prickly pear; and kabocha squash.

Not sure how to add excitement to the menu? Here are a few suggestions:

Make your own salad bar
For a dinner one night this week put together a salad bar and invite everyone to create their own salads. Include at least two vegetables that may not usually be on the menu – beetroot, radicchio or artichoke hearts, for instance. Warm up a loaf of crusty wholegrain bread. For pudding scoop up a selection of colourful sorbets topped with berries.

Give a taco party
Tacos are a terrific way to serve up lots of vegetables – tomatoes, lettuce, peppers and onions – and provide a balanced meal all in one. Put

out the components and let everyone make up their own. Help yourself to as much salsa as you want and don't forget to dab on some guacamole, even a little soured cream if you like. Look back to pages 220 to 221 for more ideas.

Slim down an old family friend
Choose a favourite casserole or bake, a pasta dish or pilaf and give it a boost by adding an extra serving of vegetables. Broccoli is terrific in a fish pie. Chickpeas make a great addition to spaghetti with tomato sauce. A good helping of green peppers can liven up, and lighten up, a bowl of chilli con carne. If fish fingers are a family favourite, serve them with a fresh tomato and onion salsa for added zest. If it helps, use a calorie counter to add up the precise calories in your adapted meal.

Order a feast of starters and side dishes
Choose a restaurant with a wide range of good starters and vegetable accompaniments and have a feast. Share the dishes with your companions and you can order practically every small dish on the menu without having to worry about portion sizes. Start with only as many dishes as there are people at the table. If you're still hungry, order more. Steer clear of fried foods, of course, and make sure the selection includes plenty of vegetables.

Exotic foods are everywhere. Try some and find out how delicious they are.

Go fish
Chances are your local fishmonger features at least a few kinds of fish you haven't tried. Be adventurous and cook something that's new for you – fresh sardines, king prawns or swordfish, for instance. Choose a recipe that involves baking or grilling, not frying. There are many low-calorie ways to give fish a burst of exotic flavour. Many supermarkets now offer spices that create the 'blackened' flavour of American Cajun cooking, for instance. A scattering of capers can also turn a plain piece of fish into something special. Spicy salsas are also terrific on fish.

Bake bread
As a special treat, take the time this weekend to bake your own loaf of bread. If you don't have a bread machine, consider investing in one. They make bread-making simple

New ways with tuna

Most tuna sandwiches are dripping with mayonnaise. But why settle for such a high-fat, ordinary-tasting treatment? In this alternative version, lemon juice, plain yogurt and Dijon mustard add moisture and a great tangy flavour.

VARIATIONS

■ For Italian tuna filling, replace the yogurt and mayonnaise with fat-free Italian dressing.

■ For Indian tuna filling, add 1 teaspoon curry powder and 2 tablespoons raisins.

■ For Tex-Mex tuna filling, replace the gherkin and mustard with 2 tablespoons salsa.

TUNA SALAD SANDWICH

Serves 2

1 can (about 200 g) tuna in water or brine, drained
1 tablespoon lemon juice
1 tablespoon plain yogurt or yogurt cheese (see page 29)
1 tablespoon reduced-fat mayonnaise
1 tablespoon finely diced gherkin
1 teaspoon Dijon mustard
1 tablespoon finely chopped onion
4 slices wholemeal bread
Lettuce and tomato

1. Place the tuna in small bowl and add the lemon juice, yogurt, mayonnaise, gherkin, mustard and onion. Mix well.

2. Line 2 bread slices with lettuce and tomato. Top each with half of the tuna mixture. Top with the other slices of bread.

per sandwich: kcals 320, fat 8 g, saturated fat 1.5 g, cholesterol 60 mg, sodium 780 mg, carbohydrate 33 g, fibre 4 g, protein 33 g, calcium 70 mg

and easy. Pop the ingredients in, and then run a couple of errands. By the time you're back, the house will be filled with the delicious aroma of freshly baked bread. Choose recipes that include wholemeal flour and, even better, whole grains like oats.

Have a pizza extravaganza

Most supermarkets sell ready-made pizza bases that make preparing a home-made pizza fast and easy. Get your family or friends together for a make-it-yourself pizza party. A few tips: include at least two vegetable toppings. Use grated cheese rather than slices and you'll get more coverage with less cheese. Try smoked mozzarella instead of plain, for even more flavour.

Make a new acquaintance

It's easy to get into a rut, especially when you go shopping. This week look a little more closely at things you've been overlooking in the greengrocers and take home a vegetable you haven't tried before. More and more supermarkets carry once-exotic leafy greens like rocket, radicchio and Swiss chard. Have you tried bulb fennel? It's delicious roasted. What about grilled parsnips? Or a fresh artichoke? If these vegetables are new to you, you're missing out on some of the world's great taste treats. This week add a new vegetable to your repertoire.

Create your own signature pasta

No other food is as versatile as pasta. It comes in a wide range of shapes and colours, from familiar spaghetti to fun shapes like wagon wheels, bow ties, shells, corkscrews, tubes and ears. And the ingredients that show up in pasta sauces are virtually limitless – from prawns or chicken to olives, artichokes, basil, diced ripe tomatoes, broad beans, tuna, capers, mushrooms, cauliflower, broccoli, Parmesan cheese ... you get the idea. Put on your chef's hat this week and create your own pasta masterpiece.

Pasta shapes and sauces

Everyone knows spaghetti goes with tomato-based sauces, but what about other noodles? In general, the lighter and more delicate the pasta is, the lighter its sauce should be. Thicker or textured pastas go best with heavier and chunkier sauces. Here's a pairing of pasta shapes and sauces:

- Angel hair (thin spaghetti): light sauces.
- Conghiglie (shells): cheese-flavoured sauces, and also good in soups.
- Farfalle (bow ties): chunky sauces.
- Fettuccine (ribbons): creamy sauces, tomato-based sauces.
- Fusilli (twisted spaghetti), ravioli (stuffed pillows), rotelle (spirals): chunky, tomato-based sauces.
- Macaroni (elbows), ziti and penne (hollow tubes): meat sauces.
- Tortellini (small stuffed dumplings): tomato-based sauces.

The food diary revisited

We've touted the virtues of keeping a food diary more than once. It's a great way to see exactly what you eat and to spot patterns that may be scuttling your efforts to lose weight, such as skipping breakfast or going overboard on snacks. From time to time while you're slimming, filling out a food diary for a day or two is also an effective way to make sure you're still on track.

As you strike out on your own this week, consider keeping a food diary for at least a couple of days. Don't let the diary stop you being adventurous. Use the form on page 309 to record what you eat – that's all. When the week is done, you can look back at the form to see how you did setting out on your own. Check on how the number of low-calorie dishes compared to the number of higher-calorie treats. Do a quick count up of the average servings of vegetables. Use what you learn from the food diary to fine-tune your food choices over the coming weeks. If you noticed yourself falling short on foods from the green-grocer, for instance, make a point of including a salad at dinner or a piece of fruit with lunch.

Travel the world

A rich variety of ethnic restaurants, from Italian and French to Indian and Chinese, and the increasing availability of ingredients from round the world, has created interest in the cuisines of different countries. This week sample a cuisine you haven't tried before, or at least one you don't eat very often. If you're an avid home cook, try preparing something from a cuisine you've never explored before. Search your library or local bookshop for a cookery book that specialises in a particular ethnic cuisine. Chances are you'll discover a world of new ingredients and tastes.

Find a new move

While you're shaking things up this week in the food department, do the same for exercise. The goal is simple: find something fun to do that you haven't done before, something that involves being active. Take the plunge at the local swimming pool. Go for a ramble in a nearby park. Take the kids boating. Go power-walking along the towpath. If you haven't given the *ChangeOne* workout on pages 236 to 237 a try, do it this week. But only if it sounds like fun.

And don't hide behind the excuse that you don't like being active. Don't tell us that you don't like strolling in a beautiful park, playing ball with the kids, walking past the shop windows in the high street or bicycling round the village. Those are the kinds of activities that make life worth living.

Strike a balance

ChangeOne is based on the simple principle that, to lose weight, you have to take in fewer calories than you burn. To maintain your weight, you have to balance calories in and calories out.

Cake for breakfast

Instead of croissants, brioche, Danish pastries and other high-calorie indulgences, try this lightened version of a moist, crumble-topped cake to start the day.

STREUSEL CAKE

Serves 16

50 g (1¾ oz) soft light brown sugar
2 tablespoons chopped walnuts
1 teaspoon ground cinnamon
300 g (10½ oz) plain flour
55 g (2 oz) unsalted butter, melted
130 g (4¾ oz) caster sugar
1 tablespoon baking powder
¾ teaspoon salt
1 egg
250 ml (8 fl oz) buttermilk
1 teaspoon grated lemon zest

1. Preheat the oven to 200ºC (400ºF, gas mark 6). Spray a 23 cm (9 in) square baking tin with cooking spray.

2. In small bowl combine the brown sugar, walnuts, cinnamon and 2 tablespoons flour. Add 1 tablespoon of the melted butter to the walnut mixture and stir until crumbly.

3. In large bowl stir together the remaining flour, the caster sugar, baking powder and salt. Make a well in the centre. Add the egg, buttermilk, lemon zest and remaining melted butter. Stir until just combined.

4. Scrape the mixture into the prepared tin. Sprinkle evenly with the walnut topping. Bake for 40 minutes or until a skewer inserted in the centre of the cake comes out clean.

5. Allow to cool, then cut into 16 squares. A serving equals 1 square. Wrap leftovers in foil and freeze for up to 1 month.

Per serving: kcals 160, fat 5 g, saturated fat 2 g, cholesterol 23 mg, sodium 236 mg, carbohydrate 43 g, fibre 1 g, protein 3 g, calcium 61 mg

VARIATIONS

Choose one of the following:

■ Add some chopped mixed dried fruit.

■ Fold in 4 tablespoons mini chocolate chips.

■ Divide the mixture in half, and stir 4 tablespoons cocoa powder into one half. Drop the mixture into the tin in spoonfuls, alternating plain and chocolate. Swirl with a knife to create a marbled pattern.

That notion of striking a balance is a powerful one and worth keeping in mind as you move forward. As far as diet goes, there are many ways to build that healthy balance. One is to watch every bite you eat. Another, more relaxed way, is to be aware of what you eat throughout the day, balancing a little indulgence here with a little restraint there. If you treat yourself to a sumptuous lunch with friends, for instance, go light on supper and try to fit in extra exercise. If there's a big birthday dinner planned in the evening, go easy on snacks and have a simple lunch.

As you've probably learned by now, one day of overdoing it on food doesn't mean the end of your diet. Cut back on portion sizes for the next day or two and you'll be able to regain your balance. Even a week of overdoing it, it turns out, won't bring your diet crashing down. Naturally, people worry about the holiday season at the end of the year, when every occasion seems to centre around food. The reality is you can enjoy yourself over the holidays without much danger of putting on a lot of weight.

Top 10 *ChangeOne* weight-loss tactics

This week, as you set out on your own to enjoy what you've achieved, let these simple but powerful directives of *ChangeOne* be your guide:

1. Eat breakfast every day – and include at least one serving of fruit.
2. Favour foods with plenty of fibre.
3. Help yourself to two servings of vegetables at lunch.
4. Keep an eye on portion sizes. If it looks oversized, divide it in half.
5. Eat slowly, savouring every bite.
6. Stop when you're satisfied.
7. Reach for a snack if you're genuinely hungry.
8. Drink plenty of water during the day, including an 8 oz glass at each meal.
9. Help yourself to two servings of vegetables at dinner.
10. Stay active!

It used to be held as a gospel truth that people typically gain about 2.3 kg (5 lb) during the holidays, but this isn't true, according to recent research from the American National Institute of Health. They tracked 200 men and women from late September to early March using weight and other health measurements. The average weight gain was about half a kilo (1 lb). And it didn't happen just over the holidays. It started in autumn and continued through March. In fact, that extra half kilo or pound may have had less to do with eating than with exercise. People who said they weren't physically active during that time typically gained about 750g (1½ lb). Those who stayed active throughout the winter months lost weight.

No, we're not advising you to throw caution to the wind when holidays or special occasions come around. It's still important to make smart choices.

Our point is that even a couple of weeks of eating more than usual isn't enough to topple your healthy diet. Become extra active, and you can counterbalance the extra food you eat. Even if you do gain weight, it's not likely to be that much. When you return to your healthier habits as the holidays end, you'll regain your balance and steadily lose any weight you might have added.

Keep your perspective

There's one more way in which keeping your balance is important as you set off from here. You've already heard about the pitfalls of all-or-nothing thinking. It's the tendency to think that a diet is working as long as you're losing weight, and that it has failed the moment you hit a plateau or gain a bit. It's the tendency of some people to think, the moment they slip-up, 'I'm a failure'. All-or-nothing thinking doesn't acknowledge anything in between and is nothing more than a skewed perspective.

One thing we hope the *ChangeOne* approach has given you is a more balanced perspective on what it takes to lose weight and keep it off. It's not an all-or-nothing proposition. It's about the choices you make every day. If you go overboard on portions one day, you have the next to restore your balance. If your weight stays on a plateau for a while, so be it. You haven't failed. The diet hasn't failed. You can give yourself a little break and then make another change or two when you feel ready. If you gain a few kilos or pounds when things at work or home are stressful, don't worry. You know what it takes to lose it again. The only way to fail is to decide that you've failed – and to give up.

Keep that in mind as you relax this week and move into the weeks ahead, and you'll be just fine. You've got what it takes to do almost anything you want. Just take it a step at a time. Keep your spirits up and your resolution firm. Stay positive. Have as much fun as you can. If you hit a rocky patch, go easy on yourself. Set your sights on a new goal. Figure out the best ways to get there. And then go for it.

Part 2

Change One

Resources

Fitness

...is the secret to lasting weight-loss success. It's that simple.

When researchers analyse the differences between dieters who keep the weight off and those who regain it, they find – time and time again – that exercise is crucial.

Was that a groan?

Okay, okay, so it's not always easy to find time to exercise during the day. And not all of us want to be gym groupies. But that shouldn't keep you from enjoying the considerable benefits of getting up and moving. You don't have to fit in a long workout session, after all; you can do a little exercise here, a little there. If you've always thought you weren't the exercise type, you may be surprised. A lot of people who lose weight discover that they like being active. It's natural to feel uneasy about exercising when you're overweight. But as you slim down, becoming physically active is a wonderful way to enjoy your new, trimmer body. And there are many benefits.

True rewards

Nothing you do for yourself has more benefits than regular exercise. Exercise burns calories. And it tones muscles, tightens up arms and trims that waistline. While you've heard a lot of convincing reasons to start exercising, there are so many more. Here are five of our favourites:

1. More energy

This may be hard to believe, but exercising will make you feel more energetic. When scientists at the University of New Orleans asked 42 volunteers to assess their moods before and after a 50 minute aerobics class, most of them said they felt less tense and less tired afterwards. And in a 1997 study, researchers found that a brisk 10 minute walk gave people more energy than eating a bar of chocolate. How can that be? Exercise boosts a hormone that increases energy. And it takes just a few workouts to improve strength and lung capacity, which in turn increases stamina. All of which means you have more energy.

2. Less stress

Just one workout can ease stress and anxiety. In a study at Indiana University, researchers used psychological tests to gauge anxiety levels in 15 volunteers before and after a 20 minute session on an exercise bicycle. The volunteers all reported feeling significantly less anxious in the hour or two after the workout. Exercise enhances the flow of brain chemicals like serotonin that are related to positive moods, and because it increases core body temperature, it can be as relaxing as a hot bath.

3. A sharper mind

Exercise can even spark creativity. Researchers at Middlesex University tested the creative thinking of 63 volunteers in two settings: after they'd done an aerobic workout and after they'd sat around watching a video. Volunteers in the experiment felt more positive and scored higher on creativity following the workout.

4. Healthier arteries

Physical activity boosts levels of high-density lipoproteins, or HDL – the so-called 'good cholesterol' – by as much as 20 per cent. HDL helps rid the body of low-density lipoproteins, or LDL – the artery-clogging kind. HDL can even pick up bad cholesterol deposited in arteries and move it to where it won't do harm. Also of benefit to the arteries: the level of fat particles in the blood, called triglycerides, falls by as much as 40 per cent after a vigorous workout. Exercising helps to convert triglycerides into fatty acids – the form in which fat can be burned for energy. You burn stored fat every time you work out – the key to keeping weight off. You also lower your level of triglycerides in the blood. And the lower your triglyceride level, studies show, the lower your risk of heart disease.

Staying active on the road

Don't let holidays or business travel stop your exercise routine. Physical activity is a great way to relieve stress and adjust to a new time zone when you're travelling. Here are some ideas to help you stay active while you're away:

- **Find fitness-friendly accommodation.** Ring ahead to make sure the hotel you're considering has a good fitness facility – or at least is in a place where you'll feel safe and comfortable going for a walk.
- **Take advantage of the local attractions.** Many places offer their own unique exercise opportunities – paths through beautiful parks or forests, beach walks, rowing on the lake or bicycle rides out of town, for example. Check the travel section of your bookshop or look on the Internet for information before you travel.

- **Pack what you'll need.** Walking shoes, gym shorts, a T-shirt, resistance bands – make a checklist of all the things you'll need to get a good workout while you're away. And be sure to pack them all.
- **Use every opportunity.** Too busy to set aside a block of time for activity? Be creative with your time and use every chance you get to be active. Walk whenever you can – between meetings, while you're waiting at the airport or simply on your way from here to there.
- **Be realistic.** If you're on a hectic business trip, don't add to the stress by trying to do too much. Managing just 15 minutes of brisk walking, along with climbing a few flights of stairs instead of taking the lift, should hold you until you get home and back to your regular routine.

5. Better defences

The moment you begin exercising, your heart starts pounding and your surging blood sends disease-fighting immune cells throughout your body, where they're able to detect trouble-makers like cold or flu viruses. Studies show that people who exercise have about half as many sick days a year as those who sit on the sofa.

Eight weeks to a better body

A walking programme is a great start. But you'll see even more results by combining an aerobic exercise like walking – the kind that burns calories and gets your heart and lungs working – with a muscle-toning programme. You'll look better, feel better and boost your metabolism.

In the following pages you'll find a simple and complete fitness programme guaranteed to give you all the benefits of exercise. Don't worry if you've never done a formal exercise programme before. We'll walk you through it step by step. For many of the exercises all you need is a pair of comfortable shoes and a place where you can stretch out. Once you hit your stride, kick your workout up another notch by adding a skipping rope and a set of resistance bands.

The *ChangeOne* fitness programme

Not sure where to begin? It's easy with the *ChangeOne* plan. Each week you'll make just one change to your activity routine. By the end of eight weeks you'll be doing all the exercise you need to keep the weight off. By tightening up lax muscles and giving your heart and lungs a workout, you'll be trimmer, slimmer and fitter.

Here's how to get into the programme:
- *If you're new to exercise,* start at Week 1.
- *If you already walk at least 15 minutes most days of the week,* start at Week 4.
- *If you walk at least 30 minutes most days,* start at Week 6.

The *ChangeOne* eight-week programme is based on walking. If you enjoy another form of aerobic exercise like bicycling or swimming, go for it. What's important is doing activities that increase your breathing rate and heart rate.

Read on for the details of the programme, sample schedules and a visual guide that will lead you through easy but effective exercise and stretching routines.

Eight week fitness programme

As with the rest of *ChangeOne*, we're only asking you to make one change a week as you progress through this eight-step road map to a regular exercise routine. Before any session, make sure you do 2 minutes of easy walking to warm up, and 2 minutes more to cool down when you finish. And remember, you should check with your doctor before starting any exercise programme.

Week 1

Aerobic: 4 sessions. Walk for at least 15 minutes four days this week. If you can't find the time or don't have the stamina to do a 15-minute walk, do two or three shorter walks that add up to 15 minutes. Walk at a pace that has you breathing hard but still able to talk.

Week 2

Aerobic: 4 sessions. Fit in a 15-minute walk four days this week. Schedule the time so that you can walk for a full 15 minutes – in the morning, during the lunch hour or after supper, for instance. If you can't find that much uninterrupted time, do several shorter walks that add up to 15 minutes.
This weekend: Schedule a leisure-time activity that involves at least 30 minutes of physical activity. Brisk walking, bicycling, working in the garden, playing cricket with the kids, swimming – whatever sounds like fun.

Week 3

Aerobic: At least 4 sessions. Increase your walks to 20 minutes. Start at an easy pace for the first 3 to 5 minutes to get your muscles loose, then walk briskly for the rest of the time. Keep a record of when you walk and how long each session takes.
This weekend: Schedule a leisure-time activity that involves at least 45 minutes of physical activity.

Week 4

Aerobic: At least 4 sessions. Increase your walks to 25 minutes; 10 minutes before you stop, pick up your pace for 5 minutes, then slow down for the last 5 minutes.
This weekend: Schedule a 45-minute leisure-time activity.
Stretching: 2 sessions. Try the eight-step stretching routine that you'll find on pages 243–246. Take your time in completing the routine, and be sure to hold each stretch as long as directed.

Week 5

Aerobic: At least 4 sessions. Increase your walks to 30 minutes. As you did last week, push yourself a little harder just before you finish. Schedule at least 45 minutes of weekend activity.

Stretching: 2 sessions. Take 10 minutes after your walk – or any time that's convenient – to do the stretching exercises you practised last week. Feel free to add as many stretching sessions as you like.

Strengthening: 1 session. This week work in the five muscle-toning exercises on pages 240–242. You don't need special equipment – just enough space to stretch out and a comfortable carpet or mat on the floor. Warm up your muscles before starting by doing some stretches or taking a brief stroll round the block. Give each exercise a try, but if one seems too difficult or uncomfortable, skip it and try another. You can always come back to it when you're feeling a little stronger.

Week 6

Aerobic: At least 4 sessions. Keep walking to at least 30 minutes. If you're looking for more of a challenge, try mixing in some intervals: 10 minutes into your walk increase your pace for 1 minute, then return to your normal pace, or just a little slower, for 2 minutes. Speed up again for 1 minute followed by another 2 minutes at your regular pace or a bit slower. Do 5 repetitions of this pattern,

15 minutes total. For an alternative to intervals, buy a skipping rope and set aside 5 to 15 minutes for jumping at the end of your walk. Do some easy-paced walking afterwards to cool down. Also, continue with the weekend activity.

Stretching: 2 sessions.

Strengthening: 2 sessions.

Week 7

Aerobic: At least 4 sessions. Increase at least two of your walks to 45 minutes. This weekend plan a fun activity that involves at least 1 hour of walking.

Stretching: 2 sessions.

Strengthening: 3 sessions. Increase your routines to at least eight exercises. Check the additional workouts on pages 247–250 for new ideas; you'll need resistance bands and a skipping rope for these.

Week 8

Aerobic: At least 4 sessions. Alternate 30- and 45-minute walks. You can increase your interval sets to 20 minutes total; or consider decreasing the recovery portion so that you do 1 minute of fast walking and then 1 minute of regular walking. This weekend plan something fun that involves at least 1 hour of activity.

Stretching: 2–3 sessions.

Strengthening: 3 sessions. If the moves are getting easier, consider adding another set.

Change
One

Eight week
fitness programme
Sample activity schedule

	MONDAY	TUESDAY	WEDNESDAY	
Week 1	Walk, 15 minutes	Off	Walk, 15 minutes	
Week 2	Walk, 15 minutes	Walk, 15 minutes	Walk, 15 minutes	
Week 3	Walk, 20 minutes	Walk, 20 minutes	Walk, 20 minutes	
Week 4	Walk, 25 minutes Stretching routine	Walk, 25 minutes	Walk, 25 minutes Stretching routine	
Week 5	Walk, 30 minutes Stretching routine	Walk, 30 minutes	Walk, 30 minutes Strength workout, 5 steps	
Week 6	Walk, 30 minutes with intervals Stretching routine	Walk, 30 minutes Strength workout, 5 steps	Walk, 30 minutes with intervals Stretching routine	
Week 7	Walk, 45 minutes Strength workout, 8 steps	Walk, 30 minutes with intervals Stretching routine	Walk, 45 minutes Strength workout, 8 steps	
Week 8	Walk, 45 minutes Strength workout, 8 steps	Walk, 30 minutes with intervals Stretching routine	Walk, 45 minutes Strength workout, 8 steps	

We've made it even easier! Here's a sample schedule for the *ChangeOne* fitness programme. Give it a try as suggested here, or adjust it to your own timetable. In either case, it's important *not* to try to memorise the programme. Copy this schedule and post it on the refrigerator with your changes pencilled in, or better still, make workout appointments on your daily calendar. Scheduling a specific time for exercise greatly increases the likelihood of your making it happen. Finally, if you don't feel ready to make the step to the next week's activity levels, just repeat your current week's activities and move ahead when it feels right.

THURSDAY	FRIDAY	SATURDAY	SUNDAY
Walk, 15 minutes	Off	Walk, 15 minutes	Off
Walk, 15 minutes	Off	Leisure-time activity, 30 minutes	Off
Walk, 20 minutes	Off	Leisure-time activity, 45 minutes	Off
Walk, 25 minutes	Off	Leisure-time activity, 45 minutes	Off
Walk, 30 minutes Stretching routine	Off	Leisure-time activity, 45 minutes	Off
Walk, 30 minutes Strength workout, 5 steps	Off	Leisure-time activity, 45 minutes	Off
Walk, 30 minutes with intervals Stretching routine	Off	Leisure-time activity, 1 hour	Stretching routine Strength workout, 8 steps
Walk, 30 minutes with intervals Stretching routine	Off	Leisure-time activity, 1 hour	Stretching routine Strength workout, 8 to 12 steps

Muscle-toning

Losing weight is only half of what it takes to win the battle of the bulge. The other half is building muscle – but we're not talking about becoming the Incredible Hulk, and you don't have to join a gym and start pumping iron. The simple exercises in this section are all you need to get started. By tightening up sagging muscles, you'll look better. Just as important, you'll boost your metabolism. Muscle tissue requires more calories for maintenance than fat does. And by strengthening your muscles, you'll increase the number of calories your body burns even while sitting still.

In this section you'll find five simple muscle-toning exercises you can do in any open space indoors or out. Take your time to get the feel of each exercise. Do 8 to 15 repetitions of each. When you can do 15 easily, wait 30 seconds and do another set. (For the wall sit, start by holding the move for 20 to 30 seconds, and then increase the amount of time as you get stronger.) Do each move slowly, steadily and consistently. Don't try to be a superhero at the beginning. It's better to start slow and build up to more repetitions or sets. That way you'll avoid becoming too sore.

1. Abdominal crunches

Lie on your back with your knees slightly bent and your lower back as flat against the floor as possible. Lightly clasp your hands behind your head, fingers loosely interlocked, and elbows pointing out. If you want to start with an easier approach, cross your arms over your chest.

Slowly curl your shoulders up until your upper back is off the ground; the small of your back should remain on the ground. Use your abdominal muscles to pull you up – don't pull your head with your arms or strain your neck. Keep your eyes on the ceiling. Pause at the top of your lift, then steadily lower yourself back to the floor using your abdominal muscles.

2. Dry swimming

Lie on your stomach, arms extended in front of you. Keeping your hips on the floor, lift your left arm and right leg at the same time.

Hold for a count of three. Return to resting position. Repeat with the right arm and left leg. If you have back trouble, skip this move.

3. Press-ups

Lie face down, with your hands on the floor, pointing forward and directly under your shoulders. Your feet should be resting on your toes. Straighten your arms as you push your entire body off the floor. Make sure that your back and legs are straight, and that you aren't bending at the waist.

Lower yourself back down until your nose almost touches the floor. Pause, then slowly straighten your arms.

If you're having trouble, push off from your knees instead of your toes.

4. Wall sit

Put your back up to a wall, placing your feet shoulder-width apart and your heels about 45 cm (18 in) from the wall. Slowly slide down the wall until your knees are bent at almost a 90-degree angle, as if you are sitting in an imaginary chair.

5. Kneeling leg curl

Start on your elbows and knees, hands and forearms flat on the floor. Extend your right leg straight back, pointing your toe down.

Raise your right foot until your leg forms a 90-degree angle. Keep your neck and shoulders relaxed. Hold the pose for a moment. Return to starting position. Do 8 to 15 repetitions, then repeat with your left leg.

Stretching

Eight simple moves

Stretching keeps muscles and joints flexible. It's also a great way to relax yourself and release tension.

The programme on the following pages combines simple stretching exercises with modified yoga poses. This series of stretches is designed to be done in sequence. But if any part feels too difficult or uncomfortable, skip it and go on to the next.

1. Side stretch

Stand up straight with your feet together, arms at chest level and fingers interlaced. Turn your palms out and raise your arms overhead. Stretch your arms, torso and legs. Relax your neck and hold for a count of five.

Now bend slowly to the right and hold for a count of five. Return to the overhead position, then gently bend to the left and hold for a count of five.

2. Forward bend

Bring your arms back down to your sides and pause. Now bend your knees and place your feet about 15 cm (6 in) apart. Then bend slowly at the waist until your chest is touching your thighs. Let your arms dangle in front and hold the position for about 20 seconds.

Slowly straighten your legs as much as is comfortably possible (you can raise your hands a little). Keep your upper body and arms relaxed and in roughly the same position, and hold again for about 20 seconds. If you need a little extra support, place your hands on a stool or block of wood.

3. Downward-facing dog

From the last position, bend your knees and place your hands on the floor. Now walk your hands forward until you're on all fours. Tuck your toes under so that the balls of your feet are on the ground. Contracting your abdominal muscles, slowly lift your hips to form an upside-down V with your body.

Keeping your back straight, gently straighten your knees and press your heels towards the floor. Hold for 20 seconds.

4. Quad stretch

Now lower yourself to the floor and lie on your left side, your left arm supporting your head. With your right hand grasp the top of your right foot and gently pull towards your bottom, feeling the muscles in the front of your thigh stretch. Your right knee should be in line with your left one. Hold for 20 seconds. Roll over and repeat the stretch with your left leg.

5. Cobra

Roll over to a resting position, face down on the floor with your legs together and the tops of your toes touching the mat or carpet. Place your hands palm down on the floor, shoulder-width apart and just in front of your head. Press up, raising your shoulders and resting on your forearms. Gaze forward or slightly up. Feel your lower back stretch. Hold for 20 seconds.

6. Child's pose

From the Cobra position, raise your midsection off the floor and slowly walk your hands back until you're sitting on your heels. The tops of your feet should be flat against the floor, and your arms should be stretched flat on the floor in front of you. Lower your shoulders and your forehead to the ground and hold for 20 seconds.

7. Hip stretch

Roll over onto your back and bend your knees, keeping your feet flat on the floor.

Straighten your left leg and roll your pelvis to the right, gently lowering your right knee as close to the floor as you can. Hold for 20 seconds, then bring your knees back to centre and repeat on the left side.

8. Corpse pose

Slowly slide your feet out until your legs are flat on the floor. Put your arms about 45 degrees from your side, palms up. Place your legs about 30 to 60 cm (1 to 2 ft) apart, and let your feet fall to the sides. Close your eyes and relax. Concentrate on releasing tension from the centre of your body outwards to your fingertips and toes.

Exercising on the go
The eight step workout for anywhere

Who needs a gym membership? With a skipping rope and resistance bands you can get a full gym-style strength and cardiovascular workout. And you can do it anywhere – at home or on the road. Again, do 8 to 15 repetitions of each exercise, and add a set when 15 gets easy. Once you add these exercises to the previous ones, you'll have a workout that tones every part of your body.

When you buy resistance bands, get a pack that contains several lengths and thicknesses. You can find a good set at most sports shops.

1. Arm curl

Stand on the band with your feet shoulder-width apart. Grasp one end of the resistance band in each hand, arms at your sides, palms facing forward.

Lift your forearms, bending at the elbow with your upper arms against your body. Hold for a moment, then return to starting position.

2. Resistance rowing

Sit on the floor with your legs straight in front of you and knees slightly bent. Loop the resistance band around your feet.

Keeping your back straight but relaxed, pull both handles of the resistance bands back to your sides, palms facing down. Hold for a moment then straighten your arms.

247

3. Chest press

Sit down and place the resistance band around your back and under your armpits. Hold one end in each hand.

Keeping your upper arms parallel to the floor and your hands about shoulder-width apart, extend arms out in front of your body and hold for a moment. Ease your arms back towards your body.

4. Band squat

Hold the ends of a resistance band in each hand and stand on top of the centre of the band, with feet hip-width apart. Bring your hands together in front of your chest so that your elbows point down and the bands wrap over your upper arms. Be sure to stand tall.

Ease your body down as if sitting on a chair. Lower yourself as far as you can without leaning your upper body more than a few centimetres forward. Be sure not to move past the point at which your thighs are parallel to the floor. Keep your head up throughout the motion. Slowly return to the starting position.

5. Tricep extension

Hold both ends of resistance band with your left hand and the doubled-up middle of the band with your right hand, feet hip-width apart. Place your left hand over the front of your right shoulder. Bend your right elbow so that your right hand is by your hip, palm facing inward. Make sure the band isn't too loose; if it is, grab the band higher up.

With your elbow stationary, straighten your right arm out behind you so that the band gets tighter as you go. Don't allow your elbow to lock. Hold for a moment. Slowly return to starting position. Switch sides, and alternate arms.

6. Calf press

Hold one end of the resistance band in each hand and sit on the floor with your legs straight in front of you. Wrap the band round the top of your right foot. Bend your right knee slightly and lift it in the air. Sit up straight. Bend your left knee for comfort if needed.

Point your toe forward as you pull back on the resistance band. Hold this position for a moment, then, while maintaining your pull on the band, straighten your foot and pull your toes back to your body. Repeat until your set is complete, then switch feet.

7. Shoulder press

Stand on one end of the resistance band and hold the handle at the other end in your left hand. Your right hand should be resting gently on your hip.

Keeping your back straight, slowly press your left arm up above your head, as if you were volunteering to answer a question. Hold for a moment, then slowly lower your arm to the starting position. Repeat until the set is complete, then switch to your right arm.

8. Skipping

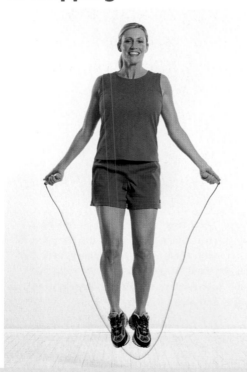

Skipping is a fabulous way to burn calories fast. It's also a great alternative to walking when the weather is foul. Make sure to wear a good pair of exercise shoes and skip on a surface with a little 'give', like a wooden floor or an exercise mat. Keep your shoulders relaxed. Skipping is strenuous, so go easy at first. If you find yourself out of breath or sweating heavily, you are overdoing it. Start with just 5 minutes of uninterrupted skipping, then work your way up.

When buying a skipping rope, make sure it is the right length for you. Gauge this by standing on the centre of the rope; the handles should reach to your armpits. For most adults, a skipping rope about 3 m (9 to 10 ft) long is adequate.

Meals
& Recipes

We hope you've had a chance to try the recipes contained in the first 12 weeks of *ChangeOne*, and that you enjoyed them, because we have lots more for you.

In the following pages, you'll find a delicious mix of fresh ideas for breakfast, lunch, supper and snacks.

You'll also discover tips, recipes, substitutions and the guidance you need to bring them to life in your own kitchen, with your own sense of style and taste.

Here is what you'll find:

Muffins and scones

What could be more inviting than a basket of muffins and scones on the breakfast table? Piping hot, they're delicious as is, or with a thin spread of butter or jam.

Café-style breakfast

1 glazed blueberry muffin or dried cranberry scone

⅛ of a melon (eg ogen or cantaloupe)

60 ml (2 fl oz) coffee mixed with 175 ml (6 fl oz) hot skimmed milk

kcals 290, fat 6 g, saturated fat 3.5 g, cholesterol 50 mg, sodium 330 mg, carbohydrate 48 g, fibre 3 g, protein 11 g, calcium 330 mg

GLAZED BLUEBERRY MUFFINS

Makes 12
280 g (10 oz) plain flour
1 tablespoon baking powder
½ teaspoon salt
100 g (3½ oz) caster sugar
**250 ml (8 fl oz) plus 1 tablespoon
  skimmed or semi-skimmed milk**
2 eggs
55 g (2 oz) butter, melted
5 tablespoons reduced-fat crème fraîche
2 teaspoons pure vanilla extract
225 g (8 oz) fresh or frozen blueberries
55 g (2 oz) icing sugar, sifted
2 teaspoons grated lemon zest

1. Preheat the oven to 200°C (400°F, gas mark 6). Line a 12-cup muffin tin with paper liners. Whisk together the flour, baking powder, salt and caster sugar in a large bowl. In another bowl, whisk the 250 ml (8 fl oz) milk with the eggs, butter, crème fraîche and vanilla extract until blended.

2. Make a well in the centre of the flour mixture. Pour in the milk mixture and stir with a fork just until blended. Do not over-mix. Fold in two-thirds of the blueberries.

3. Spoon the mixture into the muffin cups and sprinkle with the remaining blueberries. Bake for about 20 minutes or until a skewer inserted in the centre of a

muffin comes out clean. Cool on a wire rack for 10 minutes.

4. Meanwhile, mix the icing sugar and lemon zest with enough of the remaining milk to make a pourable glaze. Drizzle the glaze over the muffins.

Instead of	Try
Crème fraîche	Lemon yogurt
Blueberries	Sliced strawberries. Sliced banana with 65 g (2¼ oz) walnuts (eliminate glaze)
	Diced apple with 65 g (2¼ oz) pecans (eliminate glaze)
	40 g (1¼ oz) sultanas and 25 g (1 oz) hazelnuts (eliminate glaze)

4. Place the scones 2.5 cm (1 in) apart on the lined baking trays. Bake for 15 minutes or until golden.

5. Meanwhile, set a wire rack on a piece of greaseproof paper. Stir the icing sugar with the orange zest and juice in a small bowl. Transfer the hot scones to the wire rack and drizzle the glaze over them.

Time saver
Bake a batch of muffins and freeze in a re-sealable plastic bag. Pull one out the night before, to thaw for a quick breakfast.

ABOUT MUFFINS AND SCONES

Moist, cake-like American-style muffins are similar to teabreads except that they are baked in a muffin tin rather than a loaf tin. Scones are drier and flakier in texture.

A *ChangeOne* muffin should be about the size of a standard paper muffin or fairy cake case. Shop-bought muffins can be two to four times that size, so if you have one of these share it with a friend, or save half for tomorrow.

TIPS FOR SMARTER BAKING

- Cut the amount of butter, margarine or oil in half, and add that same weight of plain yogurt, reduced-fat crème fraîche or apple purée.
- Switch from full-fat soured cream to reduced-fat crème fraîche.
- Cut down the amount of sugar by a third.

DRIED CRANBERRY SCONES WITH ORANGE GLAZE

Makes 18
420 g (15 oz) plain flour
1 1/2 teaspoons baking powder
1/2 teaspoon salt
50 g (1 3/4 oz) caster sugar
300 g (10 1/2 oz) plain yogurt
85 g (3 oz) butter, melted
1 egg, lightly beaten
140 g (5 oz) sweetened dried cranberries
55 g (2 oz) icing sugar, sifted
1 teaspoon grated orange zest
1 tablespoon orange juice

1. Preheat the oven to 200°C (400°F, gas mark 6). Line 2 baking trays with baking parchment.

2. Sift the flour, baking powder, salt and sugar into a large bowl and make a well in the centre. In another bowl, mix together the yogurt, butter and egg. Pour into the well. Stir with a fork until moistened, then stir in cranberries. Flour your hands and gently knead the dough in the bowl just until it comes together.

3. Lightly sprinkle a work surface with flour. Turn out the dough and pat into a 23 cm (9 in) square about 2.5 cm (1 in) thick. Cut into nine 7.5 cm (3 in) squares with a knife. Cut each square into 2 triangles, to make 18 scones.

Smoothie breakfast

Shakes, batidas, smoothies – no matter what you call them, these frosty combinations of fruit and milk or yogurt refresh and nourish.

1 tropical smoothie (tall tumbler)

1 toasted English muffin half spread with 1 teaspoon (thumb tip) peanut butter

kcals 300, fat 5 g, saturated fat 1 g, cholesterol 5 mg, sodium 241 mg, carbohydrate 54 g, fibre 4 g, protein 11 g, calcium 300 mg

TROPICAL SMOOTHIE

Serves 4

1 mango, cut into cubes
1 banana, cut into large chunks
150 g (5½ oz) fresh pineapple chunks
1 kiwi fruit, peeled and sliced
500 ml (16 fl oz) plain fat-free or low-fat yogurt
1 mugful of ice cubes

1. Combine the mango, banana, pineapple, kiwi, yogurt and ice cubes in a blender. Whiz until smooth and thick.

2. Pour into 4 tall glasses.

3. Freeze leftovers in sealable plastic containers. To thaw, microwave for 30 to 60 seconds and stir to blend.

HEALTH TIP

When buying a freshly made smoothie from a café, be sure to ask them to use plain low-fat yogurt or skimmed or semi-skimmed milk.

The hearty frittata

This no-fuss Italian egg dish – really a thick, flat omelette – is cooked in a frying pan on the cooker, then finished off under the grill.

12.5 cm (5 in) wedge vegetable frittata (calculator)

75 g (2½ oz) fresh blueberries (2 golf balls)

1 slice wholemeal toast

kcals 280, fat 10 g, saturated fat 4 g, cholesterol 275 mg, sodium 490 mg, carbohydrate 28 g, fibre 5 g, protein 19 g, calcium 150 mg

VEGETABLE FRITTATA

Serves 4

115 g (4 oz) button mushrooms, trimmed and thinly sliced
½ small red onion, sliced
5 eggs
4 egg whites
1 teaspoon chopped fresh herbs (eg thyme, oregano or basil)
¼ teaspoon salt
¼ teaspoon freshly ground black pepper
4 medium tomatoes, thinly sliced
50 g (1¾ oz) mozzarella cheese, grated

1. Preheat the grill. Coat a 23 or 25 cm (9 or 10 in) ovenproof non-stick frying pan with cooking spray and set over medium-high heat. Sauté mushrooms and onion for about 5 minutes or until tender. Transfer to a plate. Wipe out the pan, coat again with cooking spray and return to the heat.

2. Whisk together the eggs, whites, herbs, salt and pepper in a mixing bowl. Pour into the hot pan. Cook, without stirring, for about 2 minutes or until the eggs begin to set, lifting up the edge of the omelette with a spatula while tilting the pan so that the uncooked egg can flow underneath.

3. Arrange the tomato slices and sautéed vegetables on top. Continue cooking for 2 to 3 minutes or until the frittata is golden brown on the base and almost set on top.

4. Sprinkle the mozzarella around the edge. Slide the pan under the grill and grill for 2 minutes or until the cheese melts and begins to brown. Cut the frittata into quarters. One serving equals one of the frittata quarters.

Fruit bread delight

Fruited breads, sometimes called 'quick breads', are a natural partner for a cup of tea, and with fresh fruit and a glass of milk they make a lovely breakfast.

1 thin slice Peach and Yogurt Loaf
(lip-balm thickness)

60 g (2¼ oz) fresh raspberries
(2 golf balls)

250 ml (8 fl oz) skimmed milk *or*
150 g (5½ oz) pot low-fat yogurt

Cup of tea or coffee

kcals 250, fat 3.5 g, saturated fat 0.5 g, cholesterol 20 mg, sodium 300 mg, carbohydrate 44 g, fibre 5 g, protein 13 g, calcium 350 mg

PEACH AND YOGURT LOAF

Serves 16
2 medium-sized fresh peaches
210 g (7½ oz) plain flour
85 g (3 oz) wholemeal flour
25 g (1 oz) toasted wheat germ
150 g (5½ oz) caster sugar
1 teaspoon bicarbonate of soda
½ teaspoon salt
125 g (4½ oz) plain yogurt
1 egg plus 2 egg whites
2 tablespoons sunflower or corn oil
1 teaspoon pure almond extract

1. Preheat the oven to 180ºC (350ºF, gas mark 4). Lightly spray a large loaf tin with cooking spray.

2. Blanch and peel the peaches, then remove the stones and chop finely.

3. Combine the plain and wholemeal flours, wheat germ, sugar, bicarbonate of soda and salt in a large bowl.

4. In another bowl mix the yogurt, egg, egg whites, oil and almond extract. Make a well in the dry ingredients and pour in the yogurt mixture. Stir until just combined. Do not overmix. Fold in the peaches.

5. Spoon the mixture into the tin and smooth the top. Bake for about 1 hour or until a skewer inserted in the centre comes out clean. Cool in the tin on a wire rack for 10 minutes, then turn out onto the rack to cool completely. One serving is one slice.

HEALTH TIP

When you order fruited bread like this at a coffee shop or café, your slice should be about the same thickness as a deck of cards. Save any extra for later.

Yogurt parfait

Very similar to an ice cream dessert, this breakfast treat is as healthy as it is delicious.

Serves 1

**150 g (5½ oz) plain or sugar-free yogurt
(dairy or soya milk)**
40 g (1¼ oz) raspberries (golf ball)
40 g (1¼ oz) diced mango (golf ball)
2 tablespoons crunchy cereal (golf ball)
**1 tablespoon shredded desiccated
coconut** (thumb)

In a tall parfait or other dessert glass, make a layer of half of the yogurt, then layers of half of the fruit and all of the cereal. Add the rest of the yogurt, then the rest of the fruit. Sprinkle the top with the coconut and serve.

kcals 250, fat 10 g, saturated fat 9 g, cholesterol 6 mg, sodium 132 mg, carbohydrate 20 g, fibre 5 g, protein 9 g, calcium 300 mg

Instead of	Try
Crunchy cereal	2 tablespoons flake cereal or puffed cereal
Raspberries and mango	85 g (3 oz) sliced peaches or 125 g (4½ oz) unsweetened apple purée
Shredded coconut	1 tablespoon chopped banana

Time saver
Stock up on frozen unsweetened berries and other frozen fruit. There is no need to thaw them ahead of time.

HEALTH TIP

In a recent study at the University of Kentucky, volunteers who ate a serving of yogurt every day lowered their blood cholesterol levels by as much as 3 per cent. That's enough to cut heart disease risk by as much as 10 per cent.

Cottage cheese melba

Don't think of cottage cheese as boring slimming food. Combined with juicy fresh peaches, toast and a delectable hot drink, it's a wonderful breakfast treat.

115 g (4 oz) low-fat cottage cheese (2 golf balls) **topped with:**

85 g (3 oz) peach slices
1 teaspoon raspberry jam*

1 slice raisin toast

Vanilla steamer* (teacup)

kcals 290, fat 4.4 g, saturated fat 2 g, cholesterol 10 mg, sodium 635 mg, carbohydrate 42 g, fibre 3 g, protein 23 g, calcium 331 mg

VANILLA STEAMER

Serves 1
175 ml (6 fl oz) skimmed or
**   semi-skimmed milk**
½ teaspoon pure vanilla extract
Artificial sweetener of choice, or
**   1 teaspoon caster sugar (adds 16 kcals)**

Put the milk in a microwave-proof mug. Stir in the vanilla extract and sweetener of choice. Heat in the microwave until warm.

Use different fruits and jams, and almond or hazelnut extract in the steamed milk.

ABOUT COTTAGE CHEESE

Cottage cheese is 'fresh', meaning that its curds have not been matured or ripened. Its moist, loose texture and mild, slightly sweet flavour make it ideal for all sorts of accompaniments, such as fruit and jam, cereals, nuts, spices and vegetables like chives and peppers. *ChangeOne* recommends low-fat ('light' or 'diet') cottage cheese. Ricotta cheese, a fresh Italian cousin made from whey (the liquid drained off from the semi-solid curds that make up cottage cheese), has a more grainy texture, as does the similar curd cheese. Both of these are low to medium-fat cheeses. The creamier-textured fromage frais and quark are available with differing amounts of fat, from 0% up to 8%.

Well-dressed baked potato

With the right toppings, a baked potato makes a healthy and satisfying main dish.

1 medium baked potato, about
  170 g (6 oz) (tennis ball) topped with:
  steamed broccoli (unlimited)
  30 g (1¼ oz) Cheddar cheese, grated
  (palmful)
Green salad (unlimited) with
  2 tablespoons fat-free dressing
  (2 salad dressing caps), or reduced-fat
  dressing (adds about 30 kcals)
75 g (2½ oz) berries in season
  (2 golf balls)

kcals 350, fat 10 g, saturated fat 6 g, cholesterol 30 mg,
sodium 568 mg, carbohydrate 45 g, fibre 8 g, protein
13 g, calcium 257 mg

Free toppings

The vegetable stuffings for your potato
are 'free' – they carry so few calories that
you can pile on as much as you wish.

Instead of	Try
Steamed broccoli	Diced tomatoes
	Chopped onions
	Steamed spinach
	Grilled mushrooms

Substitute toppings

You can swap the cheese for any of
these other toppings with about the
same number of calories:

Instead of	Try
Grated Cheddar	85 g (3 oz) canned beans (kidney, etc) or chilli con carne
	125 g (4½ oz) low-fat cottage cheese

Soups

For a hearty, sustaining meal in the middle of the day, enjoy a mug of soup paired with a simple sandwich and a piece of fruit.

Soup and sandwich

Hearty split pea *or* cream of asparagus soup (coffee mug)

1 Bavarian sandwich

1 orange, apple or peach

kcals 400, fat 10 g, saturated fat 5 g, cholesterol 42 mg, sodium 653 mg, carbohydrate 60 g, fibre 7 g, protein 25 g, calcium 232 mg

HEARTY SPLIT PEA SOUP

Serves 6
1 teaspoon olive oil
1 tablespoon stock
1 large onion, finely chopped
3 cloves garlic, crushed
2 carrots, halved lengthways and thinly sliced across
150 g (5½ oz) split peas
2 tablespoons tomato purée
225 g (8 oz) smoked turkey breast, diced
½ teaspoon salt
½ teaspoon freshly ground black pepper
½ teaspoon dried sage
1 litre (1¾ pints) water

50 g (1¾ oz) small pasta shapes
25 g (1 oz) Parmesan cheese, grated

1. Heat the oil and stock in a large non-stick saucepan over medium heat. Add the onion and garlic and cook, stirring frequently, for about 7 minutes or until the onion is golden brown. Add the carrots and cook for a further 5 minutes or until just tender.

2. Stir in the split peas, tomato purée, turkey breast, salt, pepper, sage and water. Bring to the boil. Reduce to a simmer, cover and cook for 30 minutes.

3. Uncover, add the pasta and cook for about 15 minutes or until the pasta and split peas are tender. Sprinkle each portion with 2 teaspoons Parmesan and serve hot. (Leftover soup will keep for 3 to 4 days in the fridge, 2 to 3 months in the freezer.)

For a Bavarian sandwich
Spread 1 thin slice pumpernickel bread with honey mustard. Top with 15 g (½ oz) mature Cheddar cheese, shaved or grated, and lettuce or frisée. Add another slice of bread.

HEALTH TIP

At a restaurant or café, keep an eye out for any high-calorie ingredients by asking how a soup is made. If necessary, skip the Parmesan topping.

CREAM OF ASPARAGUS SOUP

Serves 4

**550 g (1 ¼ lb) asparagus, tough ends
trimmed**
1½ teaspoons olive oil
4 spring onions, thinly sliced
**225 g (8 oz) boiling potatoes, peeled and
thinly sliced**
400 ml (14 fl oz) water
1 teaspoon dried tarragon
¾ teaspoon salt
¼ teaspoon freshly ground black pepper
125 ml (4 fl oz) semi-skimmed milk

1. Cut 10 thin asparagus spears into thirds
and reserve for the garnish. Cut the rest of
the asparagus into 1 cm (½ in) lengths.

2. Heat the oil in a medium non-stick
saucepan over low heat. Add the spring
onions and cook, stirring frequently, for
about 2 minutes or until tender. Stir in the
potatoes and chopped asparagus.

3. Add the water, tarragon, salt and pepper,
and bring to the boil. Reduce to a simmer,
cover and cook for about 10 minutes or
until the potatoes and asparagus are tender.

4. Transfer to a food processor and blend
until smooth. Return to the saucepan and
stir in the milk and reserved asparagus.
Cook over low heat for 3 minutes or until
the soup is heated through and the
asparagus pieces are tender. Serve hot.

SMART SOUP CHOICES

If you want a soup that's substantial
enough to be a meal in itself, try one
made from pulses (split peas, beans,
lentils) or packed with vegetables, beans
and pasta. On the other hand, if you
prefer a broth-based soup – chicken and
rice, hot and sour, miso – you'll want to
pair it with a sandwich or salad. And
what about 'creamed' soups? No surprise
here: unless you know otherwise, assume
that they are indeed made with cream
and are high in calories.

CREAMY SOUPS WITHOUT CREAM

Try these variations (one at a time) for a
soup that tastes creamy but still stays
faithful to your *ChangeOne* plan:

■ Add two peeled potatoes when cooking the other ingredients.
■ Add up to 250 ml (8 fl oz) evaporated
skimmed milk and heat through.
■ Stir in 115 g (4 oz) plain yogurt or
reduced-fat crème fraîche just before
serving.
■ Grate 45 g (1½ oz) Cheddar cheese
and stir in to melt just before serving.

Instead of	Try
In split pea soup:	
Split peas	Lentils
Split peas	Canned beans
Smoked turkey	Smoked ham
In cream of asparagus soup:	
Asparagus	Broccoli
Asparagus and potatoes	Carrots and sweet potato

Caesar salads

Now hugely popular, Caesar salads are readily available with all sorts of toppings – grilled chicken breast, grilled fresh tuna and tiger prawns and, here, grilled turkey.

Time saver
Wrap and refrigerate leftover grilled meat or fish for your next day's Caesar salad.

Turkey Caesar lunch

Grilled turkey Caesar salad (2 cricket balls)

115 g (4 oz) fresh fruit salad (2 golf balls)

kcals 325, fat 15 g, saturated fat 4 g, cholesterol 40 mg, sodium 568 mg, carbohydrate 25 g, fibre 3 g, protein 24 g, calcium 155 mg

GRILLED TURKEY CAESAR SALAD

Serves 4

2 garlic cloves, peeled
3 tablespoons lemon juice
2 tablespoons plain low-fat yogurt
1 tablespoon olive oil
350 g (12½ oz) boneless, skinless turkey breast (fillet)
¼ teaspoon salt
½ teaspoon freshly ground black pepper
1 large romaine or cos lettuce, torn into bite-size pieces
150 g (5½ oz) croutons (see right)
25 g (1 oz) Parmesan cheese

1. Preheat the grill or heat a ridged cast-iron grill pan. Finely crush the garlic cloves until paste-like. Put the garlic paste, lemon juice, yogurt and oil into a screwtop jar and shake until blended.

2. Sprinkle the turkey with the salt and pepper and lightly coat with cooking spray. Grill for 4 to 5 minutes on each side or until cooked through. Cut across the grain into 1 cm (½ in) thick slices.

3. Toss together the lettuce, croutons and turkey in a large bowl.

4. Shake the dressing to mix. Drizzle over the salad and toss lightly. Divide evenly among four plates. Shave strips of Parmesan with a vegetable peeler over the salads.

Instead of	Try
Grilled turkey breast	Grilled chicken fillet (85 g/3 oz per portion for this and all below)
	Grilled tuna
	Canned water-packed tuna, drained
	Grilled tofu cubes
	Grilled salmon
	Grilled steak
	Cooked peeled prawns

ABOUT CAESAR SALAD

Legend has it that Caesar salad was invented by Caesar Cardini, a restaurant owner in Tijuana, Mexico, for a group of visiting movie stars. Then there are those who credit Caesar's brother, Alex, with the concoction. Whoever dreamed it up, the salad has become a classic. The original Caesar contained romaine lettuce, tossed at the table with a dressing of raw egg, lemon juice, garlic, olive oil and Worcestershire sauce, and was adorned with croutons and Parmesan cheese.

CROUTONS

■ To make croutons: cut 150 g (5½ oz) day-old bread (crusty white bread, French bread, ciabatta, rye, etc) into 2 cm (¾ in) cubes and toss in a bowl with 2 tablespoons olive oil. Spread out on a baking sheet and bake at 200°C (400°F, gas mark 6) for about 10 minutes or until crisp and golden. Allow to cool slightly before using.

■ For garlic croutons, use garlic-flavoured oil. For herb croutons, toss the hot, freshly baked croutons with finely chopped fresh herbs such as parsley, basil and mint.

■ When buying croutons, compare brands and choose the one that is lowest in calories.

HEALTH TIP

When you're eating out, ask for dressing to be served separately, if possible, so that you can control the amount on the salad. Classic Caesar dressing is made with lots of olive oil. As with all standard salad dressings, it contains a lot of calories – about 100 – in each tablespoon. If the salad only comes ready-dressed, you may want to revise your choice.

Chilli

This family favourite comes from the south-western USA, where cowboys created stick-to-your-ribs dishes from beans, meat, peppers and any other ingredients they had to hand. Whether with meat or meatless, it makes a filling and tasty lunch.

Chilli with cheese and tortilla

Vegetable chilli (2 cricket balls)

1 corn tortilla, warmed

Green salad (unlimited) with 2 tablespoons fat-free dressing (2 salad dressing caps), or reduced-fat dressing (adds about 30 kcals)

kcals 330, fat 8 g, saturated fat 2.5 g, cholesterol 10 mg, sodium 2000 mg,
carbohydrate 49 g, fibre 17 g, protein 20 g, calcium 320 mg

VEGETABLE CHILLI

Serves 4

1 green pepper, finely chopped
1 onion, finely chopped
2 large garlic cloves, crushed
2 cans (about 400 g each) red kidney beans, drained and rinsed
2 cans (about 400 g each) chopped plum tomatoes
½ teaspoon chilli powder
½ teaspoon freshly ground black pepper
½ teaspoon ground cumin
¼ teaspoon ground cinnamon
55 g (2 oz) reduced-fat Cheddar cheese, grated
4 tablespoons plain low-fat yogurt
75 g (2½ oz) diced avocado

1. Lightly coat a large non-stick saucepan with cooking spray and set over medium-high heat. Add the green pepper, onion and garlic and sauté for 8 to 10 minutes or until the onion is browned.

2. Stir in the beans, tomatoes with their juice, chilli powder, black pepper, cumin and cinnamon. Simmer for 10 minutes.

3. Ladle into four bowls. Sprinkle 2 tablespoons of cheese over each bowl and top each with 1 tablespoon of yogurt and one-quarter of the diced avocado.

Instead of	Try
Green pepper	Chopped carrots
Red kidney beans	Black beans
	Very lean minced beef (sauté with the vegetables until browned)
Canned tomatoes	Diced fresh tomatoes

ABOUT CHILLI

Classic chilli con carne contains beans and beef in a seasoned tomato sauce. Texas-style chilli is all meat and chillies, without beans and tomatoes. White chilli is made with white beans and chicken or turkey breast, and no tomatoes. Chilli with cheese, as here, is called 'chile con queso' in Spanish.

TIPS FOR USING CANNED AND DRIED BEANS

■ Canned beans cut down preparation time by several hours. Use just one type, or mix two or three varieties.

■ Drain and thoroughly rinse canned beans to reduce their saltiness before using. Rinsing can also help to remove some of the sugars that cause unpleasant side effects such as wind and bloating.

■ To use dried beans, first soak them overnight in water to cover. Drain them and put in a pan with fresh water. Bring to the boil and boil hard for 10 minutes. Then reduce the heat and simmer until the beans are tender (1 to 3 hours).

ABOUT CHILLI TOPPINGS

Toppings can add lots of flavour to chilli without loads of calories. You can enjoy unlimited amounts of chopped onions, diced tomatoes, chopped fresh coriander, salsa and diced green chillies.

Wrap it up

Flour tortillas wrapped round a variety of fillings make a great alternative to a traditional bread sandwich as a hearty, diet-friendly lunch.

1 roasted vegetable wrap

Green salad (unlimited) with
2 tablespoons (2 salad dressing caps)
fat-free dressing

115 g (4 oz) diced honeydew melon
(2 golf balls), topped with a mint leaf

kcals 300, fat 8 g, saturated fat 1.5 g, cholesterol 56 mg, sodium 1843 mg, carbohydrate 55 g, fibre 5 g, protein 11 g, calcium 220 mg

ROASTED VEGETABLE WRAPS WITH CHIVE SAUCE

Serves 4
1 tablespoon olive oil
1 tablespoon rice vinegar
1 teaspoon chopped fresh rosemary
1 garlic clove, crushed
¼ teaspoon salt
2 courgettes, 450 g (1 lb) total weight
2 large red peppers
1 large red onion
4 x 17.5 cm (7 in) flour tortillas

Yogurt cheese made from 170 g (6 oz) plain fat-free yogurt (see page 29)
¼ teaspoon onion and chive seasoning
1 tablespoon snipped fresh chives

1. Preheat the oven to 230°C (450°F, gas mark 8). Lightly coat a baking tray with cooking spray. Whisk together the oil, vinegar, rosemary, garlic and salt in a small bowl. Cut each courgette across in half, then lengthways into 5 mm (¼ in) slices. Cut each red pepper into 8 strips. Cut the onion into 16 wedges.

2. Toss the vegetables and oil mixture in the baking tray. Roast, tossing frequently, for 30 minutes or until brown and tender. Sprinkle the tortillas with a little water, stack and wrap in foil, then heat in the oven with the vegetables for the last 5 minutes.

3. Combine the yogurt cheese, chives and onion seasoning in a small bowl. Spread evenly on the tortillas and top with the vegetables. Fold in the sides of the tortillas and roll up. Cut each one into 3 pieces.

Russian salads

Try a lighter way with Russian salad by dressing diced vegetables with vinaigrette instead of mayonnaise, and adding beans, fish or meat for a filling dish.

Fresh Russian salad (cricket ball)

1 wholemeal pitta bread
  (dessert plate)

85 g (3 oz) grapes (2 golf balls)

kcals 330, fat 5 g, saturated fat 1 g, cholesterol 0 g, sodium 1471 mg, carbohydrate 67 g, fibre 10 g, protein 11 g, calcium 40 mg

FRESH RUSSIAN SALAD

Serves 6

60 g (2¼ oz) chopped red pepper
60 g (2¼ oz) chopped green pepper
75 g (2½ oz) chopped cucumber
85 g (3 oz) diced red onion
250 g (8½ oz) diced plum tomatoes
160 g (5¾ oz) fresh, canned or frozen sweetcorn kernels
170 g (6 oz) drained canned black or red kidney beans
2 tablespoons red wine vinegar
1 tablespoon olive oil
1 tablespoon lime juice
2 tablespoons chopped fresh coriander
1 chilli, finely chopped (optional)

Combine all the ingredients in a large bowl and stir gently to mix.

ABOUT RUSSIAN SALADS

A Russian salad can be made with just about any vegetables, fresh, cooked or canned (see some ideas below). Mix the salad in a ratio of four parts of diced vegetables, or more if you wish, with one part of beans or other pulses, fish or meat. Then ring the changes with flavourings and seasonings for salads to suit the seasons and your taste.

Instead of	Try
Red and green peppers	Green and yellow courgettes
Cucumber	Celery
Kidney beans	Cooked peeled prawns Diced cooked ham Smoked turkey breast Chickpeas
Lime juice, chilli and coriander	Lemon juice, garlic and basil

Sautéed chicken fillets

Chicken fillets (boneless, skinless chicken breasts) are the most convenient type of chicken you can buy, and it's worth keeping a supply in your freezer. They can be sliced while frozen for stir-frying, or thawed to use whole – as they are, or pounded thin for escalopes. To keep this lean meat moist, pair it with a sauce.

Chicken sauté supper

Chicken and caramelised onion sauté –
 1 chicken fillet (palm) with onions (2 golf balls)

Spinach fettuccine or tagliatelle (tennis ball)

Tossed salad (unlimited) – mixed greens topped with tomato wedges, dressed with ½ teaspoon (thumbnail) olive oil, balsamic vinegar (unlimited) and freshly ground black pepper

kcals 430, fat 10 g, saturated fat 2 g, cholesterol 66 mg, sodium 292 mg, carbohydrate 49 g, fibre 5 g, protein 37 g, calcium 73 mg

CHICKEN AND CARAMELISED ONION SAUTÉ

Serves 4

700 g (1½ lb) Spanish onions
4 skinless chicken fillets, 115g to 140 g
  (4 oz to 5 oz) each
½ teaspoon salt
½ teaspoon freshly ground black pepper
4 teaspoons olive oil
2 tablespoons caster sugar
5 tablespoons chicken stock
1 teaspoon chopped fresh rosemary
1 teaspoon chopped fresh thyme
1 tablespoon red wine vinegar

1. Cut each onion into 6 wedges. Sprinkle the chicken fillets with ¼ teaspoon salt and ¼ teaspoon pepper.

2. Coat a large non-stick frying pan with cooking spray. Add 2 teaspoons olive oil and heat over medium-high heat for about 30 seconds. Add the chicken and sauté for about 3 minutes on each side or until browned. Transfer to a plate.

3. Reduce the heat to medium and add the remaining oil to the pan. Then add the onions and sprinkle with 1 tablespoon sugar and the remaining salt and pepper. Sauté for about 8 minutes or until the onions turn golden brown and caramelise. Stir frequently, breaking the onions apart as they cook. Add the stock and boil until it evaporates.

4. Stir in the rosemary, thyme and remaining sugar. Return the chicken to the pan and sprinkle with the vinegar. Cook, uncovered, for a further 4 minutes or until the chicken is cooked through (when a fillet is pierced the juices that run out should be clear).

Instead of	Try
Onions	Red onions, leeks, spring or salad onions or shallots

ABOUT CHICKEN AND OTHER POULTRY

Chicken is the most popular type of poultry and, like turkey, is endlessly versatile. Both chicken and turkey are very lean – turkey is the lower in fat and calories – and most of their fat is in the skin. Lean duck, without skin and fat, has about the same amount of fat as lamb. Here is a calorie and fat comparison, based on an 85 g (3 oz) cooked portion, without skin and bone:

	Kcals	Fat (grams)
Turkey breast	114	0.6
Duck breast	119	2.1
Chicken breast	140	3.0
Duck leg meat	151	5.1
Turkey leg meat	159	6.1
Chicken leg meat	174	8.2
Goose	202	10.8

SKIN ON OR OFF?

It's best not to eat the skin of poultry – it can add almost a teaspoon of fat per 85 g (3 oz) serving – but it can be removed either before or after cooking.

Skin off: Skinless chicken fillets are great in simmered or sautéed dishes where they are cooked with other moist ingredients or in a sauce.

Skin on: Chicken in its skin is perfect for roasting. The skin helps to keep the chicken moist, and a thin membrane between the skin and the flesh prevents the fat from getting into the meat.

ABOUT SPINACH PASTA

Pasta can be coloured and flavoured with a wide variety of vegetable purées and pastes, such as spinach (green), tomato or beetroot (red) and carrot (orange). There's not enough of the vegetable in it to make a nutritional difference, but it looks and tastes great.

Barbecued steak

Brushed with a zesty barbecue sauce and then grilled in the kitchen or cooked outdoors over hot coals, lean steak makes a delectable sandwich filling. Add some crunchy fresh coleslaw and tomatoes for a fabulous meal.

Steak barbecue supper

1 barbecued steak roll

Colourful coleslaw (cupped palmful)

Tomatoes and salad greens such as watercress (unlimited)

kcals 400, fat 10 g, saturated fat 2 g, cholesterol 52 mg, sodium 940 mg, carbohydrate 42 g, fibre 4 g, protein 27 g, calcium 100 mg

BARBECUED STEAK ROLLS

Serves 4

5 tablespoons tomato ketchup
1 tablespoon red wine vinegar
2 teaspoons soft light brown sugar
½ teaspoon ground ginger
½ teaspoon made English mustard
350 g (12½ oz) lean sirloin or rump steak
4 medium bread rolls, baps or buns (55 g/2 oz each), split open

1. Preheat the grill or heat a ridged cast-iron grill pan. Mix together the ketchup, vinegar, sugar, ginger and mustard. Brush one side of the steak with this sauce.

2. Grill for 4 minutes. Turn the steak over, brush with the sauce and grill for a further 3 to 4 minutes or until cooked to your taste.

3. Slice the steak thinly and divide into 4 equal portions (refrigerate extra). Serve in the rolls, with the coleslaw.

Note: The steaks can also be cooked on a barbecue (see opposite).

ABOUT BARBECUE SAUCE

Barbecue sauce adds much more taste than it does calories. Our recipe is based on a popular version from Kansas City in the USA. Another good variation is a dry seasoning mixture of paprika, onion powder, garlic powder and dry mustard.

COLOURFUL COLESLAW

Serves 4

100 g (3½ oz) shredded green cabbage
100 g (3½ oz) shredded red cabbage
55 g (2 oz) shredded Chinese leaves
55 g (2 oz) shredded carrots
4 tablespoons reduced-fat mayonnaise
1½ teaspoons Dijon mustard
1 tablespoon red wine vinegar
1½ teaspoons caster sugar
**Salt and freshly ground black pepper
   to taste**

1. Combine all the ingredients and mix well. Chill for at least 1 hour.

2. Before serving, divide into 4 equal portions. Refrigerate any extra, but note that cabbage wilts and 'shrinks' down the longer it is marinated.

3. The coleslaw can be served separately, or on the sandwich (as pictured). To save a few calories, serve the dressing alongside and use a small amount as a condiment on the sandwich, or drizzled on top of the shredded vegetables.

Portion bonus: Increase all ingredients except mayonnaise.

Instead of beef

Chicken and pork work well with the zestiness of barbecue sauce. To make these sandwiches with chicken:

- Use about 450 g (1 lb) of skinless chicken fillets or skinless, boneless thigh meat.
- Cut the chicken into strips and combine with the sauce.
- Cook in a 180°C (350°F, gas mark 4) oven, or simmer on the stove, for about 15 minutes.

To make the sandwiches with pork:

- Choose a lean cut such as fillet, slit in half lengthways and opened up like a book.
- Cook as for the steak, brushing with sauce and grilling until well done.

What we call barbecuing in the UK – cooking meat, fish and vegetables over charcoal outdoors – is not true barbecue in the American sense of the word.
In the USA, particularly in states such as North Carolina and Kansas, barbecue refers to slow-cooking pork, chicken or beef over indirect heat (not right on top of the coals or wood) in a special barbecue pit. During cooking, the meat or poultry is basted with a rich and piquant sauce. While the smoky juiciness of this kind of barbecued meat is unique, you can enjoy a replica of the barbecue flavour by basting your meat, poultry or fish with a zesty sauce and cooking it under the grill, on a ridged cast-iron grill pan or over hot charcoal.

TIPS FOR BARBECUING OVER CHARCOAL

Meat or chicken that are charred on the outside and barely done on the inside are all too common. They're also unhealthy. The undercooked meat can house harmful bacteria, and the charred parts of the skin contain cancer-causing compounds. The culprit is direct heat – the coals are too hot when the food is put on to cook. The solution: make sure coals are ash-covered grey before you cook, or use indirect heat.

- On a gas grill, turn on only one or two burners, leaving part of the grill top unheated.
- On a charcoal grill, arrange the coals along the 'wall' of the grill.
- Place the meat or chicken in the centre of the barbecue grid (you may want to put a drip pan under meat) or on the unlit side of a gas grill.
- Cover the barbecue kettle and cook until the meat is done to your taste or until chicken is thoroughly cooked – on an instant-read thermometer this is 75°C (170°C) for thigh meat and 71°C (160°F) for breast. During cooking, open the lid to baste frequently.

Braised beef

Think of a succulent joint of beef simmering slowly with vegetables and wine, and your mouth waters and you can almost smell the savoury aromas. Make this on an afternoon when you have several hours spare for the beef to cook to perfection.

Braised beef supper

85 g (3 oz) wine-braised beef (pack of cards) with vegetables (tennis ball)

Steamed broccoli (unlimited)

1 small slice crusty bread (palm size)

kcals 350, fat 6 g, saturated fat 2 g, cholesterol 66 mg, sodium 500 mg, carbohydrate 40 g, fibre 5 g, protein 28 g, calcium 286 mg

WINE-BRAISED BEEF

Serves 12

- **1 boneless beef joint (eg chuck, topside), weighing about 1.35 kg (3 lb), trimmed and tied into shape**
- **1 ½ teaspoons salt**
- **1 ½ teaspoons freshly ground black pepper**
- **8 large carrots, cut into 5 cm (2 in) chunks**
- **2 onions, coarsely chopped**
- **4 garlic cloves, crushed**
- **2 cans (about 400 g each) whole plum tomatoes**

55 g (2 oz) fresh basil, chopped
2 cups dry red wine or beef stock
900 g (2 lb) small new potatoes,
  scrubbed
2 teaspoons cornflour mixed with
  2 tablespoons water

1. Preheat the oven to 170ºC (325ºF, gas mark 3). Rub the beef with 1 teaspoon each salt and pepper. Put into a large flameproof casserole over medium-high heat and sear on all sides. Transfer to a plate.

2. Add the carrots, onions and garlic to the fat remaining in the casserole and sauté for about 8 minutes or until the onions are browned. Stir in the tomatoes with their juice, half of the basil, and the remaining salt and pepper. Cook for 5 minutes, breaking up the tomatoes with a spoon.

3. Return the beef to the casserole. Add the wine or stock and enough water to come 5 cm (2 in) up the side of the pot. Bring to the boil. Cover with foil and then with the lid to create a tight seal. Transfer to the oven and braise for 1 hour, turning the meat once.

4. Add the potatoes and remaining basil, plus additional water if needed to come 5 cm (2 in) up the side of the pot. Braise for a further 1 hour or until the meat and vegetables are tender.

5. Cut the beef into small chunks and arrange on a platter with the vegetables. Strain the braising liquid into a saucepan and bring to a simmer. Whisk in the cornflour mixture and bring to the boil. Simmer for 1 minute or until thickened. Ladle over the beef and vegetables, and serve.

6. Divide leftovers into individual portions. Cover and keep in the fridge for 1 to 2 days, or in the freezer for up to a month.

Portion bonus: Braise extra vegetables (except potatoes) with the beef to enhance the flavour and fill your plate.

TIPS FOR TENDER MEAT

- Keep liquid in the casserole at the right level.
- Cover the pot with foil and then the lid to create a tighter seal.
- Braise gently in a warm oven, or on top of the cooker on a low heat.
- Allow enough time for cooking; don't turn up the heat to hurry things along.
- Cook until the beef is 'fork tender': insert a large double-pronged fork into the thickest part of the joint. If the fork goes in easily and pulls out just as easily, the meat is done.

ABOUT BUYING BEEF FOR BRAISING

Lean muscular joints require long, moist cooking methods, as in this recipe, to make them tender and succulent. The best joints to use for braising are boned and rolled: blade and chuck, silverside and topside. Brisket is also excellent braised, but it is more fatty than the other braising joints.

TIPS FOR GREAT GRAVY

Meat cooked with moist heat creates delicious cooking juices that you can turn into gravy. After removing the joint and vegetables from the pot, pour the cooking juices into a gravy separator or measuring jug so that you can remove the fat. Or use a baster to suction off the liquid from under the thin layer of fat. Thicken by adding cornflour (as above) or plain flour (1 to 2 tablespoons) and gently simmering while stirring. Or omit the thickening and serve the flavoursome juices just as they are.

Meat loaf

There are almost as many different types of meat loaf as there are people who love eating it. Traditionally an economical dish, meat loaf can make minced meat grand with endless additions and flavours.

Hearty meat loaf supper

1 slice homestyle meat loaf, 2.5 cm (1 in) thick (index finger, to first joint)

Parsleyed egg noodles (tennis ball)

Steamed baby courgettes (unlimited), drizzled with 1 teaspoon (thumb tip) olive oil

kcals 430, fat 14 g, saturated fat 6 g, cholesterol 99 mg, sodium 345 mg, carbohydrate 42 g, fibre 4 g, protein 35 g, calcium 53 mg

HOMESTYLE MEAT LOAF

Serves 8

2 large onions, chopped
2 large celery sticks, chopped
1 large green pepper, chopped
3 garlic cloves, crushed
1 kg (2¼ lb) lean minced beef
45 g (1½ oz) fresh wholemeal breadcrumbs (about 2 slices)
1 egg
½ teaspoon freshly ground black pepper
1 can (about 400 g) chopped tomatoes
4 tablespoons tomato ketchup

1. Preheat the oven to 180ºC (350ºF, gas mark 4). Lightly coat a 33 x 23 cm (13 x 9 in) ovenproof dish and a large non-stick frying pan with cooking spray. Set the pan over medium-high heat and sauté the onions, celery, green pepper and garlic for about 5 minutes or until softened. Transfer the vegetables to a large bowl.

2. Add the beef, breadcrumbs, egg and pepper to the vegetables and mix well with your hands. Combine the tomatoes and ketchup in a small bowl. Add half to the meat mixture and mix again.

3. Transfer the meat mixture to the oven-proof dish and shape into a 25 x 17.5 cm (10 x 7 in) loaf, mounding it slightly in the centre. Make a lengthways groove down the centre with the side of your hand. Pour the remaining tomato mixture into the groove. Bake the meat loaf for 1¼ hours. Allow to stand for 10 minutes before cutting across into 8 equal slices.

4. Cover and refrigerate leftovers (they are delicious cold in a sandwich), or wrap in foil and freeze for up to 1 month.

To make parsleyed egg noodles
For 8 portions, cook a 350 g packet of egg noodles according to packet directions. Drain, reserving 4 tablespoons of the cooking water. Place the noodles in a bowl, add the reserved cooking water and 4 tablespoons of chopped parsley, and then toss to mix.

Instead of	Try
Minced beef	Minced lean pork
	Equal parts beef, pork and veal
	Minced lean lamb
	Minced turkey
	Soya (TVP) mince

TIPS FOR STRETCHING MEAT LOAF

Meat loaf is designed to be 'stretched' to serve more people. You can make it go further with one of the following added to 1 kg (2¼ lb) minced meat:
- 45 g (1½ oz) fresh breadcrumbs, preferably wholemeal
- 115 g (4 oz) grated carrots and/or potatoes
- 45 g (1½ oz) rolled or porridge oats
- 25 g (1 oz) quick cooking rice

ABOUT BABY VEGETABLES

Baby vegetables are miniature versions of varieties such as courgettes, fennel and carrots. Some are truly young, while others are bred to be tiny when full grown. Select baby veg that feel firm to the touch, as softness can mean a vegetable is past its prime. To steam, cook in a steamer basket for about 5 minutes, or in the microwave for about 2 minutes, until tender. Drizzle with a little olive oil, season with salt and freshly ground black pepper, and add chopped fresh herbs if you like.

TIPS FOR COOKING MEAT LOAF

The perfect meat loaf should be moist but not wet, satisfying but not too high in calories. Start with minced meat that is at least 90 per cent lean, or minced from a lean cut by the butcher. Add ingredients that moisten the mixture, like tomato ketchup or tomato sauce, as well as ingredients that hold moisture, such as breadcrumbs. You can shape the loaf 'freeform' and cook in an ovenproof dish, as here, or pack the mixture into a loaf tin, in which case gently pour off any fat from around the meat loaf at the end of cooking.

Roast pork

Pigs have been on a slimming diet too, and while they're losing we're winning.
Today's pork is leaner and more flavourful than ever – perfect for a Chinese dish.

Chinese-style pork supper

85 g (3 oz) sweet-and-sour glazed pork
  with pineapple (pack of cards)

100 g (3½ oz) cooked basmati rice (tennis ball)

Steamed patty pan squash (unlimited)

kcals 440, fat 10 g, saturated fat 3 g, cholesterol 78 mg,
sodium 400 mg, carbohydrate 61 g, fibre 2 g, protein 27 g, calcium 50 mg

SWEET-AND-SOUR GLAZED PORK WITH PINEAPPLE

Serves 4

1 can (about 425 g) pineapple pieces in natural juice
100 g (3½ oz) redcurrant jelly
2 tablespoons plus 2 teaspoons Dijon mustard
¾ teaspoon salt
1 tablespoon lemon juice
450 g (1 lb) trimmed pork fillet

1. Preheat the oven to 200ºC (400ºF, gas mark 6). Drain the pineapple, reserving the juice, and set aside.

2. Combine the pineapple juice, redcurrant jelly, 2 tablespoons of the mustard and ¼ teaspoon salt in a small saucepan. Cook over medium heat for 5 minutes, stirring frequently, until the jelly has melted and the mixture is slightly syrupy and reduced to 150 ml (¼ pint). Allow to cool to room temperature. Measure out 2 tablespoons of the mixture for basting and reserve the rest in the saucepan for the sauce.

3. Place the pork in a small roasting tin. Sprinkle with the lemon juice and remaining salt, and brush with the basting mixture. Roast the pork, basting every 10 minutes with the pan juices, for about 30 minutes or until cooked through.

4. Meanwhile, combine the pineapple with the remaining 2 teaspoons mustard in a small bowl.

5. Allow the cooked pork to stand for 10 minutes before slicing. Serve with the reserved sauce (reheated briefly) and the pineapple and mustard mixture.

ABOUT PORK

Pork loin, chops and fillet or tenderloin are the leanest cuts, being from the part of the animal that gets the most exercise. But what's good news for lowering calories can be bad news for taste. These lean cuts are easy to over-cook because they have very little fat to keep them moist. It's best to buy thicker cuts that are less apt to dry out during cooking, and to divide them into portions when cooked.

TO COOK SQUASH

If you can't find patty pan squash, you can substitute courgettes (green or yellow, or a mixture). Pick small to medium-sized squashes that feel firm to the touch – very large ones can be dry. Rinse well. Cut into 1 cm (½ in) slices, then cut each slice into thirds or quarters (if baby squashes, just halve them). To cook, place in a microwave-proof bowl, cover with a plate and microwave for 2 minutes. Uncover, stir, re-cover and microwave for an additional minute. If not yet fully cooked – a fork won't go in easily – microwave in 1 minute intervals until done. To steam conventionally, put the prepared squash in a steamer basket and cook for 5 to 8 minutes until tender.

ABOUT BASMATI RICE

Basmati rice is a slim-grained, full-flavoured rice grown only in northern India and Pakistan. It is widely available in supermarkets. Rinse well before cooking to get rid of the starchy powder left over from milling, then cook according to the packet instructions.

Grilled fish

Fish is growing in popularity, and for good reason: it's low in saturated fat – the fat contained in oily fish is the heart-healthy type – and packed with vitamins and minerals. Nutritionists recommend that you eat fish at least twice a week.

Fish from the grill

1 soy-basted halibut steak (chequebook)

Grilled mixed onions – 2 onion halves plus 2 spring onions

Ziti and courgettes (2 tennis balls)

kcals 440, fat 7 g, saturated fat 2 g, cholesterol 78 mg, sodium 2000 mg, carbohydrate 63 g, fibre 4 g, protein 38 g, calcium 171 mg

SOY-BASTED HALIBUT STEAKS

Serves 4

3 small spring onions
4 tablespoons soy sauce
100 g (3½ oz) reduced-sugar apricot jam
3 tablespoons tomato ketchup
1 tablespoon red wine vinegar
4 halibut steaks, 140 g (5 oz) each

1. Preheat the grill. Thinly slice the spring onions on the diagonal. Set aside in a bowl.

2. Combine the soy sauce, jam, ketchup and vinegar in a small bowl. Measure out 5 tablespoons and set aside for the sauce.

3. Place the halibut steaks on the grill rack and brush with the remaining soy mixture. Grill, about 10 cm (4 in) from the heat, for about 5 minutes or until browned and cooked through. Do not turn.

4. Spoon the reserved soy mixture over the fish. Serve hot, with the sliced spring onions for sprinkling over the fish.

GRILLED MIXED ONIONS

Serves 4
4 small red onions
8 spring onions

1. Slice the red onions in half lengthways. Place the red and spring onions on a baking tray and spray all sides with cooking spray, or brush lightly with olive oil.

2. Cook under the grill (alongside the fish steaks if there is room on the grill rack) until tender and browned, turning once.

ZITI AND COURGETTES

Serves 4
170 g (6 oz) ziti or other pasta shapes
 such as rigatoni or penne
2 courgettes
2 teaspoons olive oil
2 tablespoons chopped fresh basil
2 tablespoons grated Parmesan cheese

1. Cook the pasta until al dente, or according to packet instructions. Drain.

2. While the pasta is cooking, cut each courgette across in half, then slice each half into eighths lengthways to make thick 'matchsticks'.

3. Place the courgettes in a microwave-proof bowl and microwave for about 3 minutes or until just tender.

4. Toss the courgettes with the hot cooked pasta and the remaining ingredients.

TIPS FOR COOKING FISH

With the exception of grilled tuna, which often is served rare, most fish should be cooked until just done, with flaky but moist flesh (but take care not to over-cook). The '10-minute rule' can help: cook fish for a total of 10 minutes for each 2.5 cm (1 in) of thickness. Steaks and large fillets may take longer to cook, while thin fillets will cook in a matter of minutes. Here are a few guidelines.

Steaks: Grilling is good for fish steaks such as halibut, salmon, shark, swordfish and tuna, which hold together well when you turn them.

Fillets: Higher-fat fish fillets like salmon, sea bass and trout won't fall apart on the grill. Baking or pan-sautéeing is best for thin fillets such as sole, plaice, red snapper and other varieties. They are more apt to fall apart on the grill.

Whole fish, large fillets: These can be grilled, steamed in a wok or fish steamer, baked or poached.

TIPS FOR ORDERING

When eating out, feel free to order any type of fish you fancy. Even though oily fish such as salmon are higher in calories than white fish, they're also packed with heart-healthy omega-3 fatty acids – the health benefits are worth the extra calories. Grilled and steamed fish are cooked with little or no extra fat, but baked or sautéed fish may be cooked with butter or served with a cheese-based or other high-fat sauce. So be sure to ask the waiter before ordering.

Chicken pies

What could be more welcoming in chilly weather than little chicken pies baked in the oven? Enjoy the *ChangeOne* version of this comfort-food favourite, made with lots of vegetables, a creamy sauce and crisp pastry top.

Chicken pie supper

1 little chicken and sweetcorn pie

Green salad (unlimited) with
2 tablespoons fat-free dressing
(2 salad dressing caps), or reduced-fat
dressing (adds about 30 kcals)

kcals 460, fat 18 g, saturated fat 6 g, cholesterol 80 mg,
sodium 435 mg, carbohydrate 45 g, fibre 5 g, protein
30 g, calcium 90 mg

LITTLE CHICKEN AND SWEETCORN PIES

Serves 4
**450 g (1 lb) skinless chicken breast
fillets**
¼ teaspoon salt
125 g (4½ oz) shortcrust pastry
**1 egg white, lightly beaten
with 1 teaspoon water**
2 carrots, thinly sliced
160 g (5¾ oz) frozen sweetcorn kernels
150 g (5½ oz) frozen peas
120 g (4 oz) frozen small white onions
125 ml (4 fl oz) evaporated skimmed milk
3 tablespoons plain flour
1½ teaspoons butter
¼ teaspoon freshly ground black pepper

1. Put the chicken fillets in a large saucepan with ⅛ teaspoon salt and enough water to cover. Bring to a simmer over medium-high heat. Reduce the heat to low and gently poach the chicken for about 15 minutes or until thoroughly cooked (the juices should run clear).

2. Transfer the chicken to a cutting board; allow to cool, then cut into bite-sized pieces. Reserve 250 ml (8 fl oz) of the poaching liquid.

3. Preheat the oven to 225°C (425°F, gas mark 7). Lightly coat a baking tray and four 250 ml (8 fl oz) capacity ovenproof dishes with cooking spray.

4. Dust the work surface lightly with flour, and roll out the shortcrust pastry to 3 mm (⅛ in) thickness. Cut out 4 squares to fit on top of the ovenproof dishes. Transfer to the baking tray and brush the pastry squares with the egg white glaze. Bake for about 12 minutes or until crisp and golden brown. Cool on a wire rack.

5. Meanwhile, cook the carrots in boiling water for about 5 minutes or until tender; drain. Put the frozen vegetables in a large sieve and rinse with hot water to thaw them; drain.

6. Whisk the evaporated milk with the flour in a small bowl until smooth. Melt the butter in a medium saucepan over medium heat. Whisk in the milk mixture and then the reserved poaching liquid. Cook for 5 minutes, stirring, until the sauce thickens and boils. Stir in the chicken, carrots, sweetcorn, peas, onions, pepper and remaining salt. Cook for 3 minutes or until heated through.

7. Divide among the 4 ovenproof dishes and bake for 15 minutes or until the filling is bubbling. Top each pie with a pastry square and serve.

ABOUT LITTLE PIES

Little pies are perfect for *ChangeOne* because they're made as individual servings. And by baking the pastry tops separately you can keep the quantity of shortcrust per serving within a healthy range. Little pies such as this are also easy to alter according to what you have on hand: you can change the chicken to turkey, tuna or even tofu without affecting the wonderful flavour of the dish. The recipe uses frozen vegetables, which are available year-round, so the pies can always be in season. If you're serving a crowd, you can double the recipe and bake the filling in one large pie dish instead of individual dishes, then top with 8 pastry squares.

Instead of	Try
Chicken fillets	Boneless, skinless chicken thighs, 350 g (12½ oz)
	Turkey fillet chunks, 450 g (1 lb); Canned tuna in water, 3 x 200 g cans, drained
	Firm tofu, 350 g (12½ oz)
Frozen sweetcorn, peas and onions	Mixed frozen vegetables, 450 g (1 lb)
Frozen sweetcorn	Fresh sweetcorn kernels shaved off the cob
	Fresh or frozen broad beans
Evaporated skimmed milk	Fresh skimmed or semi-skimmed milk

Super side dishes

The beauty of *ChangeOne* is its adaptability: you can mix and match main courses and side dishes for an infinite number of meal combinations.

BARLEY PILAF WITH HERBS

Serves 4

1½ teaspoons olive oil
2 smoked turkey rashers, coarsely
    chopped
1 onion, finely chopped
2 cloves garlic, crushed
2 carrots, thinly sliced
100 g (3½ oz) pearl barley
½ teaspoon salt
½ teaspoon dried sage
½ teaspoon dried thyme
550 ml (18 fl oz) water
½ teaspoon grated lemon zest
½ teaspoon freshly ground black pepper
50 g (1¾ oz) Parmesan cheese, grated

1. Heat the oil in a medium saucepan over medium heat. Add the turkey rashers and cook for 2 minutes. Add the onion and garlic and cook for a further 5 minutes or until the onion is tender and golden brown.

2. Add the carrots and cook for 5 minutes or until tender.

3. Add the barley, stirring to combine. Add the salt, sage, thyme and water, and bring to the boil. Reduce to a simmer and cook, stirring frequently, for about 45 minutes or until the barley is tender.

4. Stir in the lemon zest, pepper and Parmesan until evenly combined.

5. Divide into 4 portions. One serving is approximately the size of a tennis ball.

kcals 170, fat 5 g, saturated fat 2 g, cholesterol 15 mg, sodium 1500 mg, carbohydrate 26 g, fibre 3 g, protein 10 g, calcium 175 mg

SUMMER RATATOUILLE

Serves 4

1 aubergine, about 700 g (1½ lb)
1 small fennel bulb
2 teaspoons olive oil
2 small yellow courgettes, about 170 g
    (6 oz) each, chopped
1 small onion, cut into thin wedges
2 tablespoons chicken stock
2 large garlic cloves, crushed
1 can (about 400 g) whole plum tomatoes
1 tablespoon chopped fresh oregano
1 teaspoon chopped fresh rosemary,
    plus sprigs for garnish
1 green pepper, chopped
¼ teaspoon salt

1. Cut the aubergine across into slices. Sprinkle on both sides with salt and spread out on a double layer of kitchen paper. Leave to drain for 15 minutes, then rinse well and pat dry with kitchen paper. Cut into cubes. Trim and chop the fennel bulb.

2. Heat 1 teaspoon oil in a large non-stick frying pan over medium-high heat. Sauté the courgettes and onion for 5 minutes or until the onion is softened. Transfer to a large bowl. Add ½ teaspoon oil and the stock to the pan. Stir in the aubergine and reduce the heat to medium. Cover and cook, stirring occasionally, for 12 minutes or until the aubergine is tender. Add to the bowl.

3. Add the remaining oil and garlic to the pan and cook for 30 seconds. Stir in the tomatoes with their juice, the fennel, oregano and chopped rosemary, breaking up the tomatoes with a spoon. Cover and simmer for 5 minutes. Stir in the green pepper and simmer, covered, for a further 7 minutes. Return all the vegetables to the pan. Sprinkle with the salt and bring to the boil. Cook, uncovered, for 3 minutes, stirring occasionally.

4. Divide into 4 portions. One serving is about the size of a cricket ball. Serve warm or cool, garnished with rosemary.

kcals 75, fat 3 g, saturated fat 0.5 g, cholesterol 0 mg, sodium 170 mg, carbohydrate 10 g, fibre 3 g, protein 10 g, calcium 52 mg

ASPARAGUS WITH CONFETTI VINAIGRETTE

Serves 4
700 g (1½ lb) asparagus
1¼ teaspoons salt
2 large red peppers, finely chopped
2 large yellow peppers, finely chopped
4 spring onions, thinly sliced
2 teaspoons fresh thyme or ½ teaspoon dried thyme
5 tablespoons chicken stock
3 tablespoons white wine vinegar
½ teaspoon freshly ground black pepper

1. Trim the asparagus. Bring 1 cm (½ in) of water to a simmer in a large non-stick frying pan over medium-high heat. Add the asparagus and 1 teaspoon salt. Simmer for 3 to 4 minutes or until the asparagus is tender. Transfer to a plate. Keep warm.

2. Wipe the pan dry. Coat with cooking spray and set over medium-high heat. Sauté the red and yellow peppers for about 4 minutes or until tender. Stir in the spring onions and thyme, and cook for a further 1 minute.

3. Stir in the stock and vinegar and bring to a simmer. Sprinkle with the pepper and remaining salt, and pour over asparagus.

4. Divide into 4 portions. One serving is approximately 5 spears.

kcals 80, fat 1 g, saturated fat 0 g, cholesterol 0 mg, sodium 750 mg, carbohydrate 17 g, fibre 6 g, protein 7 g, calcium 64 mg

MANGETOUT AND APPLES WITH GINGER

Serves 4
2 teaspoons olive oil
2 tablespoons peeled and finely chopped fresh root ginger
3 cloves garlic, crushed
450 g (1 lb) mangetout, strings removed
2 crisp red dessert apples, unpeeled, cut into thin wedges
½ teaspoon salt

1. Heat the oil in a large non-stick frying pan over low heat. Add ginger and garlic, and cook for 2 minutes or until tender.

2. Add the mangetout, apples and salt, and cook, stirring frequently, for about 7 minutes or until the mangetout are tender but still crisp.

3. Divide into 4 portions. One serving is approximately the size of a tennis ball.

kcals 80, fat 2 g, saturated fat 0 g, cholesterol 0 mg, sodium 250 mg, carbohydrate 12 g, fibre 6 g, protein 4 g, calcium 52 mg

Chocolate

Who doesn't love chocolate? Its unique rich flavour has been popular for centuries. But not only is it sweet, it contains plant chemicals that actually promote good health. Used judiciously, chocolate can be a part of your *ChangeOne* programme.

CHOCOLATE SNACKING CAKE

Makes 36 pieces
185 g (6½ oz) plain flour
1½ teaspoons baking powder
½ teaspoon salt
**90 g (3¼ oz) plus 2 teaspoons
 cocoa powder**
4 tablespoons buttermilk
1 tablespoon instant espresso powder
200 g (7 oz) caster sugar
110 g (3¾ oz) soft light brown sugar
**125 g (4½ oz) unsweetened apple purée
 (see below right)**
2 teaspoons pure vanilla extract
2 egg whites
**60 g (2¼ oz) plain dark chocolate,
 finely chopped**
1 tablespoon icing sugar

1. Preheat the oven to 170°C (325°F, gas mark 3). Line a 20 cm (8 in) square cake tin with foil, leaving a 2.5 cm (1 in) overhang. Sift the flour, baking powder and all but 2 teaspoons cocoa into a small bowl. Gently heat the buttermilk and espresso in a small saucepan until the espresso is dissolved.

2. Mix together the caster and brown sugars, apple sauce, buttermilk mixture and vanilla extract in a medium bowl. Stir in the flour mixture just until blended. Whisk the egg whites in a large bowl until soft peaks form. Fold the egg whites into the cake mixture together with the chocolate.

3. Scrape the mixture into the tin. Bake for 35 minutes or just until set. Cool in the tin on a wire rack for 15 minutes, then lift out the cake and set on the rack to cool completely. Sift the icing sugar and remaining cocoa over the cake. Cut into 36 squares. One serving is 1 square.

4. Wrap leftover cake in foil and freeze for up to 1 month.

TIPS FOR LIGHTENING UP CAKES AND DESSERTS

- Look for recipes that call for a fruit purée, such as prune or apple. Or add it in place of up to half the weight of fat and sugar in a recipe. To make prune or apple purée, roughly chop ready-to-eat prunes or dried apples (or apricots) and put in a pan with water to cover. Cover and simmer until very soft, then purée in a blender or food processor. Fresh apple purée can be made in the same way, using thinly sliced dessert apples and 1 tablespoon water per apple.
- Use buttermilk, plain low-fat yogurt, fromage frais or reduced-fat crème fraîche in place of soured cream.

BROWNIE BITES

Makes 16

95 g (3¹/₄ oz) plain flour
30 g (1¹/₄ oz) cocoa powder
2 tablespoons cornflour
1 teaspoon baking powder
¹/₄ teaspoon bicarbonate of soda
¹/₄ teaspoon salt
220 g (scant 8 oz) soft light brown sugar
4 tablespoons prune purée (see left)
2 tablespoons plain fat-free yogurt
2 tablespoons sunflower or corn oil
1 egg
3 tablespoons chopped plain chocolate
65 g (2¹/₄ oz) walnuts, coarsely chopped

1. Preheat the oven to 180°C (350°F, gas mark 4). Spray a 20 cm (8 in) square cake tin with cooking spray.

2. Stir together the flour, cocoa powder, cornflour, baking powder, bicarbonate of soda and salt in a medium bowl. Set aside.

3. Beat together the brown sugar, prune purée, yogurt, oil and egg in a large bowl using an electric mixer. Stir in the flour mixture just until combined.

4. Pour the mixture into the tin. Scatter the chocolate and walnuts on top. Bake for 18 to 20 minutes or until a skewer inserted in the centre comes out dry but with a few crumbs sticking to it, and the sides of the cake are pulling away from the tin. Cool in the tin on a wire rack. Cut into 16 brownies, each 5 cm (2 in) square. One serving equals 1 brownie.

5. Wrap extra brownies in foil and freeze for up to 1 month.

CHOCOLATE-DIPPED STRAWBERRIES

Makes 350 g (12¹/₂ oz)

350 g (12¹/₂ oz) strawberries (8 to 12 medium strawberries), rinsed and dried completely
115 g (4 oz) plain dark chocolate, chopped

1. Line a tray with baking parchment.

2. Heat the chocolate in the microwave on medium for about 30 seconds or until melted. Stir well until smooth.

3. Holding each strawberry by its stalk, or on a fork, dip into the chocolate. Allow excess chocolate to drip off, then gently place on the parchment.

4. When all the strawberries have been dipped, chill for about 30 minutes or until the chocolate hardens.

5. One serving equals 1 strawberry. Keep leftovers in the fridge for up to 1 day.

Note: Make chocolate-dipped banana slices or dried apricots in the same way.

Biscuits and cookies

In *ChangeOne* there's no need to give up biscuits and cookies. You can enjoy them without worry if you remember portion control and have just one or two – as long as they're small. Here are some of our favourites. For each, one serving equals a *ChangeOne* snack or sweet portion.

CHOCOLATE CHIP AND OAT COOKIES

Makes 36

140 g (5 oz) plain flour
1/2 teaspoon bicarbonate of soda
1/2 teaspoon salt
80 g (2³/4 oz) rolled oats
50 g (1³/4 oz) butter
150 g (5¹/2 oz) soft light brown sugar
100 g (3¹/2 oz) caster sugar
1 egg
1¹/2 teaspoons pure vanilla extract
5 tablespoons reduced-fat crème fraîche
125 g (4¹/2 oz) chocolate chips

1. Preheat the oven to 190ºC (375ºF, gas mark 5). Line two large baking sheets with baking parchment. Sift the flour, bicarbonate of soda and salt into a medium bowl. Stir in the oats.

2. Cream the butter with the brown and caster sugars in a large bowl using an electric mixer. Add the egg and vanilla extract and beat for about 3 minutes or until light and creamy. Blend in the crème fraîche with a wooden spoon, then add the flour mixture all at once and stir until combined (don't overmix or the cookies may be tough). Stir in the chocolate chips.

3. Drop heaping teaspoonfuls of the mixture 5 cm (2 in) apart on the baking sheets. Bake for about 10 minutes or until the cookies are golden. Cool on the baking sheets for 2 minutes, then transfer to wire racks to cool completely.

4. Store the cookies in an airtight container for up to 2 weeks or in the freezer for up to 3 months.

TIPS FOR USING HIGHER-CALORIE INGREDIENTS

- Ingredients like chocolate, nuts and butter make biscuits and cookies all the more delicious.
- Use mini chocolate chips (or chop up chocolate quite finely), as small pieces will spread throughout the mixture.
- A little goes a long way when you add sliced or finely chopped nuts. To bring out their flavour, toast them first in a frying pan, or in the microwave for 1 to 2 minutes.
- Just a little butter – 15 to 25 g (½ to 1 oz) – will add rich flavour without too many extra calories in each biscuit or cookie.

CRISP PECAN BISCUITS

Makes 72
250 g (8½ oz) plain flour
½ teaspoon ground cinnamon
¼ teaspoon salt
¼ teaspoon bicarbonate of soda
50 g (1¾ oz) butter, softened
140 g (5 oz) caster sugar
75 g (2½ oz) soft light brown sugar
1 egg
1 tablespoon pure vanilla extract
5 tablespoons reduced-fat crème fraîche
40 g (1¼ oz) pecan nuts, chopped and toasted

1. Sift the flour, cinnamon, bicarbonate of soda and salt into a medium bowl. Cream the butter with the caster and brown sugars in a large bowl using an electric mixer until light and fluffy. Add the egg and vanilla extract and beat until well blended. Using a wooden spoon, stir in the flour mixture, then the crème fraîche and pecans.

2. Spread a large sheet of cling film on the work surface and sprinkle lightly with flour. Turn the dough onto the film and shape into a 38 cm (15 in) log. Wrap in the cling film and chill for 2 hours or until firm.

3. Preheat the oven to 190°C (375°F, gas mark 5). Cut the log across into rounds 5 mm (¼ in) thick. Working in batches, place 1 cm (½ in) apart on ungreased baking sheets and bake for 8 minutes or just until crisp and golden brown around the edges. Transfer to wire racks to cool completely.

4. One serving is 2 biscuits. Store in an airtight container for up to 2 weeks or freeze for up to 3 months.

COCOA WALNUT MERINGUES

Makes 36
40 g (1¼ oz) walnut halves
4 teaspoons cocoa powder
¼ teaspoon ground cinnamon
60 g (2¼ oz) plus 2 tablespoons icing sugar
2 egg whites
Pinch of salt

1. Preheat the oven to 150°C (300°F, gas mark 2). Line 2 baking sheets with baking parchment. Toast the walnuts in a small frying pan, stirring frequently, until crisp and fragrant. When cool enough to handle, chop them coarsely.

2. Sift together the cocoa powder, cinnamon and all but 2 tablespoons of the icing sugar onto a sheet of greaseproof paper.

3. Whisk the egg whites with the salt in a large bowl until stiff peaks form. With a rubber spatula, gently fold in the cocoa mixture and then the walnuts.

4. Drop by generous teaspoonfuls onto the baking sheets, spacing the meringues 2.5 cm (1 in) apart. Bake for about 20 minutes or until set. Remove and cool on a wire rack. Dust with the reserved icing sugar just before serving.

5. One serving is 4 or 5 meringues. Store at room temperature in an airtight container.

Snacks

As you know, smart snacking helps to hold off between-meal hunger. Here are a few more make-it-yourself snacks to try in addition to the snacks in Week 3. All but the roasted pepper pinwheels will keep well in an airtight container, so you can have them on hand to enjoy each day. Each serving provides about 100 kcals.

CURRY-SPICED FRUITS, NUTS AND SEEDS

Makes 32 servings
1 tablespoon curry powder
2 teaspoons finely chopped fresh ginger
1 large egg white
25 g (1 oz) fine or medium oatmeal
150 g (5½ oz) blanched almonds
150 g (5½ oz) pecan nut halves
150 g (5½ oz) brazil nuts
55 g (2 oz) pumpkin seeds
55 g (2 oz) sunflower seeds
75 g (2½ oz) sultanas
75 g (2½ oz) dried cranberries

1. Preheat the oven to 130°C (250°F, gas mark ½). Mix together the curry powder, ginger, egg white and oatmeal in a large bowl. Add all the nuts and seeds, and toss well to coat.

2. Transfer to a baking tin, spreading out evenly. Bake for about 1 hour, stirring occasionally, until lightly browned and crisp. Leave to cool in the tin.

3. Tip the nuts and seeds into a bowl. Add the sultanas and cranberries and mix well.

4. One serving is 25 g (1 oz). Store in an airtight tin for up to 2 weeks.

ROASTED PEPPER PINWHEELS

Makes 8 pieces
1 red pepper, cut lengthways into flat panels (about 4, depending on shape of pepper)
55 g (2 oz) canned chickpeas, rinsed and drained
1 tablespoon plain fat-free yogurt
½ teaspoon toasted sesame oil
½ teaspoon grated lemon zest
2 teaspoons lemon juice
2 teaspoons water
Pinch of salt
1 flour tortilla (20 cm/8 in diameter), plain or flavoured
100 g (3½ oz) mixed salad greens

1. Preheat the grill. Grill the pepper pieces, skin side up, until charred. Transfer to a plate. When cool enough to handle, peel and cut into 1 cm (½ in) wide strips.

2. Combine the chickpeas, yogurt, sesame oil, lemon zest and juice, water and salt in a food processor and blend until smooth.

3. Spread the mixture evenly over one side of the tortilla, leaving a 1 cm (½ in) border clear all round. Top with the salad greens and roasted peppers. Roll up the tortilla like a Swiss roll.

4. Wrap tightly in foil or cling film and chill for at least 1 hour, but no more than 4 hours. The roll will get softer and easier to slice as it sits in the refrigerator; if left longer than 4 hours it will become soggy. To serve, unwrap and cut across into 8 pieces (each 2.5 cm/1 in wide).

5. One serving equals 2 pieces. The pinwheels do not keep well and should be eaten the day they are made.

SESAME PITTA CRISPS

Makes 36 pitta crisps
6 pitta breads
2 tablespoons olive oil
2 tablespoons sesame seeds

1. Preheat the grill to high. Spread out the pitta breads on a baking tray. Using 1 tablespoon of the olive oil, brush the top side of each pitta with oil. Sprinkle over half of the sesame seeds.

2. Grill for 1 minute or until the bread and the seeds are golden brown.

3. Turn the pittas over and brush with the remaining olive oil. Sprinkle over the rest of the sesame seeds. Grill for 1 minute or until bread and seeds are golden brown.

4. Using scissors, quickly cut the hot pitta breads across into 6 fingers. Leave to cool and become crisp.

5. One serving equals 3 pitta crisps. Store in an airtight tin for 1 to 2 days.

PARMESAN TWISTS

Makes 40 twists
85 g (3 oz) plain wholemeal flour
85 g (3 oz) plain white flour
¼ teaspoon salt
45 g (1½ oz) butter
45 g (1½ oz) Parmesan cheese, grated
1 large egg
2 tablespoons semi-skimmed milk
1 teaspoon paprika
1 tablespoon poppy seeds

1. Preheat the oven to 180°C (350°F, gas mark 4). Sift the flours and salt into a bowl, and add the bran from the sieve. Rub in the butter, then stir in the Parmesan.

2. Whisk the egg and milk together. Reserve 1 teaspoon of the mixture and stir the rest into the flour mixture to make a firm dough. Knead briefly until smooth.

3. Sprinkle the paprika over a floured surface, then roll out the dough to a square just larger than 20 cm (8 in) on all sides. Brush with the reserved egg mixture and sprinkle over the poppy seeds.

4. Cut the square of dough in half, then cut into 10 cm (4 in) sticks that are about 1 cm (½ in) wide. Twist the sticks and place on a baking sheet lined with baking parchment.

5. Bake for 15 minutes or until lightly browned and crisp. Cool on the baking sheets for a few minutes, then transfer to a wire rack to cool completely.

6. One serving equals 3 twists. Store in an airtight tin for up to 5 days.

TORTILLA CHIPS

Serves 8
8 corn tortillas, about 300 g (10½ oz)
4 teaspoons corn oil
Seasoning (eg ground cumin, or salt and freshly ground black pepper)

1. Preheat the oven to 170°C (325°F, gas mark 3). Brush each tortilla with ½ teaspoon oil and sprinkle with seasoning.

2. Using kitchen scissors, cut each tortilla into wedges. Spread out on a large baking sheet.

3. Bake for 15 minutes or until crisp and firm. Transfer to a wire rack to cool. One serving equals chips from 1 tortilla.

4. Store in an airtight tin for 1 to 2 days.

Fruit desserts

What could be more refreshing than a fruit-based dessert? Fruit adds colour and flavour to so many sweet dishes, together with weight-controlling fibre, vitamins and a whole host of other beneficial nutrients. Your family and friends will never know that you've lightened up the sweet course with these 100-kcal portions.

MELON SALAD WITH RASPBERRY VINAIGRETTE

Serves 4

- **1 tablespoon hulled pumpkin seeds**
- **4 tablespoons no-sugar seedless raspberry spread**
- **1 tablespoon balsamic vinegar**
- **2 teaspoons lemon juice**
- **¼ teaspoon ground cinnamon**
- **1 large cantaloupe or other orange-fleshed melon, cut into 8 wedges**
- **145 g (5¼ oz) blueberries**

1. Toast the pumpkin seeds in a small, heavy frying pan over medium heat for about 5 minutes or until they begin to pop. Set aside to cool.

2. Whisk together the raspberry spread, vinegar, lemon juice and cinnamon in a large bowl. Add the melon and blueberries and toss to combine. Sprinkle with the seeds.

3. One serving equals 2 cantaloupe wedges, a golf ball-size serving of blueberries, and 1 teaspoon (thumb tip) of pumpkin seeds.

ABOUT MELON

Melons – cantaloupe, Charentais, ogen, honeydew and watermelon – are among the lowest-calorie fruits because they have a high water content and less sugar than other fruits. Orange-fleshed melon is rich in vitamins C and A, two important nutrients that you get mainly from fruits and vegetables. A serving of melon cubes about the size of a fist contains between 45 and 60 kcals.

BLUEBERRY MOUSSE

Serves 4

125 ml (4 fl oz) semi-skimmed milk
2 tablespoons dried skimmed milk
425 g (15 oz) blueberries
**50 g (1¾ oz) plus 1 teaspoon caster
  sugar**
Pinch of salt
115 g (4 oz) plain fat-free yogurt
1½ teaspoons powdered gelatine
2 tablespoons cold water

1. Combine the milk and dried milk in a
small bowl and whisk until well blended.
Place in the freezer for up to 30 minutes.

2. Reserve 75 g (2½ oz) of the blueberries,
and combine the rest with the 50 g (1¾ oz)
sugar and the salt in a medium saucepan
over low heat. Bring to a simmer, stirring
to dissolve the sugar, then cook for 10
minutes or until the berries have broken
up and the mixture has reduced to about
250 ml (8 fl oz). Cool to room temperature,
then stir in three-quarters of the yogurt.

3. Sprinkle the gelatine over the cold water
in a heatproof measuring jug. Soften for
5 minutes, then set in a saucepan of
simmering water for 2 minutes or until the
gelatine has dissolved completely. Cool.

4. Whisk the chilled milk until thick and
soft peaks form. Whisk in the remaining
teaspoon sugar and the gelatine mixture.
Fold into the blueberry mixture.

5. Spoon into 4 dessert bowls or glasses.
Chill for 2 hours or until set. Just before
serving, top with the remaining yogurt and
the reserved blueberries.

ABOUT FAT-FREE AND REDUCED-FAT DAIRY PRODUCTS

Fat-free and reduced-fat dairy products
can be used to make creamy desserts
with far fewer calories than recipes
with cream. In this recipe, a mixture of
semi-skimmed milk and dried skimmed
milk is chilled, then whisked to a fluffy
consistency. The gelatine helps to keep
the whisked milk firm. A measure of
250 ml (8 fl oz) of the whisked milk
mixture supplies around 58 kcals; the
same quantity of whipped cream has
over 400! You can also use fromage frais
in the same way as the milk mixture.

TIPS FOR USING GELATINE

- Gelatine helps to 'set' desserts made
  with lower-fat dairy products instead
  of whipped or double cream.
- Use only the amount called for in the
  recipe. More is not better – you'd end
  up with a rubbery texture.
- When warming softened gelatine stir
  well until all the granules dissolve.
  Undissolved gelatine will give a
  dessert a grainy texture.
- Refrigerate desserts made with
  gelatine, but do not freeze: freezing
  will cause them to separate.

ABOUT BERRIES

You can make this dessert with your
favourite berries, whether they're
blueberries, strawberries, raspberries,
blackberries or a combination. All have
healthful qualities. Blueberries supply the
most antioxidants – naturally occurring
plant compounds that help to protect the
body's cells from damage, guarding
against cancer and keeping blood vessels
sound. Strawberries are lowest in calories
and richest in vitamin C. Raspberries and
blackberries supply the most fibre.

FRUIT BOATS WITH ORANGE AND BALSAMIC GLAZE

Serves 4

4 tablespoons balsamic vinegar
¼ teaspoon grated orange zest
2 tablespoons orange juice
2 teaspoons soft light brown sugar
1 large cantaloupe or other melon
350 g (12½ oz) strawberries, hulled
and quartered
150 g (5½ oz) blueberries
150 g (5½ oz) raspberries
2 kiwi fruits, peeled, halved, and cut
into thin wedges

1. To make the glaze, combine the vinegar, orange zest and juice, and brown sugar in a microwave-proof dish. Microwave on high for 2 to 3 minutes or until syrupy. Or cook over medium-high heat in a small saucepan, for 4 to 5 minutes. Set aside.

2. Cut the melon into quarters, discard seeds and scoop out balls of flesh, leaving a thin layer of flesh on the rind that you'll use as boats. Put the melon balls, strawberries, blueberries, raspberries and kiwi fruit in a large bowl.

3. Drizzle over the glaze. Toss to coat the fruit evenly. Spoon into the 4 melon boats and serve immediately.

FRUIT AND HEALTH

Fruits (and vegetables) are extremely important to good health and well-being. This is reflected in the '5-a-Day' recommendation – to eat at least five servings of fruits and vegetables every day (a total of about 400 g/14 oz edible part). Fruits and vegetables offer a unique package of plant compounds, called phytochemicals, that are linked to lower risks of heart disease, high blood pressure, stroke, certain cancers and other long-term ailments. The evidence so far is that you get these benefits mainly from eating real fruits and vegetables, and much less so from taking vitamin and mineral supplements.

Meal Plans and Shopping Guide

It's a vicious circle: if you don't know what you are going to be cooking in the week ahead, you can't shop for food effectively. And if you are not shopping effectively, it becomes very difficult to cook and eat well. As we've said a few times, eating well takes a little planning.

We're here to help. This section includes detailed weekly meal plans, plus strategies to buy and stock food.

Following a rigid eating plan may seem unappealing, but give it a look. At worst you'll get a quick overview of the *ChangeOne* programme. And you may even stumble on a day or week that's worth a try.

Each day's meal plan falls into or near our 1300-calorie target. For those in the 1600 Club, remember as you look at these plans that you can double your starch or grain at breakfast; and you can double your protein at lunch or dinner, *or* add an extra serving of starch or grain at dinner.

And don't forget to check out the shopping strategies that follow the meal plans. You'll find tips and advice that will improve even the best-organised kitchen.

Week 1	Monday	Tuesday	Wednesday	
Breakfast	**Yogurt parfait** (page 257) • Yogurt layered with crunchy cereal, fruit and coconut	**Bagel delight** (page 29) • Half bagel topped with cream cheese and jam • Yogurt with sliced ripe peach	**Breakfast on the go** (page 30) • Cereal bar • Yogurt topped with blueberries	
Lunch	**Chef's salad** (page 44) • Green salad topped with sliced turkey breast, ham and cheese • Crusty wholegrain roll • Diced melon	**Soup and sandwich** (page 260) • Hearty split pea soup • Bavarian sandwich • Seasonal fruit	**EATING OUT** **Friendly fast food** (page 50) • Hamburger with lettuce, tomato and condiments • Tossed green salad	
Snack	Baked tortilla chips dipped in salsa	Cocoa made with skimmed milk	Baked apple (page 72)	
Supper	**Fish from the grill** (page 278) • Soy-basted halibut steaks, accompanied by grilled mixed onions • Ziti and courgettes	**Beef stew supper** (page 92) • Beef stew • Egg noodles	**Chinese-style pork supper** (page 276) • Sweet-and-sour glazed pork with pineapple • Fluffy white basmati rice • Steamed patty pan squash	
Snack/ Dessert	Blueberry mousse (page 291)	Fruit juice lolly	Yogurt smoothie	

Thursday	Friday	Saturday	Sunday
A perfect bowl of cereal (page 32) • Bran flakes topped with raisins and chopped nuts • Skimmed or semi-skimmed milk	**Cottage cheese melba** (page 258) • Cottage cheese with fresh peaches • Raisin toast • Vanilla steamer	**Pancakes with berries** (page 24) • Vanilla pancakes topped with maple syrup and sliced strawberries • Skimmed or semi-skimmed milk	**Streusel cake** (page 227) Skimmed or semi-skimmed milk # Brunch Hummus and pitta Crudités platter (raw vegetables)
Pitta pizza (page 39) • Pitta bread topped with tomato sauce, cheese and grilled vegetables • Green salad • Apple	**Soup and salad** (page 40) • Vegetable soup with breadsticks • Green salad topped with chicken • Green or red grapes	**Deli sandwich** (page 52) • Turkey and Gruyère cheese sandwich • Shredded vegetables • Melon salad	**The Sunday omelette** (page 130) • Vegetable cheese omelette • Chunky oven chips • Melon wedge Orange juice (juice glass)
Frozen yogurt	Oatcake with low-fat cottage cheese	Pot of plain yogurt topped with fruit	
EATING OUT **Italian** (page 112) • Melon with Parma ham • Pasta arrabiata with Parmesan cheese • Mixed salad • Fresh figs	**Storecupboard supper** (page 156) • Chickpea and pasta stew • Garlic bread	**EATING OUT** **Chinese** (page 114) • Hot and sour soup • Prawns stir fried with ginger and spring onions • Plain boiled rice • Fresh pineapple	**Hearty meat loaf supper** (page 274) • Homestyle meat loaf • Parsleyed egg noodles • Steamed baby courgettes
Brownie bites (page 285)	Skimmed or semi-skimmed latte	Microwave popcorn	

Week 2	Monday	Tuesday	Wednesday	
Breakfast	**Smoothie breakfast** (page 254) • Tropical smoothie • Toasted English muffin half, with peanut butter	**A perfect bowl of cereal** (page 32) • Bran flakes topped with raisins and chopped nuts • Skimmed or semi-skimmed milk	**Egg on a roll** (page 23) • Scrambled egg on a wholemeal roll • Fresh fruit salad • Skimmed or semi-skimmed milk	
Lunch	**Tuna salad sandwich** (page 224) • Tuna salad sandwich • Carrot and celery sticks • Banana	**Turkey Caesar lunch** (page 262) • Grilled turkey Caesar salad • Fresh fruit salad	**Well-dressed baked potato** (page 259) • Baked potato stuffed with broccoli and cheese • Mixed green salad • Seasonal berries	
Snack		Chocolate chip and oat cookies (page 286) with skimmed or semi-skimmed milk	Frozen yogurt	
Supper	**Chicken sauté supper** (page 268) • Chicken and caramelised onion sauté • Spinach fettuccine • Tossed salad	**Braised beef supper** (page 272) • Wine-braised beef with vegetables • Steamed broccoli • Crusty bread	**Pasta primavera supper** (page 98) • Pasta primavera • Italian salad	
Snack/ Dessert	Fruit boats with orange and balsamic glaze (page 292)	Apple	Pineapple chunks	

Thursday	Friday	Saturday	Sunday
Café-style breakfast (page 252) • Glazed blueberry muffin • Melon wedge • Coffee and hot milk	**Breakfast on the go** (page 30) • Cereal bar • Yogurt topped with blueberries	**Yogurt parfait** (page 257) • Yogurt layered with crunchy cereal, fruit and coconut	**Pancakes with berries** (page 24) • Vanilla pancakes topped with maple syrup and sliced strawberries • Skimmed or semi-skimmed milk
Russian salad (page 267) • Fresh Russian salad • Wholemeal pitta • Grapes	**Deli sandwich** (page 52) • Turkey and Gruyère cheese sandwich • Shredded vegetables • Melon salad	**Tex-Mex wrap** (page 55) • Flour tortilla wrapped round chicken, beans and condiments • Orange	**Wrap it up** (page 266) • Roasted vegetable wraps with chive sauce • Green salad • Honeydew melon
Peanut butter on a rice cake	Strawberry smoothie	Rich tea biscuits with skimmed or semi-skimmed milk	Pretzel sticks and reduced-fat Cheddar cheese
EATING OUT **Family restaurant** (page 120) • Tomato soup • Grilled chicken with potato wedges and tomato salsa • Large mixed salad with low-fat dressing • Ice cream with strawberries	**Chicken pie supper** (page 280) • Little chicken and sweetcorn pies • Green salad	**Weekend grilling** (page 138) • Crudités platter • Spicy chicken • Grilled summer vegetables • Warm potato salad with Dijon vinaigrette • Sesame breadsticks	**Steak barbecue supper** (page 270) • Barbecued steak rolls • Colourful coleslaw • Tomatoes and salad greens
Almond-flavoured milk	Brownie bites (page 285)	Chocolate snacking cake (page 284)	Blueberry mousse (page 291)

Week 3	Monday	Tuesday	Wednesday	
Breakfast	**Fruit bread delight** (page 256) • 1 slice peach and yogurt loaf • Fresh raspberries • Skimmed milk or low-fat yogurt	**Café-style breakfast** (page 252) • Glazed blueberry muffin • Melon wedge • Coffee and hot milk	**Yogurt parfait** (page 257) • Yogurt layered with crunchy cereal, fruit and coconut	
Lunch	**Soup and sandwich** (page 260) • Hearty split pea soup • Bavarian sandwich • Seasonal fruit	**Chilli with cheese and tortilla** (page 264) • Vegetable chilli • Corn tortilla • Green salad • Banana	**EATING OUT** **Friendly fast food** (page 50) • Hamburger with lettuce, tomato, and condiments • Tossed green salad	
Snack	Rice cake with peanut butter	Digestive biscuit and hot cocoa made with skimmed milk	Breadsticks with tomato salsa	
Supper	**Fish parcels with Spanish rice** (page 100) • Sea bass and sugarsnaps • Spanish rice	**EATING OUT** **Indian** (page 118) • 1 vegetable samosa plus salad • Tandoori king prawns • Lentil dhal • Fresh fruit salad	**Italian style stir-fry** (page 90) • Chicken and broccoli stir-fry • Orzo or basmati rice	
Snack/ Dessert	Brownie bites (page 285)		Frozen yogurt	

Thursday	Friday	Saturday	Sunday
Breakfast on the go (page 30) • Cereal bar • Yogurt topped with blueberries	**Bagel delight** (page 29) • Half bagel topped with cream cheese and jam • Yogurt with sliced ripe peach	**Hearty frittata** (page 255) • Vegetable frittata • 1 slice wholemeal toast • Fresh blueberries	**Pancakes with berries** (page 24) • Vanilla pancakes topped with maple syrup and sliced strawberries • Skimmed or semi-skimmed milk
Pitta pizza (page 39) • Pitta bread topped with tomato sauce, cheese and grilled vegetables • Green salad • Apple	**Deli sandwich** (page 52) • Turkey and Gruyère cheese sandwich • Shredded vegetables • Melon salad	**Soup and salad** (page 40) • Vegetable soup with breadsticks • Green salad topped with chicken • Green or red grapes	**Fishcake brunch** (page 132) • Crab cakes • Tossed salad • Crusty bread roll • Seasonal berries • Crisp pecan biscuits (page 287)
Mixed dried fruit	Curry-spiced fruits, nuts and seeds (page 288)	Pot of fat-free yogurt	Mixed nuts
Chicken, beans and rice (page 159) • Quick beans and rice • Grilled chicken fillet • Green salad	**Thai noodle salad** (page 102) • Thai noodle salad	**Tuna bake supper** (page 162) • Tuna noodle bake • Rocket salad	**EATING OUT** **Italian** (page 112) • Tomato bruschetta • Small portion of spaghetti with seafood • Granita
Frozen yogurt	Fresh fruit	Chocolate chip and oat cookies (page 286)	Fresh fruit salad

Week 4	Monday	Tuesday	Wednesday	
Breakfast	**Egg on a roll** (page 23) • Scrambled egg on a wholemeal roll • Fresh fruit salad • Skimmed or semi-skimmed milk	**Smoothie breakfast** (page 254) • Tropical smoothie • Toasted English muffin half, with peanut butter	**A perfect bowl of cereal** (page 32) • Bran flakes topped with raisins and chopped nuts • Skimmed or semi-skimmed milk	
Lunch	**Turkey Caesar lunch** (page 262) • Grilled turkey Caesar salad • Fresh fruit salad	**Tex-Mex wrap** (page 55) • Flour tortilla wrapped round chicken, beans and condiments • Orange	**Chef's salad** (page 44) • Green salad topped with sliced turkey breast, ham and cheese • Crusty wholegrain roll • Diced melon	
Snack	Cocoa made with skimmed milk	Mixed nuts	Crisp pecan biscuits (page 287)	
Supper	**Italian style stir-fry** (page 90) • Chicken and broccoli stir-fry • Orzo or basmati rice	**Pasta primavera supper** (page 98) • Pasta primavera • Italian salad	**EATING OUT** **Bistro and pub** (page 116) • Moules marinères • Smoked haddock fish cakes • Large mixed salad • Summer pudding or fresh berries	
Snack/ Dessert	Fruit boats with orange and balsamic glaze (page 292)	Fresh fruit salad		

Thursday	Friday	Saturday	Sunday
Breakfast on the go (page 30) • Cereal bar • Yogurt topped with blueberries	**Yogurt parfait** (page 257) • Yogurt layered with crunchy cereal, fruit and coconut	**Cottage cheese melba** (page 258) • Cottage cheese with fresh peaches • Raisin toast • Vanilla steamer	**Bagel delight** (page 29) • Half bagel topped with cream cheese and jam • Yogurt with sliced ripe peach
Pitta pizza (page 39) • Pitta bread topped with tomato sauce, cheese and grilled vegetables • Green salad • Apple	**Well-dressed baked potato** (page 259) • Baked potato stuffed with broccoli and cheese • Mixed green salad • Seasonal berries	**Wrap it up** (page 266) • Roasted vegetable wraps with chive sauce • Green salad • Honeydew melon	**Soup and salad** (page 40) • Vegetable soup with breadsticks • Green salad topped with chicken • Green or red grapes
Mixed dried fruit	Tortilla chips (page 284)	Crudités	Sesame pitta crisps (page 284)
Chicken sauté supper (page 268) • Chicken and caramelised onion sauté • Spinach fettuccine • Tossed salad	**Prawn kebab feast** (page 88) • Prawn and pepper kebabs • Sesame broccoli • Wild and white rice	**Fish from the grill** (page 278) • Soy-basted halibut steaks, accompanied by grilled mixed onions • Ziti and courgettes	**Steak barbecue supper** (page 270) • Barbecued steak roll • Coleslaw • Tomatoes and salad greens
Frozen yogurt	Sorbet	Blueberry mousse (page 291)	Fruit juice lolly

Shopping strategies

Putting *ChangeOne* into action at the supermarket is easy with our guide to sensible shopping lists that will ensure you're never without the essentials.

Chances are, you already have many of the ingredients for the sample meals in our four-week plan. It is surprisingly easy to cook with flavour and richness when you have a good collection of condiments, herbs and spices, stocks, canned beans and baking supplies close by. They're part of the basic provisions – the storecupboard, refrigerator and freezer items to keep always on hand – that you'll see in the comprehensive list on the next two pages.

ChangeOne meals also call for lots of perishable foods such as fruits, vegetables, meats and dairy products. That's where a good checklist comes in handy. For your convenience, we've designed a *ChangeOne* shopping plan that takes care of these foods in two categories: long-life and short-life.

Supermarkets stock their produce separately from dairy, meats and seafood, so that's the way for you to set up efficient checklists for your *ChangeOne* shopping plan.

Long-life items such as apples, onions and other foodstuffs you can store in a cool larder or in the refrigerator – they keep for a while and are good to have to hand all the time.

Fruits and vegetables
- Apples
- Kiwi fruit
- Lemons and limes
- Melons (uncut)
- Oranges
- Cabbage
- Carrots
- Celery
- Garlic
- Onions and spring onions
- Potatoes
- Pumpkin and other squash

Dairy products, meat and seafood
- Butter
- Cheeses, hard and dry (eg Parmesan)
- Yogurt
- Beef (in the freezer)
- Chicken joints (in the freezer)
- Salami, hard Italian
- Salmon (in the freezer)

Short-life items such as lettuce, milk and uncooked meats – they keep only a few days in the refrigerator and are best bought and used for a specific recipe.

Fruits and vegetables
- Berries in season
- Grapes
- Mangoes
- Peaches
- Courgettes
- Cucumbers
- Lettuce and salad greens
- Peppers, red and green
- Tomatoes

Dairy products, meat and seafood
- Cheeses, medium (eg Cheddar, mozzarella)
- Cheeses, soft (eg ricotta, cottage)
- Milk
- Cooked deli meats
- Meats and seafood, uncooked

The *ChangeOne* shopping plan

Monthly. Around the same time every month, check and replenish your kitchen staples.

Twice monthly. Replenish long-life fruits and vegetables, dairy products, meat and seafood as needed.

Weekly to twice weekly. Pick up short-life items for that week's meals.

A few general tips can simplify your shopping even more:

- Plan a whole week's recipes and write your shopping list. Then check your storecupboard and refrigerator for items you will need that week.
- You're the best judge of how much of each item you'll need, based on the number of people you're cooking for and the substitutions you make for individual ingredients or entire meals.
- You can substitute just about any fruit or vegetable for another, so feel free to buy the ones you like or are in season, and be creative with the meals.

If you find you're not going to use fresh meat, poultry or fish within a day of buying it, you should freeze it.

Sample shopping list

Based on our approach, your shopping list for Week 2 of the meal plans might look like this:

QTY	PRODUCE
	Bananas
	Blueberries
	Fresh fruit salad
	Mango
	Raspberries
	Strawberries
	Broccoli
	Fresh coriander
	Aubergine
	Fennel
	Fresh herbs, assorted
	Guacamole
	Lettuce
	Red, green and yellow peppers
	Tomatoes
	Courgettes
	Cucumber

QTY	DAIRY, MEAT AND BREAD
	Buttermilk
	Cheese, cheddar
	Cheese, ricotta
	Milk, skimmed or semi-skimmed
	Crème fraîche, reduced-fat
	Lean cooked ham
	Prawns
	Sirloin or rump steak
	Turkey breast fillet, skinless
	Rolls, wholemeal
	Pitta breads

Kitchen essentials

Well-chosen kitchen tools can be a slimmer's friend. Here are some top choices.

1. Good sharp knives Any professional chef will tell you that good knives are essential. A sharp knife takes the drudgery out of chopping and dicing. If yours won't cut butter, it's time to sharpen them up or invest in a new set.

2. Measuring jug and spoons Essential tools to prevent 'portion creep'.

3. Kitchen scales Another vital way to keep portions in check, as well as to weigh ingredients for recipes.

4. Non-stick frying pan With a good heavy frying pan, you can use less oil or butter for cooking.

5. Heavy griddle pan Also ideal for cooking succlent meat and fish with a minimum of added fat.

6. Salad spinner A must-have for salad lovers. A spinner makes it easy to dry salad leaves without bruising them.

7. Vegetable peeler A good sharp peeler that's easy to hold makes a dull task much faster and easier. Choose a peeler that feels good in your hand.

8. Kitchen scissors Removing chicken skin, trimming bacon rashers – these come in handy so often.

9. Vegetable steamer Use a collapsable metal steamer rack that fits into a saucepan or a special steamer pan. Make sure you have one big enough for a variety of vegetables.

10. Individual serving-size storage containers With small containers and freezer bags, you can store leftovers or divide jumbo packets into smaller portions in advance.

Clockwise from top right: vegetable steamer, wok, and ridged cast-iron grill or griddle pan.

11. Blender You can whip up yogurt and fruit smoothies, fruit ices and all kinds of savoury sauces. Blenders are also great for home-made soups. A hand-held blender saves on washing-up.

12. Wok If you love stir-fries, this is the pan to have. By distributing heat evenly over the cooking surfaces, woks allow you to cook very fast. A non-stick wok will need less oil.

13. Timer Accurate timers with loud alarms give you a break from the kitchen and prevent disasters.

14. Cheese grater Hard cheeses like Parmesan and pecorino have lots of

flavour so a little can go a long way. Grate them finely or shave into fine curls. Use the grater for lemon zest too.

15. Microwave If you're in a hurry to reheat leftovers, or thaw something from the freezer, a microwave is a real boon.

16. Bulletin board, or wipe-clean notice board This is a great way to keep track of what you're running low on, so you won't be caught short when preparing a meal or looking for a quick healthy snack.

Tips for storing food

In our *ChangeOne* recipes, we often suggest you dish out that meal's servings, and then immediately package and refrigerate the leftovers. That will prevent you from serving unnecessary second helpings, and guarantees you'll have meals in correct portions available at any time.

The trick of smart storage is to get food sealed quickly and thoroughly to minimise bacteria, and then to refrigerate the food quickly to prevent any bacteria from multiplying. Here are more storage tips, along with safe refrigeration times for everyday foods:

- Ensure containers have tight seals. The less air that circulates around the food, the less chance of bacterial growth.
- Use a shallow container for hot leftovers so they will cool more rapidly. Don't worry about putting warm containers in the refrigerator: rapid cooling doesn't affect the food. The only issue is that the container will warm the refrigerator very slightly.
- If you're not going to eat leftovers in the time specified in this table, freeze them. With freezing, you get zero bacteria growth, but also risk 'freezer burn', which occurs when the moisture in the food gets drawn out by the dry environment. To minimise this, put the sealed container in another sealed container (freezer bags are good).

Food	Use within...
Yogurt, cottage cheese	7 days
Hard cheeses	6–12 weeks unopened; 1 week opened
Cheese spreads	3–4 weeks
Eggs, in shell	3 weeks
Eggs, hard-boiled	1 week
Beef or pork joints, steaks, chops, uncooked	3–5 days
Beef or pork joints, steaks, chops, cooked	3–4 days
Minced beef, uncooked	1–2 days
Stewing meat, uncooked	1–2 days
Poultry, uncooked	1–2 days
Poultry, cooked	3–4 days
Sausages, uncooked	1–2 days
Ham slices, cooked	3–4 days
Deli meats	3–5 days
Fresh fish, uncooked	1–2 days
Prawns, scallops, crab meat	2–3 days
Deli salads	3–5 days

And remember:
Many foods are stamped with a suggested sell-by date; but that isn't necessarily the last day you can safely eat them. Once opened, refrigerated food may spoil before the date on the package, so use caution.

Personal Tools

Throughout *ChangeOne*, we've asked you to write things down. How's the weight-loss progressing? What are your current goals? What did you eat today? What activities did you do?

But the truth is, few of us are in the habit of writing down such things. So we've tried to make it easier for you.

On the following pages are all the guides you need to progress through *ChangeOne*.

Each of these forms was conceived to be as simple to use as possible. They ask the tough questions, but in easily answerable ways. So give them a try. They take just a few minutes. You are free to make as many photocopies of each form as you need to track your progress.

Here's what you'll find:

- The *ChangeOne* Contract
- Hunger profile
- Daily food diary
- Daily activity log
- Personal time analyser
- Progress log
- Your healthy weight calculator

Change One Contract

ChangeOne start date: _____

I VOW TO MYSELF that over the next three months I will learn and practise the eating habits necessary to lose weight and improve my health. I put forth the following goals:

Intermediate weight target: _____

Ultimate weight target: _____

HOW I EXPECT MY LIFE TO IMPROVE: _____

_____

_____

_____

HOW I EXPECT MY HEALTH TO IMPROVE: _____

_____

_____

_____

IN ADDITION to weekly weigh-ins on the scales, I will track my progress by the two methods I will list below (for example, clothing size, appearance, energy, notches in a belt, or self-confidence):

1. _____

2. _____

I HEREBY AFFIRM that the goals I have set meet the TRIM test. Each one is Time-bound, Realistic, Inspiring and Measurable.

I agree to review my progress and re-evaluate my strategies for reaching my goals every two weeks during the programme.

I agree to keep this contract as a reminder of my commitment.

Signed: _____

Witnessed by (optional): _____

Date:

Hunger profile

Instructions: Make a copy of this form and carry it with you during the day. Every time you get hungry, record the time, how you felt (tired, bored, ravenous, stressed-out, just plain hungry), what you ate or what you did instead of eating (took a walk, distracted yourself with work). This will help you to determine your eating habits – both good and bad – and make it easier to adjust your meal and snack times for healthy weight loss.

	TIME	HOW I FELT	WHAT I ATE	WHAT I DID
MORNING				
AFTERNOON				
EVENING				

Date: _____

Daily food diary

Instructions: First, write down what you eat. Next, estimate portions as carefully as you can, based on what you've learned throughout *ChangeOne*. For example, if one egg is the recommended portion at breakfast, and you eat two, then write in 'two portions'. Keep a copy of the form with you and fill it in as soon after a snack or meal as you can.

Adding up calories is optional. We don't recommend that *ChangeOne* participants worry about calories – managing portion sizes will take care of that. But if you really want to see how you are doing, here's how to find calorie information:

- For *ChangeOne* meals, use calorie counts that we provide;
- For *ChangeOne* snacks and desserts, estimate 100 kcals per portion;
- For other snacks and prepared foods, use their nutrition labels.

	WHAT I ATE	ESTIMATED PORTIONS	CALORIES
BREAKFAST			
LUNCH			
SUPPER			
SNACKS			
		TOTAL KCALS (optional):	

309

Date:

Daily activity log

Instructions: Use this form to track daily exercise. Include all activities of 5 minutes or more in duration and estimate their intensity. As general guidelines, light activities could be dusting, ironing, playing croquet. Moderate activities include playing golf, raking the lawn, walking, washing the car or dancing. Strenuous activities could be aerobic dance, jogging, bicycling, swimming, hiking with a backpack, and playing tennis. When you're done, add up the number of minutes you spent doing light, moderate, and strenuous activities.

	WHAT I DID	TIME SPENT IN MINUTES PER INTENSITY		
AM		Light	Moderate	Strenuous
6:00				
7:00				
8:00				
9:00				
10:00				
11:00				
PM				
12:00				
13:00				
14:00				
15:00				
16:00				
17:00				
18:00				
19:00				
20:00				
21:00				
22:00				
23:00				
24:00				
AM				
1:00				
2:00				
3:00				
4:00				
5:00				
	TOTAL MINUTES:			

Date: _____

Personal time analyser

Instructions: On at least one weekday and one weekend day, keep track of how you spend your time. Make a copy of this form and keep one with you on a particular day. In the two columns to the right, estimate in minutes how much time you spent being active and how much time you spent being inactive. 'Active' means anything that requires you to get up and move around. 'Inactive' includes sitting, lying down or standing.

TIME	ACTIVITIES/TASKS	ACTIVE	INACTIVE
AM			
6:00			
7:00			
8:00			
9:00			
10:00			
11:00			
PM			
12:00			
13:00			
14:00			
15:00			
16:00			
17:00			
18:00			
19:00			
20:00			
21:00			
22:00			
23:00			
24:00			
AM			
1:00			
2:00			
3:00			
4:00			
5:00			
	TOTAL MINUTES:		

Progress log

Instructions: Once a week, record your weight and estimate how much time you spend being active. Jot down notes on any problems or issues you're facing. Try to weigh yourself and fill in the form at the same time each week.

Week of: _____ **Weight:** _____   **NOTES**

AVERAGE DAILY ACTIVITY   **HOW I'M FEELING**   _____
❑ 45 minutes or more   ❑ Great   _____
❑ 30 minutes   ❑ Okay   _____
❑ Less than 30 minutes   ❑ Stressed out   _____
                                 ❑ Discouraged   _____
                                 ❑ _____   _____

Week of: _____ **Weight:** _____   **NOTES**

AVERAGE DAILY ACTIVITY   **HOW I'M FEELING**   _____
❑ 45 minutes or more   ❑ Great   _____
❑ 30 minutes   ❑ Okay   _____
❑ Less than 30 minutes   ❑ Stressed out   _____
                                 ❑ Discouraged   _____
                                 ❑ _____   _____

Week of: _____ **Weight:** _____   **NOTES**

AVERAGE DAILY ACTIVITY   **HOW I'M FEELING**   _____
❑ 45 minutes or more   ❑ Great   _____
❑ 30 minutes   ❑ Okay   _____
❑ Less than 30 minutes   ❑ Stressed out   _____
                                 ❑ Discouraged   _____
                                 ❑ _____   _____

Week of: _____ **Weight:** _____   **NOTES**

AVERAGE DAILY ACTIVITY   **HOW I'M FEELING**   _____
❑ 45 minutes or more   ❑ Great   _____
❑ 30 minutes   ❑ Okay   _____
❑ Less than 30 minutes   ❑ Stressed out   _____
                                 ❑ Discouraged   _____
                                 ❑ _____   _____

	WEEK 1	WEEK 2	WEEK 3	WEEK 4
+3.6 kg (8 lb)				
+2.7 kg (6 lb)				
+1.8 kg (4 lb)				
+1 kg (2 lb)				
_____ STARTING WEIGHT				
−1 kg (2 lb)				
−1.8 kg (4 lb)				
−2.7 kg (6 lb)				
−3.6 kg (8 lb)				

At the end of the month, use this graph to chart weight changes during the month.

Your healthy weight calculator

What's your ideal weight? The answer depends on your body type. Researchers use a scale called Body Mass Index, or BMI, which assigns a number based on a combination of height and weight. Essentially, the number indicates whether you are carrying a healthy or unhealthy level of body fat.

To find your BMI on the chart below, locate your height in inches in the column on the left hand side. Then move your finger across the horizontal row of numbers to find your weight. Finally, locate the number directly above the row where your weight appears, in the column marked BMI at the top of the chart.

You'll notice that the BMI chart gives a wide range of weights that fall within the normal category. The normal BMI weight range for someone who is 5 foot 7 inches, or 67 inches, is between 8 stone 9 lb and 11 stone 5 lb, for instance. The reason: people have different body types, some slender, some stocky, some small-boned, some large.

The BMI index isn't foolproof. It tends to overestimate body fat in athletes and people with very muscular builds. It tends to underestimate body fat in older people, who have usually lost muscle mass.

	NORMAL						OVERWEIGHT					OBESE								
BMI	**19**	**20**	**21**	**22**	**23**	**24**	**25**	**26**	**27**	**28**	**29**	**30**	**31**	**32**	**33**	**34**	**35**	**36**	**37**	**38**
HEIGHT (FT & IN)	BODY WEIGHT IN STONES AND POUNDS																			
4'10	6'7	6'12	7'2	7'7	7'12	8'3	8'7	8'12	9'3	9'8	9'12	10'3	10'8	10'13	11'4	11'8	11'13	12'4	12'9	12'13
4'11	6'11	7'1	7'6	7'11	8'2	8'7	8'12	9'2	9'7	9'12	10'3	10'8	10'13	11'4	11'9	12'0	12'5	12'10	13'1	13'6
5'0	6'13	7'4	7'9	8'0	8'6	8'11	9'2	9'7	9'12	10'3	10'8	10'13	11'4	11'9	12'0	12'6	12'11	13'2	13'7	13'12
5'1	7'2	7'8	7'13	8'4	8'10	9'1	9'6	9'11	10'3	10'8	10'13	11'4	11'10	12'1	12'6	12'12	13'3	13'8	13'13	14'5
5'2	7'6	7'11	8'3	8'8	9'0	9'5	9'10	10'2	10'7	10'13	11'4	11'10	12'1	12'7	12'12	13'4	13'9	14'1	14'7	14'12
5'3	7'9	8'1	8'6	8'12	9'4	9'9	10'1	10'6	10'12	11'4	11'9	12'1	12'7	12'12	13'4	13'10	14'1	14'7	14'12	15'4
5'4	7'12	8'4	8'10	9'2	9'8	10'0	10'5	10'11	11'3	11'9	12'1	12'7	12'13	13'4	13'10	14'2	14'8	15'0	15'6	15'11
5'5	8'2	8'8	9'0	9'6	9'12	10'4	10'10	11'2	11'8	12'0	12'6	12'12	13'4	13'10	14'2	14'8	15'0	15'6	15'13	16'5
5'6	8'6	8'12	9'4	9'10	10'2	10'8	11'1	11'7	11'13	12'5	12'11	13'4	13'10	14'2	14'8	15'1	15'7	15'13	16'6	16'11
5'7	8'9	9'1	9'8	10'0	10'6	10'13	11'5	11'12	12'4	12'10	13'3	13'9	14'2	14'8	15'1	15'7	15'13	16'6	16'12	17'5
5'8	8'13	9'5	9'12	10'4	10'11	11'4	11'10	12'3	12'9	13'2	13'8	14'1	14'7	15'0	15'6	15'13	16'6	16'12	17'5	17'12
5'9	9'2	9'9	10'2	10'9	11'1	11'8	12'1	12'8	13'0	13'7	14'0	14'7	14'13	15'6	15'13	16'6	16'12	17'5	17'12	18'5
5'10	9'6	9'13	10'6	10'13	11'6	11'13	12'6	12'13	13'6	13'13	14'6	14'13	15'6	15'12	16'5	16'12	17'5	17'12	18'5	18'12
5'11	9'10	10'3	10'10	11'3	11'11	12'4	12'11	13'4	13'11	14'4	14'12	15'5	15'12	16'4	16'11	17'4	17'12	18'6	18'13	19'6
6'0	10'0	10'7	11'0	11'8	12'1	12'9	13'2	13'9	14'3	14'10	15'3	15'11	16'4	16'11	17'4	17'12	18'5	18'13	19'6	19'13
6'1	10'4	10'11	11'5	11'12	12'6	13'0	13'7	14'1	14'8	15'2	15'9	16'3	16'11	17'4	17'12	18'5	18'13	19'6	20'0	20'8
6'2	10'8	11'1	11'11	12'3	12'11	13'4	13'12	14'6	15'0	15'8	16'1	16'9	17'3	17'11	18'4	18'12	19'6	20'0	20'7	21'1
6'3	10'12	11'6	12'0	12'8	13'2	13'10	14'4	14'12	15'6	16'0	16'8	17'2	17'10	18'4	18'12	19'6	19'13	20'7	21'1	21'9
6'4	11'2	11'10	12'4	12'12	13'7	14'1	14'9	15'3	15'11	16'6	17'0	17'8	18'2	18'11	19'5	19'13	20'7	21'1	21'10	22'4

Remember that losing even a few kilos or pounds when you're overweight will make you healthier, reducing your risk of heart disease and diabetes. Trying to bring your weight down to a normal BMI is a terrific goal. But if you have a long way to go to get there, set some milestones along the way. Reward yourself at each step, and don't get discouraged. Every little bit helps.

Recipe index

General index

Entries in *italics* refer to recipes.

Origination: Colour Systems Limited, London
Printing and binding: Mateu Cromo, Madrid, Spain

FOR READER'S DIGEST UK
John Andrews, Liz Edwards, Penelope Grose, Kate Harris,
Fiona McIntosh, Jane McKenna, Lisa Thomas, Rachel Weaver

READER'S DIGEST GENERAL BOOKS

Editorial Director
Cortina Butler

Art Director
Nick Clark

Executive Editor
Julian Browne

Development Editor
Ruth Binney

Managing Editor
Alastair Holmes

Picture Resource Manager
Martin Smith

Style Editor
Ron Pankhurst

ISBN 0 276 42768 8
Book Code 400-159-01
Concept Code US9100/IC

Visit our web site at www.readersdigest.co.uk